WILL
AMERICA
CHANGE?

Ziauddin Sardar
Merryl Wyn Davies

ICON BOOKS

327·73

Published in the UK in 2008 by Icon Books Ltd,
The Old Dairy, Brook Road, Thriplow,
Cambridge SG8 7RG
email: info@iconbooks.co.uk
www.iconbooks.co.uk

Parts of this text were originally published
under the title *Why Do People Hate America?*
by Icon Books Ltd in 2002, 2004

Sold in the UK, Europe, South Africa and Asia
by Faber & Faber Ltd, 3 Queen Square,
London WC1N 3AU or their agents

Distributed in the UK, Europe, South Africa and Asia
by TBS Ltd, TBS Distribution Centre, Colchester Road
Frating Green, Colchester CO7 7DW

This edition published in Australia in 2008
by Allen & Unwin Pty Ltd,
PO Box 8500, 83 Alexander Street,
Crows Nest, NSW 2065

Distributed in Canada by
Penguin Books Canada,
90 Eglinton Avenue East, Suite 700,
Toronto, Ontario M4P 2YE

ISBN: 978-184046-879-3

Typesetting in 10pt Sabon by Wayzgoose

Printed and bound in the UK by
CPI Bookmarque, Croydon CR0 4TD

Contents

About the authors

Ziauddin Sardar is a prominent journalist and author. Prolific and polymathic, he is a columnist on the *New Statesman* and a familiar radio and television personality.

Merryl Wyn Davies is a writer, anthropologist and former producer of religious programmes for the BBC.

Acknowledgement

Many friends generously shared their thoughts and suggestions over the course of our engagement with America. We thank them and hope we have made constructive use of their invaluable input. A special thanks to Huw Rowlands who has been an attentive and even interested sounding board as this book took shape. Our most sincere thanks and gratitude go to Duncan Heath at Icon Books who has been enormously supportive, unfailingly encouraging and endlessly patient; without such nurturing, this book might never have reached completion.

CHAPTER ONE

Beyond Ground Zero

Will America change? The answer depends on the Ground Zero from which change is measured. An America, changed by 9-11, that seeks to restore its default settings to the year 2000 will find it has hardly moved in resolving its difficulties with the world.

The world's problems with America centre on its changelessness – the consistency of ideas and policy that span successive administrations irrespective of their position on the domestic political spectrum. For the world, morning in America is always the dawn of Groundhog Day, a repeat performance as in the movie of that name where a hapless reporter wakes to discover that he must keep reliving the traditional day foretelling the end of winter and coming of spring. The cycle is broken only when the central character becomes aware of his shortcomings and reforms his own behaviour towards other people.[1] Likewise, American policy follows a recurrent pattern driven by a consistent set of attitudes and ideas from which the world reaps consistently negative consequences that ultimately serve only American interests – which may, however, not be in the long-term best interests of the US either. An America that genuinely seeks to resolve these problems needs a different Ground Zero, one centred on the very idea of America, the premises on which it interacts with the world. From that Ground Zero, the question is: Can America be changed?

What kind of change will Americans opt for? Though the question affects the lives of everyone, everywhere around the globe, the only people who can provide an answer are the voting public of the United States of America. How America debates and conceives of change, what kind of change Americans can believe in – or more importantly, what kind of change Americans are prepared to see enacted – will determine the problems or opportunities the rest of the world has to come to terms with. What America thinks needs changing is of vital concern to people everywhere, for what can or cannot be changed in America will set the agenda for the global future.

A perceptible groundswell for change is a recurrent feature of the American political landscape, erupting on the right as often as the left, spurred by Republicans as much as by Democrats, and is the perennial condition of the populace independent of these poles. The change theme did not materialise merely for the 2008 campaign. It helped George W. Bush to power as much as it now mobilises those who disown what Bush's policies have meant for America. And it prompts a recurrent question. In all the mood swings and electoral upheavals over the decades – how much has America really changed in its relationship to the rest of the world?

What is different today is the prominence that ordinary Americans place on the issue of their country's problems with the world. It is more than the Iraq question, the reaction against, or die-hard support for, an unpopular war. Whether the issue is domestic or foreign policy, the public perceives that all is not well with the world, accompanied by a feeling that America might have a hand in, or even be responsible for the trouble. At no time in recent history have Americans been so aware of their involvement in the world beyond their borders. In no previous election were politicians at such pains to promise to repair America's relations with the world.

But if the world is so much with them, how well fitted is American society or its political process to debate their nation's place in the world, its role and relations with other countries? We, the disenfranchised people of the world, are entitled to ask, 'What is the world to America?' Ultimately, starkly different visions of how America should operate within the global community appeal in the same language and imagery to the same idea of America to motivate or be the objective of change. The world at large remains the chaotic backdrop against which America expresses the ideal of itself. Detailed consideration of the global, regional and bilateral difficulties in which American action can, should or will change is hard to find. Study after study reports how little ordinary Americans, especially the young, actually know of basic geography, world history or current affairs in other countries. Politicians assure the American public that they will reclaim the country's global leadership and restore America's moral authority. But what do those pledges mean to the average American, especially when they are presented in the language of nationalist self-flattery to confirm American exceptionalism despite the far-from-exceptional operation of American power during the Bush years? How much confidence can the rest of the world have that choices made by American voters will address the real issues and deliver remedial change in how America affects their lives?

America is indisputably what former secretary of state Madeleine Albright described as the 'indispensable nation'; it is the greatest accumulation of military, economic, political and cultural power the world has ever seen, the sole hyperpower. But does reclaiming global leadership mean reassertion of a refurbished benign American empire – is that a recipe to resolve its problems with the world? Is the indisputable power to go it alone, to consider its own national security within its own view of geo-political strategy a superior imperative, one overriding the well-being of other nations, any basis to claim moral authority – even with the blemishes of abuses of power, not to mention international law, removed?

The American heretic Ambrose Bierce wrote: 'War is God's

way of teaching Americans geography.'² It's a great one-liner, but putting things right around the globe needs more than basic geography. Wars, rumours of war and volatile instability are a direct legacy of the Bush years which have hardened antipathies and suspicions of America while leaving mega global problems – from climate change to arms control, and nuclear proliferation to poverty eradication – in a dangerous limbo. That the world is in a mess is no great insight. But all global problems come with local antecedents and specifics, they appear in distinctive forms with their own local dynamics, constraints and expression. How is complexity refined and focused in America as an electoral change agenda?

Serious debate about how America can or should interact with the world needs to be informed by the kind of familiarity the rest of the world has with America. America's multifaceted image of itself is on display, on sale, at work, setting the benchmarks, creating the fashion and avidly consumed, parodied and promulgated in even the remotest corners of the globe – such is the reach and potency of its power and domination, not least in the realm of global popular culture. People living anywhere beyond America are vicarious Americans, participants in aspects of American ways of life, since American news dominates the global news agenda. Ordinary Americans have no comparable exposure to the rest of the world, and many, perhaps most, have no sense of lacking some essential component necessary for the responsible exercise of political judgement. Paradoxically, the very medium that familiarises the world with America simultaneously provides most Americans with their image and idea of the world. But the American media consumed on Main Street – beyond the Beltway and the chattering class – replicates an asymmetrical vision, a way of looking through the wrong end of a telescope, that does not serve the interests of informed political debate. Without knowing the world, how can Americans determine what is the best way to repair their relations with it? How can they choose between the promises of the different worldviews on offer?

It is futile to argue against facts: America is the indispensable nation. Its accumulations of power as the largest economy, the pre-eminent consumer of global resources and production, the most technologically sophisticated society, the most extensive military establishment and arsenal ever assembled at unimaginable cost, make it the fulcrum of global diplomacy on all issues from energy and food security to climate change and everything between. American wealth and power give it a decisive voice in all international bodies on which the fate of nations depends, whether it is the policy of the International Monetary Fund or the United Nations. There is no getting away from, going around or simply ignoring the indispensable nation.

The question for Americans to determine is: What does (or should) their indispensability consist of? What is the distinction between leadership and engagement? Does the world need more of the theory that what's good for America is good for the world? Or does the world long for America to participate in collective decision-making based on listening to and learning from others, a negotiation between nations and people with huge disparities of wealth and power, but acknowledging the equal validity of different interests and opinions? Instead of undermining global institutions according to its own interests and ideology, should America be a driving force empowering them for the common good? These are alternative models of leadership, very different in what they mean for America and the world. And when it comes to moral authority, what can (or should) be the basis of a global moral order? Can there ever be a case for the unquestioned assertion of innate superior moral authority? Or does moral authority derive from judgements about how power and influence has been exercised? Should moral authority come after careful consideration of the facts, weighing of the consequences of policy and action for all parties concerned, rather than presuming the perennial pure and benign intentions, no matter what they do, of the most powerful? Would Americans, and the rest of the world, not be better served by acknowledging that all nations are less than perfect, morally ambiguous actors on the world stage, rather than being required to endorse the concept that might makes one nation more right than any other? Is the American public ready to question these differences with any degree of self-criticism? Are Americans ready to consider the idea that to restore the promise of America they may need to reconsider the very idea of America?

America's problem with the world is inseparable from defining and understanding the world's problems with America. This proposition is neither un-American nor anti-American. Unless you know the problem, there can be no effective solution. And the problem lies in how we come to terms with the realities of an increasingly interconnected and interdependent world. It depends on determining whether the events of the Bush years, the years since 9-11, have carried Americans beyond the pained question of 'Why do they hate us?' to a clearer appreciation of how American power and the exercise of that power impacts on the daily life of ordinary people around the globe.

The history of America's relations with the world did not begin on 9-11, 2001. But the Ground Zero created by the monstrous carnage of the attacks on the World Trade Center and Pentagon diagnoses the response to that national trauma as the immediate problem demanding solutions. It produced a rush to declare a badly defined war on terror that made militarism the centre-point of response; it was too easily stampeded down the side-track of an illegal war founded on a false prospectus against the wrong, in the sense of not culpable for 9-11, target in the wrong place, with no planning or strategy for post-war reconstruction, which was, in the event, catastrophically mishandled. It diagnoses the problem of war wielded as unquestionable justification for an assault on civil liberties with the abandonment of normal lawful standards of operation at home and abroad: illegal wiretaps; invasive snooping on the everyday lives of law-abiding citizens; the redefinition of torture; 'extraordinary rendition' to facilitate torture; the routine practice of torture by

American service personnel; and the indefinite incarceration in legal limbo of so-called illegal combatants, many of whom after years of imprisonment in dire conditions, and without apology or explanation, have simply been returned home without ever being charged with any wrong-doing. Then there is the death and destruction visited on uncounted innocent Afghan and Iraqi civilians, a legacy of horror and trauma for families and communities every bit as acute as the scars of 9-11, that outstrips by hundreds of thousands the number of victims of 9-11. Promised freedom and democracy, they have inherited displacement, worsened or unimproved conditions that have handed Afghanistan back to warlords and drug-traffickers and made Iraq a weakened basketcase where a lost generation with little or no access to education will be prey to global and regional pressures that make nonsense of the idea of national autonomy. More American soldiers have died in pursuit of these mismanaged wars than there were victims of 9-11, and tens of thousands more have received horrific, permanent, life-changing injuries. The fixation with homeland security has generated untestable doomsday scenarios beyond any risk analysis as the baseline of policy and preparedness, prompting the rebirth of 'Star Wars' with its threat of destabilisation in Eastern Europe, yet leaving porous American borders and fears about port security to further sour Americans' view of foreigners and foreigners' views of Americans. The financial cost, immediate and long-term, of these policies produces numbers with unimaginable strings of noughts and keeps on mounting while tax-cutting, the credit squeeze and threats to global liquidity push the American economy towards recession with knock-on effects worldwide. Focus on the wrong war has deflected attention from innumerable international issues, from the festering sore of the Palestine/Israel peace process to global trade negotiations and co-ordinated efforts on climate change.

There can be no doubt that Ground Zero 9-11 leaves a legacy worthy of a change agenda. But the dust clouds of that event did not stop history in its tracks. Workable solutions need to face up to a more telling question than wondering what has gone wrong in the Bush years. Ground Zero 9-11 offers the easy conclusion that Bush, his administration and policies are an aberration. However, the real problem is the continuity of approach that underpins the Bush policies. For all the talk of pre-emptive preventative war, the disdain for global opinion and gerrymandering of coalitions of the willing, the architecture of American response, the dynamic of Bush's policy carries forward the thrust of the Clinton administration which refined the essence of the Bush senior years which ... and so on. There is a consistency evident in America's response to the world founded on policies pursued and positions taken over the preceding decades. Meaningful change needs a different Ground Zero, one that seriously debates the recurrence of the devastating consequences of American policies around the world and wrestles with the causes of the consistent attitudes that sour America's relations with the world.

On September 11, 2001 a shell-shocked woman emerged from the infernal fumes enveloping lower Manhattan. She turned to a waiting television reporter and asked: 'Why do they hate us?' Her words were taken up by ordinary people, experts and commentators, politicians and President George W. Bush. Most often they were used as a self-evident assertion of fact, a statement about the animus behind such an enormity of evil. As people who shared the experience of 9-11 with a global television audience, we, the authors, heard something different. We heard a cry of pain and incomprehension that was also a plea for explanation. In the coming days we watched town-hall meetings on American TV where again and again we picked up this same theme. There seemed to be a hunger among ordinary people for more information to help them understand how and why their country became a target. The glib assertion – 'They hate us' – seemed to be wielded to short-circuit the question and the debate that so many Americans appeared to want. We decided to take the question seriously and began writing *Why*

Do People Hate America? Like those who posed the question in America, we were not looking for justification for the indefensible, but we were intent on making clear the context that made such a monstrous act possible. Our answer was concerned with consistency; the consistency of outcomes, of deeds of commission and omission in America's impact on the rest of the world. In the words of T. S. Eliot, we tried to show how 'sin grows with doing good'[3] – how policies presented to the American public as virtuous and selfless have very different implications for the lives of people in other countries; how Americans' conviction of their country's good intentions and benevolence in practice operates to restrict the freedoms, undermine the hopes and deny the prosperity of ordinary people beyond its shores.

Back in 2001 we felt the need to argue the case that America had a problem with the world because of actions, not envy. We further argued, on the basis of past actions, that the world had legitimate cause to fear that American response to 9-11 would adopt the wrong approach not because of George W. Bush and the ascendancy of neo-conservative ideology but because of the consistency of American attitudes and ideas about itself and towards the rest of the world. After the Bush years, any delicacy in arguing that there is substance for the world's disquiet about, or even hate for, American foreign policy seems entirely superfluous. Whether they blame the policy or the mismanagement of policy, Americans are as aware as people everywhere that the world has become a more dangerous place for Americans and for everyone else. It is no longer a problem that has to be made clear. What remains problematic is what needs to change and how much America can or will be changed. In posing these questions we return in revised form to much of the material contained in *Why Do People Hate America?* We do this to weave together the continuity between events, policy and attitudes before and after 9-11, the better to question whether America is ready for change.

History is a process of reassessment; it considers events in light of before and after, prologue and response. Time and reflection offer the opportunity to focus more clearly not only on what went wrong but why policies were bound to be misconceived. Only by interweaving the critique that we, along with others, offered then can we highlight how clearly it predicted the consequences that have flowed from America's response to 9-11. Only by reviewing the continuities of policies and attitudes before and after 9-11 can we turn attention to what was ignored and suggest why it prevented an effective American constituency from backing a different course. From these continuities, familiar policy responses emerge; America set its usual course according to unchanged premises. In pursuing its objectives, American policy generates the same division of opinion at home and abroad. Only by integrating what could have been known and should have been relevant back then is it possible to make this pattern visible. Also, it clarifies the options being offered to the American electorate as a promise of change: what merely restores the status quo that produced 9-11; what is mere cosmetic change that leaves the underlying problems in place; and what might begin a genuine debate about what can and should be changed, and what meaningful change entails. 'Will America change?' is of concern to people everywhere. Whether America can be changed is the darkest cloud of doubt and fear looming over the global future.

America's national conversation is the loudest aside in human history, a stage whisper that reverberates around the globe. America disproportionately dominates the world's attention. Events in America that are essentially local make the news everywhere: a tornado that devastates a small town; an ice storm that brings down power lines; the tripping of an electrical grid that shuts down air conditioners and deep freezes; these will get more global news coverage than mass starvation, dearth, death and war in most of Africa, South America or Asia. What is Anna Nicole Smith to the world that her end made news far beyond the US, in places where her career never registered? An American travelling the world – albeit a novel proposition in a country where the vast majority never even apply for a passport – will never be far from news of home. Turn on the television anywhere and images of America are readily available. Conversely, a foreigner coming to America could be forgiven for wondering if the rest of the world exists – except when Americans are involved. The question is more complex than a nation of continental proportions that generates an abundance of material made available through American media outlets and their domination of the global media market. It cannot be reduced to the market force of the unit costs of mass production, nor is it mere curious fascination on the part of the rest of the world. It is a kind of strategic necessity. What America thinks, knows, cares about and experiences is an insight into the constituent elements of the way of life by which its power and domination are constructed and sustained. Knowing America seems the best way to access how its policies are made and how American opinion will affect the rest of the world. And in a world where the majority of people get their news and views via television, what America tunes into has a direct bearing on what the rest of the world is about to receive. American television is in many senses more than just programming, the listings of what's on. The conundrums of American history, current events and social concerns all make their way into TV drama and comedy; the back-chat between the so-familiar characters in TV series is a reflection of conventional American information and attitudes. The storylines, plot devices, stock characters and talk are there because they resonate with American audiences – and that is exactly what makes them relevant to audiences around the world. The global television marketplace is less a window on the world than an opening into the American mindset. How Americans talk among themselves, in the realm of politics or popular culture, speaks volumes to the rest of the world. But what is heard often conveys very different meaning to a worldwide audience. It is in that disparity that America's problem with the world and the world's problems with America are located. And so we use television and films to explore the issues that bear on the question, 'Will America change?', and that affect the reckoning of whether and how America can be changed.

The whole world saw and experienced 9-11 through television. Television showed us what happened; it also archives, retrieves and replays the experience. It is a paradox of the new media that one of its principal sources of income is making these archives, the back catalogue, instantly and ever more widely available. The accessibility of the archive through syndication, repeats and distribution for the home market make films and television a continuous flow of influence that not only shows us what was, but continues to make relevant the ways we thought about what happened.

★

On 3 October 2001, barely three weeks after the terrorist attacks on New York and Washington, NBC aired a special episode of the television series *The West Wing*. Introduced by the regular cast members, the audience of 'Isaac and Ishmael', as the episode was titled, were urged to donate money to the victims of 9-11; profits from the programme were also donated to this cause. The one-off special is a creative – in the sense of imaginary – attempt to come to terms with real events, a demonstration of how American television mediates what matters to Americans. *The West Wing* does not bring the real 9-11 into its virtual world – that would be an effrontery too far. But it does not need to; we all know what this episode is about. What is important is the way in which the programme deals with the issues. It was and is a remarkable compendium of the themes and information that preoccupied America's national debate on how to make sense of and respond to 9-11.

The West Wing was described by *Time* magazine as 'a national civics lesson'. The show represents a particular vision of American liberal values and democratic culture. It won nine Emmys in its first season (more than any other programme, ever) and continued to be honoured over the course of its seven seasons in production. The series is the continuing story of President Bartlet, a liberal Democrat of impeccable credentials, who exists in a parallel universe to US politics. *The West Wing*'s storylines offer a virtual mirror, a running commentary on and, over time, intriguing counterpoints to the actual political domain. Like any real administration in the White House, President Bartlet and his staff struggle to cope with personal problems, scandals, lobby groups, ethical dilemmas of power, domestic issues and global politics. In 'Isaac and Ishmael' the perspective of liberal Hollywood was at one with that of conservatives, neo-cons and even Christian fundamentalists.

As befits a national civics lesson, the main thrust of the episode centres on a group of high school students, part of a programme called Presidential Classroom, caught up in a security alert while visiting the White House. Alarm bells ring, a security lock-down commences. The students are directed to the Mess – 'it's where we eat lunch' – a location provided with tables, chairs and a white board, where the series' cast of regular characters whiles away the time by providing the lesson for the day. A second storyline, explaining the security alert, is interwoven with the classroom. The FBI receives information about a terrorist calling himself Yaarun Nabi, which translates as 'friend of the Prophet', we are told. He uses a number of aliases, among which is Raqim Ali. A search of databases reveals five potential suspects with that name, one of whom is an Arab American member of the White House staff. The alarm bells are on his account; he is bundled into a darkened room for urgent questioning, and provides the audience with an alternative civics lesson. When Leo McGarry, the Chief of Staff, is informed that a potential terrorist may be on the premises, he looks stunned and mutters: 'Well ... it was only a matter of time, huh?' The first proposition made by *The West Wing*, as by American society, is self-evident: the menace of terrorism is more than a potential threat – it is an inevitability, an enormity merely waiting to happen, intent on reaching into the centre of American life, virtual or real.

The Presidential Classroom's discussion begins with a decidedly oblique question. One of the students asks Josh Lyman, Deputy Chief of Staff: 'So ... what's the deal with everyone trying to kill you?' Before we get to the substance of debate about actual mass murder we are offered asides about fictional attempted murder that honour the conventions of series television. In a previous storyline of this parallel universe, Lyman was shot and critically injured. We are referred back to an episode within the fictional timeline in this special offering which is explicitly designed to stand outside that timeline to set a context: the aside is there to contextualise terror. First, it provides an opportunity, through a long digression on the part of Lyman, to acknowledge the human impact of violence. In a world in which people feel as strongly, if not more so, about fictional characters as real ones, we are given an acknowledgement of emotional trauma, however trite that may seem in the circumstances. Second, and more importantly, it is there to provide a modicum of balance while highlighting a theme central to the analysis. In the two-part story that opened *The West Wing*'s second season ('In the Shadow of Two Gunmen', first aired on 4 October 2000), Lyman was shot when gunmen opened fire on the presidential party during a visit to Virginia. The intended target of the assassination was President Bartlet's aide Charlie Young, who happens to be black, as punishment for dating Zoey, the president's daughter. The gunmen were members of a neo-Nazi group called West Virginia White Pride. The aside reminds the audience that terror not only can but on numerous occasions has had an American incarnation; hatred is not the exclusive preserve of one kind of group or society. On another level, it reinforces the implication that racial hatred is the most pernicious and enduring of hatreds, the recurring theme of this

special episode. Thirdly, we are being r[...]
of the series and its command of a simple la[...]
its most obvious usual suspects. In the earlie[...]
White House Situation Room scrambles to deal wit[...]
ing, the status report notes that the whereabouts of Osa[...]
Laden are not immediately known, and that there is conc[...]
about a front-line build-up of Iraqi Revolutionary Guards.
Whatever was happening in the real world, this West Wing had
its finger firmly on the hot-button issues.

The special episode then moves swiftly to the obvious question: 'So why is everyone trying to kill us?' As convenor of this
civics class, Lyman argues that not everyone is bent on violence
towards Americans, but most definitely all Americans are
targets. The question, he insists, must be refined. He writes his
test question on the white board: 'Islamic extremist is to Islam
as — is to Christianity'; and provides his own answer: 'KKK.'
'That's what we're talking about – the [Ku Klux] Klan gone
medieval and global. It could not have less to do with Islamic
men and women of faith, of whom there are millions and millions' – including those in the American armed services, police
and fire departments, he adds. The analogy, heavy on the racial
theme, once made is never explored, making it hard to see how
it helps anyone to understand better the source and nature of the
threat.

The specific question becomes: 'Why are Islamic extremists
trying to kill us?' Discussion of this question serves one prime
function, to differentiate Us from Them, because the differences,
everyone accepts, explain the motive that unleashes terror. What
defines America is what terrorists are against, which is the
straightforward proposition on which all marshalling of information and discussion turns. For the students in the show, the
difference between Us and Them is simply 'freedom and democracy'. Theirs is exactly the analysis that dominated the
American national conversation, reiterated at every opportunity
by President Bush.

uch simplistic analysis,
 sophisticated form. The
both urbane and worldly-
American values as open-
rogramme's favourite ethic,
: 'It's probably a good idea to
specific complaints.' Indeed, it
not one much favoured either by
al clamour. The 'complaints' he
rica supports'; 'US troops in Saudi
Iraq'; and 'support for Egypt'. And
we are to   these complaints every day. Since we
can assume that   ity Chief of Staff is not in daily contact
with terrorists or Islamic extremists, these cannot be the only people voicing these 'complaints'. These are substantive issues, actual
long-standing features of American foreign policy that attract
repeated complaint. In which case, it might be a suitable place
to begin an instructive exploration of these issues, even if 'complaint' seems a distinctly neutral term for such contentious policy
issues. It might, for example, be significant to consider the fact
that such 'complaint' comes from many different sources –
Americans, Europeans, people and governments across the
Third World – as well as from Muslims. When such 'complaints'
are made so often, from so many sources, might they not contribute to the creation of terrorism, or the conditions in which
terrorism festers and recruits? So, *The West Wing* acknowledges
the existence of the critique we explored in *Why Do People
Hate America?* But this West Wing, the acme of liberal open-
mindedness and plurality, responds in keeping with the unanimous mainstream of American debate. Lyman definitively tells
the class: 'I think they are wrong.' Pause for reflection is stopped
dead in its tracks; it is superfluous distraction, it need not detain
our civics class. As in the real world, the opportunity to be self-
critical, to examine the actual consequences and outcomes of
American foreign policy, is raised merely to be dismissed.

What explains terrorists, what defines their difference, is solely concerned with the nature and history of their beliefs – this is the essence of the lesson we are to be given. So what is Islamic extremism? 'It is strict adherence to a particular interpretation of 7th-century Islamic law, as practised by the Prophet Muhammad.' And Lyman adds for emphasis: 'When I say "strict adherence", I'm not kidding around.' With a single bound, at the very beginning of the civics lesson, we have been plunged into the sort of misinformation that is seriously detrimental to reasoned judgement. Islam was first preached by the Prophet Muhammad in the 7th century, in which case, by this definition, terrorism is original to Islam. If strict adherence to Islam 'as practised by the Prophet Muhammad' is what makes an extremist – and we have already been told that extremism has nothing to do with millions of Muslim men and women of faith – then what exactly is the connection between these many millions and their faith, or indeed the Prophet Muhammad? Presumably these millions are less than strict in their adherence. The implicit assumption behind this assertion – as common among ordinary people as among opinion-formers, commentators, specialists and academics – cedes authenticity solely to the extremists. No matter what caveats are offered, exactly as Lyman states them, the opinions and understanding of millions and millions of Muslims are disempowered, rendered voiceless and invisible because they are not an authentic expression of 'real' Islam. Islam is as it is defined by non-Muslims, based on what can only be described as pure ignorance.

The practice of the Prophet Muhammad is second only to the Qur'an itself and is essential for all Muslims. It is referred to and revered by all as a guide and example of how to live; it provides the moral values and ethics of Islam, as well as such vital details as how to pray and what form prayer should take. Furthermore, all Islamic schools of law, which actually developed after the 7th century, as well as all shades of opinion and interpretation among all Muslims, are grounded in, refer to, and are justified by reasoning based on the practice of the Prophet Muhammad. What is being asserted and offered is a distinction that can only generate confusion and the inability to distinguish an Islamic extremist from any other Muslim. Moreover, in this analysis *The West Wing* is consistent with the equally erroneous, and more offensively expressed, opinions of televangelists Pat Robertson and Jerry Falwell, who went so far as to argue that the Prophet Muhammad himself was a terrorist![4] Where this unanimous perspective leads joins up the elements of the civics lesson so far. It leads to the conclusions such as those set out in a lengthy article by the military historian Victor Davis Hanson, in *City Journal*. 'They hate us', he wrote, 'because their culture is backward and corrupt' and because 'they are envious of our power and prestige'. For Hanson, democracy, consensual governance, constitution, freedom and citizenship are all European (Greek and Latin) inventions; they have nothing to do with the rest of the world in general and the Muslim world in particular. This is the sophisticated face of racism dressed in the robes of scholarship.[5]

Of course, *The West Wing* could not be *that* coarse and jingoistic. But having defined the difference between Them and Us in terms supposedly original to the nature of Islam, it leaves few options. Indeed, essentially the same point is made when *The West Wing* uses the Taliban to exemplify the difference: men forced to pray and grow their beards to a certain length, women denied education and employment and publicly stoned for crimes like not wearing a veil, the banning of films and television. The essence of the difference between Them and Us is lack of personal choice. 'There's nothing wrong with a religion whose laws say a man's got to wear a beard or cover his head or wear a collar. It's when violation of these laws becomes a crime against the state, and not your parents, that we are talking about lack of choice', Toby Ziegler, the Communications Director, asserts when he joins the discussion.

Furthermore, if the KKK provides a good religious analogy

for Islamic extremists, there is also a political analogy. Here *The West Wing* quotes directly from a widely circulated letter written by the Afghan American, Tamim Ansary.[6] The political analogy for the Taliban is the Nazis, and the people of Afghanistan are the Jews in the concentration camps. Opposing the Nazis was a good thing, so by analogy, a war against the Taliban must be equally justified. Once the reductive argument about the nature of Islam is accepted, there is neither basis nor need to investigate the origins of a movement such as the Taliban. If it derives directly from Islam, then it has nothing to do with the specifics of the recent history of Afghanistan; it is unnecessary to enquire why such an appalling ideology was actually welcomed when it took control: because it brought security to ordinary people across large areas of the country. And, taking nothing from the oppressive nature of their rule, it is irrelevant to consider that the Taliban effectively banned the production of opium poppies; or to wonder whether the opinion of the *ulema*, the Taliban religious scholars, that the attack of 9-11 was against Islamic law might open an alternative avenue for negotiated solutions. If Taliban equals Nazi, war is inevitable, eradication by military means the only answer, and so it remains despite the subsequent failure to bring security, change or development to Afghanistan. Indeed, the military solution has empowered the very local warlords from whom the people sought deliverance by the Taliban, having failed to prevent the explosion of poppy production and heroin trafficking and eventually generating a resurgence of Taliban-led resistance.

Simply and irrevocably, the Taliban stand for all Islamic extremists, and by analogy all Islamic extremists are terrorists. Which leads the students gathered in the virtual universe of *The West Wing* to the next question: 'What was the first act of terrorism?' We are told that a secret cult led by the fanatical Mullah, Hasan ibn al-Sabah, committed the first act of terrorism in the 11th century. Al-Sabah's followers, who were taught to believe in nothing and dare all, carried out swift and treacherous murders of fellow Muslims and did so in a state of religious ecstasy induced by hashish and with the promise of Paradise. So not only is extremism original to Islam, but the first terrorists were Muslims who preyed upon Muslims. The history of the world before the 11th century then becomes devoid of any kind of terrorism! What this piece of potted history also leaves out is the fact that the *hashshashin*, from which comes the word 'assassin', arose in the context of the Crusades; they were employed as much by the Crusaders as by various Muslim groups jostling for power. It is one thing to use the antics of the Old Man of the Mountain, as al-Sabah was known, to understand and locate the nefarious activities of bin Laden. It is quite another to suggest that Muslim history is the origin and prime source of assassins and terrorists. And an assassin is not a terrorist; there is a distinction between the terms and the actions they imply. The assassins committed individual acts of political murder: their targets were kings and viziers with whom they had a particular grievance. The term 'terrorist' was first coined by Edmund Burke to refer to those who conducted The Terror, the bloody, guillotine-wielding phase of that campaign for liberty, equality and fraternity known as the French Revolution – the origin of the term being, therefore, state terror. Assassination is politically motivated murder directed at specific individuals, and is not designed to kill innocent bystanders. Terrorism is politically motivated aggression; it defines whole classes of people or nations as enemies who are collectively responsible and guilty. Where no one is innocent, everyone is a potential target by design, though not necessarily by intent in each specific instance. Terrorism and assassination are tactics, the use of violence to intimidate and coerce for political ends. If the tactic is the only point of definition, then the specifics of the history and conditions in which it arises; the objectives for which it is employed – to oppose state oppression, to foment revolution within a particular state, to destabilise capitalism; and the difference between state terror and its use by non-state groups – all are irrelevant. What results is a grand amalgam justifying the declaration of a total universal war on terrorism – the strategic response of the Bush administration.

In *The West Wing*'s discussion of terrorism, Sam Seaborn, introduced to the class as the resident White House expert on the subject, is asked what strikes him most about terrorism. 'Its 100 per cent failure rate', he replies without hesitation. This was perhaps intended as a reassurance for a worried public, but it hardly passes muster as an examination of the history of terrorism. The complete failure rate of terrorism comes about, says Seaborn, because: (1) terrorists 'always fail in what they are after'; and (2) 'they pretty much always succeed in strengthening whatever it is they're against'. Not even a group of high school children can fail to demur at this. What about the IRA? Well, says Sam, the Brits and the Protestants are still there. This is hardly a precise reflection of the political objectives of the IRA. It forgets that 'Brits out' is now, and has long been, an accepted proposition that will be determined by the votes of Protestant and Catholic citizens of Ulster. Nor does it recognise the complex story of the rise of Sinn Fein, who adopted an explicit policy of the gun and the ballot box which eventually became an entirely electoral policy and led to their participation in the Good Friday Agreement. If terrorism is a 100 per cent failure, one wonders what we should make of the power-sharing agreement, brokered in association with the US government, in which a member of the IRA Military Council, Martin McGuinness, is now deputy first minister of Northern Ireland. A tangential point, but a far from irrelevant one, is also glossed over: during the 30 years of 'the Troubles' in Northern Ireland, much of the money that funded IRA terrorism was raised in the US. The Basque extremists, says Seaborn, have had no results. Again, this ignores the considerable accommodations that Spain has made in granting greater regional autonomy, including to the Basque area. And 'the Red Brigades, Baader-Meinhof and the Weathermen sought to overthrow capitalism and capitalism's doing fine', Seaborn adds. Well, true enough, but unquiet lies the theory that wears the crown, and the criticisms of capitalism have not gone away.

Each of these assertions is open to serious question, as is the purpose for which political violence was used in each historical context by these different groups. *The West Wing* sidesteps completely any consideration that, ultimately, campaigns of terrorism lead to a political process of negotiation, accommodation and rapprochement, and result in change. In historical terms, terrorists frequently, if not usually, achieve 'what they are after'; and almost always affect and ultimately change 'whatever it is they're against'. The record of independence campaigns that employed terrorism as a tactic against colonial powers is extensive. Without Mau Mau, would Jomo Kenyatta have become the first prime minister of an independent Kenya? And both Menachem Begin and Itzak Shamir went from being active terrorists against the British Mandate to being prime ministers of Israel.

Seamlessly, *The West Wing*'s discussion moves on to non-violent protest, which presumably is considered a related subject, although the nature of the relationship is worth more discussion and thought than simply lumping everything in one pot. More than anything else in the aftermath of 9-11, this is a relationship that we have to clarify. We need to consider the distinctions between people and groups with similar – or even the same – objectives who nevertheless generate different campaigns, different policies and different kinds of mobilisation. How has the war on terror affected the worldwide Muslim community with its own indigenous movements for change and reform? Has a militarised campaign allegedly designed to 'liberate' the women of Afghanistan done more than the women-led campaign in Morocco that produced a new national family law based on a reinterpretation by Islamic scholars of traditional Sharia, Islamic law? How have reform movements across the Muslim world that have long argued for strengthening Islamic institutions of civic society been constrained by an onslaught perceived on the streets as directed solely at Muslims and based in large measure on antipathy to and crude misunderstanding of Islam? Has the space for peaceful reform, for better understanding, mutual respect and negotiated support for the advance of Islamic democratic agents been advanced or hindered? *The West Wing* simply notes that non-violent protest worked for Gandhi and the civil rights movement. So terrorism, in this view, is many things – a broad enough term to bracket everything from the unmentioned al-Qaeda to Gandhi and the American revolutionaries at the Boston Tea Party (who we are told declared war most courteously), and still warrant the judgement that it always fails.

From such potent illogic which obscures far more than it either reasons with or clarifies, we now move on to the awkward choices that terrorism presents to society: the balance between liberty and safety. One of the students quotes Benjamin Franklin's aphorism: 'They that can give up essential liberty to obtain a little temporary safety deserve neither liberty nor safety.' *The West Wing* offers a strident defence of the national security state, presented by C.J. Cregg, the press secretary. The liberal objections are voiced by Toby Ziegler. The essence of the discussion is to convince the students that human spies are needed, phone-tapping may be required, and certain cherished liberties may have to be compromised if the citizens of America are to feel safe. (What the Patriot Act agenda has contributed to national safety is questionable, but what it has done to undermine the safety, security and freedom from discrimination of American Muslims – those ordinary millions who serve the nation – is clear: 76 per cent of young Arab Americans surveyed in July 2007 said they had personally been discriminated against.[7]) C.J.'s argument is that the reality of terrorism presents a clear and present danger, and to combat it effectively America needs partners who may not be great believers in freedom and democracy, or that much different from the Taliban. In other words, to defeat terrorism one must resort to exactly those policies that form the 'complaint' from so many sources which argues that such double standards promote yet more terrorism. When so much substantive detail has already been swept aside, it is hardly surprising that the most recurrent feature of America's problem with the world is advocated as the only solution.

C. J. admits that this agenda has consequences for free speech and doesn't begin to wrestle with the problem of people being 'lynched by the patriotism police for voicing an opinion'. Nevertheless, she insists, we need to acknowledge that covert actions of the CIA variety are not only necessary and expedient, but their success and effectiveness speaks for itself. C. J. lists the triumphs of the recent past: the Soviets never crossed the Elbe, the North Koreans stayed behind the 38th parallel and the millennium passed off peacefully. Not only is this a highly con-tentious list of debatable 'triumphs', it is also very partial. It neglects any criticism of covert American support for terrorism and death squads across South America (such as funding the Contras in Nicaragua), as well as in other parts of the world, to advance its own national security interests – another aspect of those 'complaints' that need not concern us. For all the inherent risks to liberty, such as blacklists, McCarthy-type witch-hunts and unlawful detentions, safety owes a debt to the sort of remedies currently needed to defeat terrorists. If all this sounds too strident, C. J. tells the students: 'Nothing is more American than coalition-building. The first thing John Wayne always did was put together a posse.' And as we know from the years since 9-11, coalition-building turned into an exercise in arm-twisting, encouragement to defy popular dissent that distorted the demo-cratic will of countries such as Britain and Australia and under-mined the credibility of major international institutions, such as the United Nations, on which much of the rest of the world pins its hopes for a more secure and peaceful future. So, for *The West Wing*, which displays its immaculate liberal credentials at every opportunity, posse law, covert operations, US interven-tions (military and otherwise) and much else besides is justifi-able in the name of safety and the American way.

Chalmers Johnson, a retired cold warrior who teaches at the University of California, has little doubt of how this 'American way' affects both national interest and safety. It is precisely these elements of American foreign policy that have generated the hatred of, and terrorism against, the United States, as he has argued in his trilogy of books: *Blowback*, *The Sorrows of Empire* and *Nemesis*.[8] In an interview on National Public Radio's *All Things Considered*, on 12 October 2001, Johnson explained the term 'blowback', coined by the CIA in the 1950s to refer to unintended consequences of covert operations that come back to haunt the United States. When the term was first used, it referred to the consequences of the CIA's attempted assassination of the then Iranian prime minister, Muhammad Mossadegh. 'The result of this egregious interference in the affairs of Iran was to bring the Shah to power and 25 years of repression and tyranny, leading finally to the holding of the entire US Embassy in Tehran hostage for over a year and the revolution of the Ayatollah Khomeini', said Johnson. The perpetual expansion of the 'American empire' and its 'overextended reach', he argued, was the root cause of 9-11 – an argument that could be made in 2001 yet has to be repudiated as offensive to the American psyche, good taste and serious political consideration when stated by Pastor Jeremiah Wright and replayed to the echo on YouTube in election season 2008.

The West Wing's definition of terrorism is much simpler: it's a product of intolerance motivated by inability to accept the programme's trademark recipe for all problems – pluralism. Pluralism, then, by its very nature is a threat to the existence of all those who strictly adhere to a system of law and practice that permits no deviation, that imposes totalitarian compliance. Those who adhere to these rigid systems are threatened not merely by the multicultural nature of American society, the existence of different faiths, races and ways of life openly practised side by side, but also by the ability to entertain a plurality of ideas on any given subject. Once again, stereotype overlays history and crowds out necessary information which it should be essential for an under-informed public to consider. The history of Muslim society and Islam as religion and law is founded on the toleration of plurality. Islam is intrinsically a pluralistic worldview, as much of its history illustrates so vividly. Moorish Spain, Spain under the rule of Muslims, was the golden age of Jewish Talmudic scholarship. When Spain was reconquered by the Most Catholic monarchs, Ferdinand and Isabella, the ethos of national racial purity required the expulsion of the Jews, who sought refuge in, and were embraced with open arms by, the Muslim Ottoman empire. The expulsion of the Jews was closely followed by Spain's expulsion of all Muslims. Pluralism, far from being an exclusive development of modern society, also has a history. One could add further that when the Crusaders captured and held Jerusalem, none but Christians were permitted to live there; while in the centuries before and after, under Muslim rule, the city was home to Christians, Jews and Muslims. The same plurality has been part of history across the Muslim world and in other parts of the non-West. It is no secret that ethnic tensions have been the 20th-century legacy in the so-called developing world. But it would be worth questioning what these humanitarian disasters owe to the legacy of colonial dispossession, the favouring of one group over another and the lack of flexibility that the modern nation state shows in accommodating traditional indigenous institutions and practices that previously sustained and peacefully mediated relations between different religions, cultures and identities. Nor has the developing world received much in the way of plurality in the policies of the US, which has sponsored uniform, one-size-fits-all prescriptions that have incited ethnic tensions and assaults, as argued so cogently by Amy Chua in her book *World on Fire*.[9] But such thoughts need not disturb the assurance of the civics class being conducted in the special episode of *The West Wing*.

The show does acknowledge that there is a problem in being a Muslim. This is demonstrated in the sub-plot, the questioning of Raqim Ali. This White House staffer with the same name as a wanted terrorist is an Arab American MIT graduate. He is bundled into an office, where he must answer for his father making a contribution to something called the Holy Land Defender, and for his participation in demonstrations protesting against the presence of American troops in Saudi Arabia. Ali explains that Saudi Arabia is home to Islam's two holiest sites, and that for him the real objective of American military intervention was protecting America's oil interest. But most of all, he objects to the double standards by which an army composed of women as well as men was sent 'to protect a Muslim dynasty where women aren't even allowed to drive a car!' Ali's objections prompt an immediate classic paternalist defence of American foreign policy in terms which are the essence of an imperialist mindset: Leo McGarry, the exceptionally nice Chief of Staff, responds, 'Maybe we can teach 'em.' There is, of course, scant evidence that the US has had much success in nurturing democratic and social change among its client states in the region. And it is certainly untrue that the only impetus for democracy and change in the Middle East comes from American tuition. On the contrary, dissident campaigners in American client states see American support for undemocratic and unrepresentative governments as the main impediment to change.

For all its liberal credentials, this sub-plot is unapologetic, explicit and emotive. Ali says that it's not uncommon for Arab Americans to be the first suspected 'when this kind of thing happens', and it's simply 'horrible'. Speaking for the masses, nice Leo retorts: 'I can't imagine why. No! I'm trying to figure out why anytime there's terrorist activity people always assume it's Arabs.' Then he works himself up to the clincher: 'It's the price you pay.' So there we have it. Being a Muslim has a price tag: an emotive ignorance that confuses Arab with Muslim, Middle East with terror (even though according to a 1997 report by the state department, terrorism originating from the Middle East is sixth in order of frequency), politics with religion, to generate the rationale for a scenario in which there is a real enemy within. Presumably, Ali must pay the same price as Japanese Americans who had the misfortune to have the face of the enemy during World War II and therefore could be interned and stripped of their property and livelihood for national security.

The sub-plot is abruptly terminated when the other Raqim Ali, the real suspect, is located in Germany, leaving the protagonist of these scenes – the nice, humane Leo – to contemplate what he has said. *The West Wing*, much like many of the foaming-at-the-mouth pundits and commentators, unreservedly declines to think of America's own history, as well as the history of its interaction with the world during the last five decades. Cosmic events, such as 9-11, do not allow you to be neutral. Cosmic events also beg for cosmic conclusions. In the closing segments of *The West Wing*, the civics class asks its final question: 'How did all this start?' By now, the First Lady has appeared in the Mess and it falls on her to come up with an answer which provides the title for this special episode: 'Isaac and Ishmael'. According to the First Lady, the problem begins with the Biblical story of Abraham and his sons. 'And so it began: the Jews, the sons of Isaac. The Arabs, the sons of Ishmael.' In which case, the attack on America is understood to be directly connected to the question of Israel, and the question of Israel is explained by a dispute with Biblical origins, a dispute that has stood through time to wreak havoc and disaster. If the dispute – far from being a territorial feud – is of Biblical origins and Biblical proportions, then it can hardly have a real political or policy-based solution. There is little that we – as individuals, Americans, people of the world – can do about it. This conventional repetition is the usual mis-statement of the Palestine/Israel dispute, whose more appropriate origins are to be found in the Balfour Declaration of 1917, the British mismanagement of its Mandate in Palestine from 1920 to 1948, and the operation of, and US support for, Israeli policy since the 1967 war. When history is simply abolished, the course suggested by Canadian justice minister Anne

McLennan – 'we have to honestly assess why we believe this is happening' and, if 'there is any necessity', to change our 'policy or approaches' – becomes redundant.[10] There is no necessity to change. When all is said and done, *The West Wing* refuses to confront the real issue and prefers to cop out.

The show ends with a final exhortation to the departing students to keep on entertaining more than one thought, precisely what the programme has avoided at every opportunity. The trouble is, thought without *information* does not advance understanding. It is the quality and accuracy of information, coupled with original thought, that unlocks meaning and provides potential answers to difficult problems. Whatever sensibilities *The West Wing* would like to believe it champions, the information at its disposal is the insurmountable flaw. This was not 'just television'. The logic and illogic, arguments and obfuscation, rationale and justification, history lessons, analysis, disinformation and gross stereotypes provided by *The West Wing* followed the same course as news coverage, commentary, analysis and debate in the real world. In this instance, the parallel reality was a mirror; it mirrored the premises and entrenched positions of America's policy, attitudes and self-image. What the virtual reflection makes clear is that the terms of debate are seen through a glass darkly, blurred, mis-shapen and imprecise. The limitations of America's national conversation propelled and incited as much as it supported without due scrutiny the Bush administration's response to 9-11.

CHAPTER TWO

'E Pluribus Unum'

According to the virtual wisdom of *The West Wing*, entertaining a plurality of ideas is deeply disturbing: it drives people crazy. In the real world it is America's failure to embrace plurality in its relations with the world that drives friend and foe crazy. The Ground Zero of America's foreign policy is constructed on a resilient consensus of national purpose, enshrined in potent national myths, effortlessly recycled and sold to a willing public. Buttressed by this self-image, America is resistant to criticism, its national conversation unwilling and unprepared to engage with readily available information, ideas or opinion that contradict its self-serving vision of reality. On Ground Zero, the wreckage of the Twin Towers, a single overarching narrative was swiftly erected to rationalise America's response to the attacks of 9-11. A global war on terror would be waged, military power would descend on Afghanistan as the prelude to a focus on an 'axis of evil' centred on Iran and personified in Iraq, designed to prevent the world's most dangerous weapons from falling into the hands of the world's worst regimes and the terrorists they sponsored. Victory by force of arms would allow America to seed a breeding ground of secular democracy that would transform the entire Middle East.

Why America has so spectacularly failed in this mission and how it confronts the problems of extracting itself from the debacle are interconnected questions. The project was designed to order the future with the hallmarks of the new American century. The Project for the New American Century, a Washington-based think tank, was founded in 1997 by, among others, Vice President Dick Cheney, Donald Rumsfeld, Paul Wolfowitz and Richard Perle. They regarded regime change in Iraq as fundamental to their plan. In a letter to President Clinton written in September 1998, they urged him to turn

> your Administration's attention to implementing a strategy for removing Saddam's regime from power. This will require a full complement of diplomatic, political and military efforts ... In any case, American policy cannot continue to be crippled by a misguided insistence on unanimity in the UN Security Council.[1]

The Director of the Project, William Kristol, explained that while this vision of the future began in Baghdad, it did not end there:

> ... it is clearly about more than Iraq. It is about more than the future of the Middle East and the war on terror. It is about what sort of role the US intends to play in the twenty-first century.[2]

As this future project falters and as politicians promise to retrieve America's global leadership from the morass, real change depends on a willingness to explore America's undiscovered country: its past. It is not that America is oblivious to the past – it is the source of imagery, a terrain filled with iconic heroes and mythic validation that sustains its vision of the future. What it is not is a territory mined for serious national debate of deeds done and their outcomes either at home or abroad. Yet scrutiny of America's past is vital to determining not only whether America can or will change, but how, and what most needs to change. Only by looking to its past can America appreciate how its current predicament arose and realise that it has faced such a predicament before. What better epitaph for America's bungling in Iraq than the conclusion: 'it was a mistake of judgement and a mistake of information.'[3] This assessment was written in 1958, before the nation committed itself to 'probably the greatest single error made by America in its history': the Vietnam war.[4] And long before the next error now generally described as the greatest in its history: the invasion of Iraq. The Ground Zero that America needs to reconnoitre is why it makes serial mistakes of judgement and information.

The 'mistake of judgement and mistake of information' was the self-diagnosis of a fictional character in *The Ugly American*, a novel as thinly veiled examination of the realities of America's policies and presence in South-East Asia. It was published in 1958, before America committed increasing numbers of 'special advisors' to Vietnam, to be succeeded by hundreds of thousands of conscript soldiers. *The Ugly American* should have been required reading for all American politicians, administrators and policy advisers in the days after 9-11. Had they stopped to ponder its moral, we might have been spared exactly the same mistakes being recounted by Rajiv Chandrasekaran in his 2007 tale of American administration inside Baghdad's Green Zone: *Imperial Life in the Emerald City*.[5]

What makes these two books required reading is not the simple parallels, though they are striking, but the insight they provide into the consistent features of America's approach to the rest of the world. Together they detail the attitudes and ideas that go into the formation of policy and that provide the context of debate that make errors of judgement and information the most likely outcome. What made the war in Iraq inevitable were systemic mistakes generated over decades. It was the culmination of a process; not the purblind mismanagement of one ideologically driven administration, but a function of the characteristic practice of American government, governance and society. Iraq is a military, political, economic and cultural error, a hyperpower failure. It is a prime example of what we call the hamburger syndrome, the way American power is processed into a conveniently dispensed package deal.

The 'ugly American' has become shorthand for how this package deal operates. But, like calling monsters 'Frankenstein', it is a misnomer, a tribute to how sloppily bestselling books are read. The monster has no name; it is the creation of Dr Frankenstein. Rather than demonstrating all that is wrong with America's attitude to the world, the character called the ugly American is the moral heart of the novel – the one who gets it right. He is a good-hearted, sensible, modest but highly success-ful hands-on engineer from the American heartland. He is effec-tive at winning hearts and minds because he concentrates on genuine transfer of appropriate technology that solves the real problems of ordinary people in far-away places by working alongside them, empowering them without imposing upon their society or culture. With his ugly, pudgy hands and dirty finger-nails, this American instinctively knows the right way forward – as dramatically as Dr Frankenstein leaves the path of reason, seduced by his arrogance.

Appropriately, the errors of judgement and information, whether in South-East Asia or the Middle East, in the pages of *The Ugly American* or *Imperial Life in the Emerald City*, begin with history. In both cases it is not that information about the history and culture of South-East Asia or the Middle East is unknown, but that the plurality of readily available information which should be an essential part of debate and scrutiny of policy is ignored. Among the first characters we meet in *The Ugly American* is John Colvin, an OSS officer parachuted into South-East Asia during World War II to organise resistance to the Japanese. To prepare for his mission he learns the native language, and through his work with the locals he learns to appreciate their culture and philosophy. After the war, he reads repeatedly that the country he served in has become a potential domino in the communist onslaught. He feels the situation must be being handled badly and writes long letters to his congress-man, who in return politely assures him that his views have been forwarded to the state department: 'But the policy of the United States did not change.'[6]

In Vietnam the situation was just so. Ho Chi Minh confided to an OSS agent that he would welcome 'a million American soldiers ... but no French' because, as the agent reported to the secretary of state, the Vietnamese were 'determined to maintain their independence [from France] even at the cost of their lives', since 'they have nothing to lose and all to gain'.[7] Indeed, anyone who cared to could read the terms in which Ho Chi Minh declared Vietnamese independence on 2 September 1945. It had a familiar ring:

> 'All men are created equal. They are endowed by their Creator with certain inalienable rights, among these are Life, Liberty, and the pursuit of Happiness' ... In a broader sense, this means: All the peoples on the earth are equal from birth, all the peoples have a right to live, to be happy and free ...
>
> We are convinced that the Allied nations which at Tehran and San Francisco have acknowledged the principles of self-determination and equality of nations, will not refuse to acknowledge the independence of Vietnam. A people who have courageously opposed French domination for more than eighty years, a people who have fought side by side with the Allies against the Fascists during these last years, such a people must be free and independent.[8]

The declaration denounced the inglorious, indeed deplorable record of French colonialism, and announced the end of monarchy and the beginning of a state not averse to elections but most of all determined to improve the lives of the population.

But it was not what the Allies who met at Tehran and San Francisco had in mind at all. In the aftermath of the defeat of Japan in 1945, the British were charged with responsibility for

Vietnam south of the 16th parallel. They reoccupied, established martial law, rearmed French and Japanese POWs to resist their erstwhile allies the Viet Minh, and opened the way for the restoration of French rule. Britain's Labour government, elected by a landslide in 1945, was committed to granting independence to India, but elsewhere – in Malaya, Burma, Vietnam and Indonesia – they worked to overthrow emerging independent states in favour of what foreign secretary Ernest Bevin described as 'the jolly old empire'.[9] Vietnam's struggle for independence had to be resumed and the Vietnamese turned for support to Russia and China.

Did support from communist Russia and communist China for the communist-led Viet Minh make Vietnam the vanguard of an oncoming tide inimical to America's national security and vital national interests that had to be stopped by all means, including force of arms? History suggests otherwise. The battle was not ideological but nationalist. In the words of General Vo Nguyen Giap, strategist of the military defeat of both the French and Americans, 'Our profoundest ideology, the pervasive feeling of our people is patriotism.' As the historian Stanley Karnow explains, Vietnam had been a battleground for thousands of years and revered 'real or mythical heroes and heroines who resisted foreign intruders, chiefly the Chinese'.[10] Even more significantly, the most recent examination of American policy on the path to war in Vietnam by Gareth Porter argues that successive American administrations were well aware that neither Russia nor China was capable of, nor committed to, openly entering the conflict on the side of the Vietnamese.[11] It was southern communists, victims of the repression of the Diem government installed and ultimately overthrown by the US, who forced the hand of the North Vietnamese. After the Korean war, fear of American power led both Russia and China to 'give up their previous policy of backing revolutionary struggles'.[12] Also, it persuaded the North Vietnamese to contemplate an almost open-ended continuation of a South Vietnamese regime in anticipation of eventual elections throughout the entire country, as set out in the Geneva Accords of 1954. The decision, by secretary of state John Foster Dulles, to abrogate America's commitment to these elections, knowing they would result in a victory for the communists, was predicated on what Porter calls the 'perils of dominance': American confidence that it could exert its power without fear of a general escalation and could even exploit the weakness and rivalry between Russia and China to its own advantage:

> One lesson of the path to war in Vietnam, however, is that war is much more likely to arise ... from conflicts involving the vigorous assertion by the United States of its power interests abroad, even in the absence of an overt challenge by another state.[13]

In which case, Porter asks whether war is most likely to arise not from states seeking to change the international balance of power, or disturb a regional status quo, but from the tendency of the United States to extend its power and influence too far and thereby provoke greater resistance and hostility to US power.[14]

The facts of Vietnam's history were easily available to successive American governments. They were collated into a report commissioned for the Pentagon in 1967 by secretary of defence Robert McNamara. But, instead of becoming the basis on which America debated its policy and involvement in Vietnam, history was obliterated by an illusory strategic framework. Successive presidents and innumerable politicians and pundits invoked the domino theory: as goes Vietnam so goes the whole of Asia, like a cascade of dominoes falling into the communist camp. Public debate was structured around this fear factor, the epic struggle with the 'evil empire' of the global communist conspiracy. The specifics of each situation, the history and dynamics of each country, were obliterated by a single soundbite, a headline-sized concept that could be sold to a public already made fearful of the 'red menace'. Yet despite frequent recourse to this image in their public pronouncements, Gareth Porter shows that no president actually believed this favoured scare story. The greatest problem for presidents from Eisenhower to Johnson was contending with their own national security bureaucracy who, in concert with the political and public mood, planned and sought to operate as if the scare theory were fact. The facts of three decades of growing US involvement in Vietnam did not enter the public domain until 1971, when Daniel Ellsberg leaked the contents of the so-called Pentagon Papers and they were reported in the *New York Times*. And 40 years on, there is still a sizeable section of American opinion which rejects the validity of the counter-arguments of history.

Yet, if detailed facts were not common currency, the American public could glean a fictional paraphrase of the plurality of attitudes in *The Ugly American*. For example, Prince Nyong, a minister in the invented country of Sarkhan, presents a common attitude to the Cold War context among citizens of the Third World when he observes:

> 'We don't want to be in the camp of either of these nations. What we desire is Sarkhan's independence and development. This means that we'll take aid and assistance from anyone who will help us, but not at any price. And not at the price of the loss of our independence.'[15]

The desire for independence, the freedom to make one's own mistakes even, is not an impenetrable objective. But it is one which resonates most strongly in countries that have experienced colonisation. Where colonisation has been imposed by a radically different culture convinced of its own superiority and bent on remaking the identity and even humanity of its colonised charges, the will to resist and determination to oppose can be adamantine. Only imperial hubris can render it invisible.

The historical evidence of such a basic proposition in fact or fiction, now long known, has had no perceptible role in shaping public debate about the subsequent course and workings of American foreign policy.

No country has more history than Iraq, the land that was the cradle of agriculture, urbanisation, writing and much more. Yet the invasion of Iraq was planned for and undertaken in indefatigable, wilful ignorance of its history, ancient or modern, and the influence of history on the attitudes of the Iraqi people. The point is examined in detail by the American scholar and founding director of the Center for Middle Eastern Studies at the University of Chicago, William R. Polk,[16] and with forensic precision by *Guardian* journalist Jonathan Steele in his book *Defeat*.[17] What America, with its profusion of Middle East Area Studies specialists, chose not to know should certainly have been obvious to Britain, which created, organised and administered the modern state of Iraq at the end of World War I; and thereby encountered determined ongoing Iraqi resistance.

The modern map of the Middle East is a contrivance manufactured from two projects for future nation-building devised by imperial powers: the Sykes-Picot agreement and the Balfour Declaration. While World War I was under way, Sir Mark Sykes and Monsieur Picot, representatives of Britain and France, reached their agreement to carve the lands of the Ottoman empire into respective spheres of influence, largely based on their countries' pre-existing regional interests. In 1917, Arthur Balfour, ex-prime minister serving as foreign secretary to the war cabinet, acquiesced to the lobbying of Lord Rothschild and committed Britain to establishing a national home for the Jews in Palestine. Iraq was in Britain's sphere. It was created from the amalgamation of three Ottoman provinces, Baghdad, Basra and Mosul, with the notable subtraction of Kuwait, a small sheikhdom on the Persian Gulf that was part of Basra province but where Britain had long been cultivating its special interests.

From the mid-18th century, Iraq had been an important

stepping stone, part of a quick communication route between Britain and its major imperial possession, India. On the outbreak of World War I, Britain immediately invaded Basra with a force drawn from its Indian army. In 1917, as they moved north, the force became trapped at Kut, where there followed one of the most ignominious defeats in British military history. It made little impression on public memory, probably because most of the troops were sepoys, Indian servicemen. By the end of the war Britain's principal interest in the region was oil, which the Anglo Persian Petroleum Company was exploiting in Persia and Kuwait. President Woodrow Wilson's high-sounding 'fourteen points', embracing the ideal of self-determination, were not meant to extend beyond Europe, a bitter lesson learned by the Middle Eastern representatives at the post-war convention. When oil was discovered in Iraq in 1927, the terms of the British Mandate, confirmed by the League of Nations, ensured that the province of Mosul would remain part of Iraq. It also ensured that Britain and America took an increasingly close interest in the country.

Britain set about administering Iraq according to the playbook of its imperial history. It disbanded the Ottoman-elected municipal councils. Then it creatively re-imagined the history and ethnography of the 'natural order' of the country, as it had done in India and elsewhere. It distributed subsidies to 'chiefs', conferring on them a status they had never previously enjoyed. It completely reordered the land distribution, effectively making those who cultivated the land serfs while granting ownership to their favoured 'chiefs' and urban merchants. Iraq was made a grossly inegalitarian society according to an imagined idea of what a pre-modern society ought to be, complete with an elite class with the makings of a European-style feudal aristocracy. Britain could then rely upon the dependent and compliant elites it had created to protect its interests while it operated its preferred colonial system of indirect rule. Britain would be the power behind the throne that was the effective voice of command.

Iraq had no monarchy. So Britain supplied it with one. Their choice was the Hashemite Prince Feisal of Mecca, in what is today Saudi Arabia. Feisal, made famous by his association with the exotic self-publicist T. E. 'Lawrence of Arabia', had been a leader of the Arab revolt against the Turks. Making him king of Iraq, a country where he was little known and had no obvious ties, was a convenient solution to Britain's Feisal problem. The French had refused to have him as king of their mandated new nation, Syria, which Feisal's Arab revolt had liberated on behalf of the allies. Meanwhile, the oriental secretary to the British civil commissioner in Iraq, Gertrude Bell, was championing her strategy for remaking Iraq. Her predilection was for Britain to work with the largely urban and Sunni nationalists to create a modernised Iraq. Her objective was to end the power of the Shia religious hierarchy, which she considered obscurantist, over the community which constituted 60 per cent of the population.

For Iraqis this new colonial order was confusing. They were perplexed by the variety of opinions they encountered in the small world of British officialdom in Baghdad, and uncertain about their implications for the future or how best to exploit the differences, as Charles Tripp has argued.[18] By the 1920s, perplexity had become open revolt, which Britain proceeded to counter with military vigour. The colonial secretary, Winston Churchill, had a definite opinion on how to deal with resistance. He advocated aerial bombardment of the insurgents using poison gas: 'I am strongly in favour of using poison gas against uncivilised tribes', he wrote.[19] The only reason his proposal was not carried out was the lack of appropriate technology at the RAF base in Habbaniyah, situated near the outskirts of Fallujah, the city which would later be the recipient of American overwhelming force, including the use of alleged chemical weaponry, after the invasion of 2003. But Britain did make liberal use of aerial bombardment of Iraqi insurgents in a brutal campaign of suppression. It prompted the then secretary for war, Sir Laming

Worthington-Evans, to issue a cautionary note which, eight decades later, the Americans would have done well to consider:

> If the Arab population realized that the peaceful control of Mesopotamia ultimately depends on our intention of bombing women and children, I'm very doubtful if we shall gain that acquiescence of the fathers and husbands of Mesopotamia to which the Secretary of State for the Colonies looks forward.[20]

Before the British invasion of 1918, Iraq had never been a single nation in the modern European sense. But that did not mean it was devoid of complex identities, politics or civil society, or not rich in collective historic experience. One might say that Iraqis have more experience of being overrun by – and observing the rise and fall of – empires than any other people on earth. Devising strategies to deal with invasions, and when appropriate oppose them, is the warp and weft of its history, as Polk argues. Iraq is the ground over which claimants for regional influence have always contended. Any Western power intervening in Iraq would be well advised to inform itself about the influence of history on the attitudes of the Iraqi people. The evidence, however, shows that Britain and America preferred to invent their own versions of what Iraqis ought to think and feel, rather than consult expertise and opinion that was readily available.

History made Iraq part of the Muslim *ummah*, the worldwide community of believers, and then of the Arab nation, the modern politico-linguistic interconnection of regional nationalist movements that shapes popular sentiment, 'the Arab street', as it overarches the boundaries of individual countries. Within and beyond its boundaries, Iraq is part of a peculiar sensitivity to invasion, colonialism and their legacy. As Muhammad Heikal, doyen of Arab journalism and noted historian, explained in the aftermath of the Persian Gulf war of 1990:

> History's influence in creating what the West says is an over-suspicious Arab attitude to Western involvement was much stronger than most people in the West realised ... the crusader, the colonist, the mercenary and the spy have all made their mark on Arab attitudes.[21]

Britain's colonial involvement in Iraq did a great deal to foster the strength of such anti-Western sentiment. Exerting its influence through the constitutional monarchy and the social order it had constructed produced endemic political instability in Iraq. Eventually, it led to the bloodbath of 1958. The young king and his uncle, the regent, were gunned down in an army coup that brought General Abdul Karim Qasim to power. Britain, just two years after the Suez debacle, had no stomach for invading Iraq yet again and retired from the scene. Its residual interest was to preserve the independence of Kuwait, to which British troops were despatched in 1961, when the sheikhdom formally declared its independence, before handing over to the Arab League.

The stage was set for America to become the dominant Western influence in the region. One clear lesson that Iran and Iraq provided for the US was the fallacy of a global communist conspiracy. In 1953 the CIA engineered the overthrow of the elected Iranian leader Muhammad Mossadegh, reinstalled the Shah and thereafter worked with him to ferret out members of the communist-controlled Tudeh party. Even when the Shah and his American backers moved to eliminate the Tudeh party, Russia refused to support its attempts to organise popular resistance. In 1958, in response to the coup in Iraq, America landed troops in Lebanon as a show of force in the Middle East. President Eisenhower did so having discounted the probability of any Soviet military reaction. Indeed, Russia denounced the Iraqi communists who sought representation in Qasim's government as 'irresponsible', even as Qasim arrested and murdered hundreds of rank-and-file members of the Communist party.

What concerned Ike, however, was the 'attitude of the people in the area' towards US intervention.[22] A wise concern, the 'attitude' was never difficult to discover, though it seems, nevertheless, to have remained a permanent mystery to successive American administrations.

In default of consulting local opinion, America continued to pursue the objective of its Basic National Security Policy, adopted in 1955, of destroying the effectiveness of the communist apparatus in the free world, which would rest largely on the action of local governments, 'although the United States should be able to help significantly through covert means'.[23] In 1959, Qasim switched from killing communists to using them to counter the influence of the Ba'ath party, and opened relations with the USSR. The CIA helped significantly by supporting a bungled assassination plot. Its members included 'a young, then unknown man from Tikrit, Saddam Hussein'.[24] Saddam was secreted out of Iraq and around the Middle East, allegedly under the auspices of the CIA, before returning to resume a career based on the use of brute force. Relentlessly, Saddam negotiated the eddies and cross-currents of Iraqi politics to achieve sole power.

Polk identifies the political strands at work in Iraq and across the region as: pan-Arabist sentiment, *qawmiyah*; straightforward nationalism, *wataniyah*; and a third force, the influence of various Islamic movements, such as the Egyptian-founded Sunni *Ikhwan al Muslimeen*, the Muslim Brotherhood, and the Shia *ad-Dawwah*, the Call. None of these tendencies was restricted to a particular country. Indeed, they were not even mutually exclusive ideas, frequently being used as alternate postures according to circumstance and operating as cross-fertilising ideals that influenced governments and popular opinion across the whole of the Middle East. All were fuelled by a desire for autonomy and by resentment, often surly and suppressed, of foreign influence which everywhere seemed to restrain the rekindling of the region's historic glories. All made independence and development central political themes, but the different tendencies also often produced deep factional differences on how and by whom these could or should be delivered. In Iraq they were further complicated by the Kurdish factions, often contending with each other and forming various alliances with and then against neighbouring states as well as successive governments in Baghdad. All of which had the effect of making Iraq the most complex nation in the region.

In 1963 a group of army officers calling themselves the National Council of the Revolutionary Command, and assisted by the CIA, overthrew Qasim's government. They secured their position, again with CIA help, through a purge that killed 'hundreds or perhaps thousands of members of Qasim's regime'.[25] A few months later, after a coup within the coup, sole power was wielded by Colonel Abdus-Salam Arif. A thorough authoritarian, Arif formed what became the Republican Guard, charged with the task of deterring anyone from conspiring against him. It did not prevent an attempted coup in September 1965, but what finally finished him was a helicopter crash in 1966. He was succeeded by his brother, Abdur-Rahman Arif, whose failure to assist other Arab states in the 1967 war with Israel provoked widespread demonstrations. This opened the way for the Ba'ath party. With the help of the United States, the Ba'ath engineered a bloodless coup while the commander of the Republican Guard was overseas.

Initially only a small part of a revolutionary coalition, the Ba'ath had to build a power base for their regime. The task fell to Saddam Hussein, who at first appeared a minor follower of General Hassan al Bakr, the president, prime minister and secretary general of the Ba'ath party, and chairman of the Revolutionary Command Council. Polk explains that Saddam made it his job to know the 'name, rank, and serial number' of virtually every adult Iraqi. This was only the first step. By using patronage and appointment to official positions, he sought to align virtually the entire adult Iraqi population with what was initially only a small cadre of Ba'athists. 'All could be co-opted, bribed, or if necessary, frightened into becoming partisans ... Saddam's single unifying aim was neither organisation nor ideology – he wavered as danger or opposition demanded ... His aim was power.'[26] By the time he pushed General Bakr aside in 1979, Saddam had made the Ba'ath a mass political party, which he then ruthlessly used to maintain his hold on absolute power.

All the phases of revolutionary Iraqi history were concerned with rejecting and rolling back the hated legacy of imperialism. Colonialism was not merely an affront to historic pride; it was also an impediment to genuine development, in Iraq and the Middle East generally as much as elsewhere across the Third World. When the Ba'ath gained control they abolished the British land settlement, and within a few years a quarter of a million farmers received sufficient land to support a family. Provision of free health and education transformed living standards. They continued tinkering with the oil concessions to foreign-owned companies, begun by previous regimes, to increase Iraq's income. After studying the problem, in 1972 Saddam proposed and pushed through the nationalisation of Iraqi oil, the most popular move he ever made. Enormously increased oil revenues made possible the virtual remaking of Iraqi society. Vast new infrastructure projects were undertaken; there was modernisation and expansion of the armed forces. Schools, universities, hospitals, factories, theatres and museums proliferated; employment became so universal that a labour shortage developed. 'Iraq was on its way to becoming the most advanced of Arab states.'[27]

But the dream of a new golden age did not last. In September 1980 the eight long years of the Iran–Iraq war began. The causes of the war are insignificant compared with the context and the fact that it provided the opportunity for America to 'help significantly, chiefly through covert means', both sides to keep fighting. The Iranian revolution of 1979 which overthrew the Shah, considered its strongest regional ally, had taken America completely by surprise. A revolution fomented by an octogenarian Shia cleric that unleashed popular support for an Islamic state had occurred entirely beyond the scope of its intelligence radar, or comprehension. The new regime headed by Ayatollah Khomeini, along with Iranian society generally, had deep suspicion and fear of American interference. For its part, America urgently needed a counterweight to the perceived scourge of Islamic fundamentalism, and in the former protégé of its intelligence community, Saddam Hussein, and his secular nationalist Ba'ath party, they seemed to have an ideal candidate in just the right place. As the war dragged on, Saddam received from America satellite images of Iranian troop deployments, he was supplied with arms, and lent or given money and foodstuffs without which the Iraqi economy would have collapsed. To underline the Reagan administration's identification with the Iraqi cause, Donald Rumsfeld visited Baghdad in December 1983, eager for friendly business and government relations, according to the declassified minutes.[28] The following month Iraq was removed from the 'terrorist list' and Iran was added.

> President Reagan had instructed government officials to do whatever was 'necessary and legal' to prevent Iraq from losing the war. To this end, the United States either supplied directly or arranged for others to supply conventional weapons, cluster bombs, anthrax and other biological weapons materials as well as components for nuclear weapons and equipment to manufacture poison gas.[29]

By the time of Rumsfeld's visit, Iraq had already used poison gas against Iranian forces in the almost static trench warfare that stretched along the border between the two countries which constituted the battlefield. No reference is made to the subject of poison gas in the minutes of Rumsfeld's visit. Nor was there any great international outcry until 1988 when the notorious aerial gas attack on the Kurdish town of Halabja, which occurred after the Iranians had overrun the area, was widely reported.

During the war the US navy was deployed to the Persian Gulf, where its actions went beyond protecting shipping in the 'tanker war'. It destroyed the Iranian navy, and shot down an Iranian civilian passenger airliner. In 1985 Iran, subject to an international weapons embargo, made a secret request to buy arms from America. President Reagan, anxious for Iran's help in gaining the release of American hostages in Lebanon, agreed. Before the story was broken by a Lebanese newspaper, *Al Shiraa*, some 1,500 missiles had been shipped to Iran. Of the $30 million Iran paid for its weapons, $18 million was diverted to fund the Contra guerrillas, the force that the US helped significantly by covert means to train, and which it funded to oppose the Sandinista government of Nicaragua.

The Iran–Iraq war was a protracted stalemate which both sides lost at enormous cost in blood and treasure. It saddled Iraq with huge debts, undermined its economy and stalled the progress of development. Saddam was in urgent need of money and turned his attention to where money oozed from the ground: Kuwait. A street corner thug Saddam might be, but his principal focus was regional politics, aspiring to be a colossus in the mould of Gamal Abdul Nasser, or a new Salah ed Din al Ayyubi, the medieval hero who hailed from his home town of Tikrit. The 12th-century leader, better known to the West as Saladin, had succeeded in uniting Arab forces to retake Jerusalem from the Crusaders and founded a dynasty that ruled Egypt, Palestine and much of Syria. By repatriating Kuwait, Saddam would wipe away the last vestige of imperialism. He was returning to a policy embraced even by Iraq's constitutional monarchs and by all subsequent regimes, a policy which had great popular support among Iraqis. Iraq not only laid territorial claim to the sheikhdom, but accused it of illegally siphoning oil from the Iraqi Rumailah oilfield and exceeding its OPEC quota, thus keeping world oil prices artificially low, and thereby impoverishing Iraq. But Saddam's career had been shaped by the realities of American influence and its significant help through covert means. So, before moving against Kuwait, he took the precaution of consulting the opinion of the Bush Snr administration.

As Saddam moved his troops up to the Kuwaiti border, a state department spokesman, asked if America planned to defend Kuwait, said: 'We do not have any defence treaties with Kuwait, and there are no special defence or security commitments to Kuwait.'[30] To make doubly sure, Saddam consulted American ambassador April Glaspie, who repeated the instruction from Washington that America took no position on frontier disputes among Arab states. On 2 August 1990 Saddam's troops crossed the border; 24 hours later he was master of Kuwait, and in the eye of an international storm that finally conferred on him the official status of monster in American public opinion.

Operation Desert Storm was mounted as an international coalition backed by UN Security Council resolutions, but led by US military forces prudentially applying all the lessons derived from their Vietnam experience. It was the kind of war the American military understood: limited and clear objectives, fought on open terrain suitable for large-scale manoeuvres by tanks, supported by overwhelming force against an overmatched enemy whose command and control infrastructure could be smashed to smithereens. Victory was unequivocal. The ground offensive lasted a matter of days during which the retreating Iraqi army endured a 'turkey shoot' on the 'road of death'. Polk estimates that Iraqi loss of life was 'immense: perhaps ten thousand civilians and thirty thousand Iraqi soldiers were killed. Proportional to the population that was more than five times the casualties suffered by America in the Vietnam war.'[31] For the American military this was a good war, a vindication of their rebuilding post-Vietnam. For America it was a good war, a defensible cause with international legitimacy that cost few American casualties – and with coalition partners picking up the bill, America even made a small profit.

Victory, however, created its own quandary. Having branded Saddam a monster in the mould of Hitler and likened his regime to the Nazis, America stopped well short of insistence on total surrender. There was no push for Baghdad. The overthrow of this pariah regime would have to rest largely on the action of the local population. President Bush was reported as saying:

> There is another way for the bloodshed to stop, and that is for the Iraqi military and the Iraqi people to take matters into their own hands, to force Saddam Hussein to step aside.[32]

In his book *A World Transformed*, Bush Snr explained: 'Had we gone the invasion route, the United States could conceivably still be an occupying power in a bitterly hostile land.'[33]

Both the Shia in the south and the Kurds in the north responded to Bush's invitation to undertake regime change. Quickly and bloodily, they found that they would not be helped significantly either by covert or overt means by America. While conscripted Iraqi troops had been devastated, the elite Republican Guard had eluded the Americans. Stormin' Norman, General Schwarzkopf, defended Iraqi weapons dumps to prevent them falling into the hands of Shia rebels and permitted Iraqi helicopter gunships to operate against poorly armed and poorly organised civilians with impunity and murderous effect. The *intifada* was put down with horrific brutality as American forces stood idly by. In the north, the Kurds too were amazed at the speed with which the Iraqi army was able to deploy and retake all the major centres. With fresh memories of Halabja in 1988, the Kurds had reason to fear what might come next. Half the Kurdish population began to flee, only to find the borders with neighbouring countries closed. A major humanitarian outcry was raised as they huddled in mountain fastnesses. Ostensibly to protect humanitarian relief flights, a no-fly zone north of the 36th parallel was established in April 1991. Belatedly, four months later, a further no-fly zone was declared south of the 36th parallel.

The Gulf war ought to have made clear that Saddam had precious little intention of employing weapons of mass destruction against anyone capable of retaliating like for like – that was not the kind of thug Saddam was. The cocktail of antidotes to potential chemical and nerve agents injected into coalition troops, along with the effects of depleted uranium shells they used on the battlefield (the long-denied Gulf war syndrome), did more harm than anything unleashed by Saddam. But America had reason to be concerned about Saddam's potential to use the facilities to produce chemical, biological and nuclear weapons that it had helped him acquire. The removal of weapons of mass destruction (WMD) became the basis of the sanctions and inspection regime imposed on Iraq by Security Council Resolution no. 687. Iraqi assets abroad were frozen, and imports and exports were banned except for medical supplies and certain foods. The administration of the boycott, which in 1995 became the 'Oil for Food' programme, did not prevent Saddam from acquiring weapons, but it succeeded in pauperising the Iraqi population. Its continuation year after year eroded earlier development and ended by making the entire population more dependent on Saddam and his regime than ever before. The nationwide rationing system of heavily subsidised basics which Saddam implemented was essential to the survival of Iraqis in the face of the collapse of the economy, whose infrastructure was devastated by war and starved of investment in reconstruction, compounded by the impossibility of getting spare parts or new equipment of any kind, since everything could be deemed by American and British officials to have potential dual use. The condition of the Iraqi people on the eve of America's 2003 invasion was no mystery. It is recorded in graphic detail in Dilip Hiro's 2003 book, *Iraq: A Report From the Inside*.[34] The effect that the sanctions regime had on the attitude of the people within Iraq and across the Middle East was not hard to gauge. Tyrannical and brutal as Saddam's regime was, Iraqis were not lacking in historical memory, nor did they have reason to demur from the attitudes openly expressed by Arab writers and politicians. The opinion of Ghassan Salame, a Lebanese minister who became an advisor to the UN in Iraq in 2003, writing in 1982, had resonance throughout the region and particular meaning for Iraqis:

> The US, as an essential part of a totally hostile world system, played a central role in stealing the Arab's oil at rock bottom prices for years. The US played with Arab destinies on a daily basis, sometimes imposing rulers who do not enjoy the confidence of their people, and defending others who had lost that confidence. Washington considered the whole region as an arena for its soldiers and its gluttonous corporations. It continuously plundered the region's resources, threatened to interfere, broke wills and brandished sanctions. Over the last four decades, Washington has played a key role – and regrettably an effective one – in smashing the unity of Arab opinion and positions whenever Arab unity was on the point of establishing itself. This happened with Eisenhower's plan for the Arabs, with Kissinger, and the two Camp David agreements.[35]

The histories of Vietnam and Iraq are not secret; even the covert connections were rumoured, reported and available for consideration. What was lacking was a lively public curiosity to discover and debate the plurality of opinions created and affected by history. History consists of the record of events differently experienced, differently remembered, which affect and influence the attitudes of peoples differently. History, examined for a plurality of perspectives, can and should provide the information on which reasoned debate and informed judgements are made. It is, in the final analysis, the only way to achieve the insight recommended in Robbie Burns' old line: 'to see ourselves as others see us.' But as *The Ugly American* and *Imperial Life in the Emerald City* demonstrate, this has not been the American way, any more than it has been the way of any imperial power in history. The exercise of overwhelming power invites that most subtle of the perils of dominance: to listen only to the opinions of those dependent on your patronage who tell you what you want to hear, to discount the views of the generality of people, and to see the world from the vantage point of one's ability to manufacture and manipulate history to one's own ends. But, as so many imperial powers have learned to their cost, dominance in and of itself cannot obliterate history entirely. And history, even among the overmatched, can find ways to debunk and derail the fondest delusions of imperial arrogance.

America is a nation built on the conviction that it is the last best hope of mankind, the future for all people. It is a self-image conducive to indifference towards other people's history and culture, an insulating justification for seeing the world only through the perspective of American interests. But confidence that if the American way is good enough for America then it must be good enough for everyone is hardly a recipe for appreciating the significance of opinions expressed by other people far from home. There is nothing inherently wrong with self-belief; the question is whether and to what degree it results in systemic patterns of behaviour and policies which prepare the way for hostility and failure. The Asian characters in *The Ugly American* explain the variety of ways in which the gamut of American policy and behaviour affronts their intelligence, ignores their sensitivities and confounds their legitimate interests to foster resentment. U Maung Swe, described as the best-known journalist in Burma, defines the problem thus:

A mysterious change comes over Americans when they go to a foreign land. They isolate themselves socially. They live pretentiously. They're loud and ostentatious. Perhaps they're frightened and defensive; or maybe they're not properly trained and make mistakes out of ignorance.[36]

The novel explores the ways in which grand strategy is mirrored in individual mistakes of ignorance that contribute to a systemic failure. There is the American ambassador who holds receptions where only American liquor is served, while local Buddhists and Muslims drink only fruit juice or water. Hence the people who might provide insight into the attitude of the people do not attend. Meanwhile Joe Bing, the quintessential loud American, assures recruits to the foreign service that they will eat the same food on their postings in Asia as they do at home. And what's more:

'We don't expect you to learn the native language. Translators are a dime a dozen overseas. And besides, it's better to make Asians learn English. Helps them too. Most of the foreigners you'll do business with speak perfect English.'[37]

Forty years on in the Green Zone in Baghdad, Chandrasekaran reports that the canteen in the Republican Palace headquarters, the only place that all the Iraqi secretaries and translators had to eat in, served nothing but standard American fare heavy on the bacon, sausage, hot dogs and pork chops – which Muslims do not eat. Even before security became a reason for huddling behind the blast walls, the hordes of neophyte Americans serving abroad were incredulous that anyone ventured beyond the 'Emerald City' which provided them with all the bars, discos and even souvenir shops they desired. And just as before, they felt no need to learn the language. The Baker Hamilton Report on American policy in Iraq noted that of the 1,000 American staff serving in its Baghdad embassy, its largest in the world, only six were fluent in Arabic.[38] Language is the passport to the kind of conversations that reveal the attitudes of the people. But

Americans in the Green Zone got their news of events in Iraq 'by watching Fox News and reading *Stars and Stripes* which was printed in Germany and flown daily to Baghdad'.[39]

> Veteran diplomats, who had worked in the Arab world or worked in post-conflict situations, wanted local cuisine in the dining room, a respect for local traditions and a local workforce. But they were in the minority.[40]

In fact most Coalition Provisional Authority (CPA) staff had never worked outside the US before; more than half were estimated to have acquired their first-ever passport in order to travel to Iraq. So perhaps one should not be too surprised by a conversation between one American staffer and an Iraqi worker about a forthcoming holiday. The festival of Eid al Fitr marks the end of the Muslim fasting month of Ramadan and is the biggest celebration in the Islamic calendar. Asked when this would occur, the Iraqi duly replied that he didn't know. Islam observes a lunar calendar, and despite the fact that calculation of the phases of the moon is a sophisticated science pioneered by Muslim scientists of the classical era, by tradition the day of Eid is announced based on actual sighting of the new moon by religious authorities. Depending on circumstances, the Eid can occur one day early or one day late and everyone eagerly anticipates the announcement. The American staffer, without asking for explanation, exploded: 'This is stupid. This is in a week and you don't know when you're going to celebrate it?' Or there was the experience of the US citizen of Lebanese descent who, when asked by one of CPA chief Paul Bremer's top aides what his religion was, replied 'Muslim'. 'Oh, you're a Muslim? But you're not like a terrorist are you?'[41]

The systemic failure highlighted by these vignettes emerges from the inward-looking self-absorption of Americans, their focus on American concerns and interests rather than on empowering other peoples' local aspirations in appropriate ways. So, *The*

Ugly American portrays an American ambassador as a political appointee more concerned about getting a judgeship back home in the US and about how his performance will be viewed in Washington, than with understanding the internal politics of the country where he serves. He is content to work with and through those dependent on and helped significantly by America. Or there is the case of a dedicated and diligent congressional visitor who, nevertheless, encounters the prudential interest of the local American embassy in ensuring that he sees only their authorised version of facts. And most of all there is a system of interest in foreign affairs rooted firmly in American national self-interest, commercial and political, that is keenly attuned to American electoral calculations. As Joe Colvin discovered, and as *Imperial Life* demonstrates, despite the facts that could be discovered on foreign ground, 'the policy of the United States did not change'.

In Iraq, the CPA administration headed by Paul Bremer worked to a script authored by neo-con verities: Iraq was to be remade as a bastion of free-market democracy. This outcome would be secured by applying American standards and American systems, whether appropriate and desired by Iraqis or not. The recruitment process for US personnel to work in Iraq had a great deal more to do with their political loyalties and Republican connections than their qualifications. Job interviews were either negligible or more concerned with eliciting their opinion on *Roe v. Wade*, the Supreme Court ruling that underpins a woman's right to an abortion, than details of their professional experience. Youngsters, just out of college with no experience, found themselves responsible for highly complex and technical transformations of infrastructure vital for Iraq's future. The preference was for grand schemes at the cutting edge of the very latest developments without questioning how useful or user-friendly these might be in the context of a country ruined by war and starved of investment for decades.

The American public were assured by Vice President Dick Cheney that their troops would be welcomed as liberators by

Iraqis. It was a conceit based on historic ignorance, that the US went on compounding with their policy of 'giving' Iraq free-market democracy by means of military occupation. Iraq had seen such things before, courtesy of Britain, and as before resisted violently. But in America and among its representatives in Iraq, the theory was: think Marshall Plan. If Saddam was Hitler, then how America took the lead in rebuilding post-war Germany, where it still maintains major military bases 60 years on, was the virtuous model of good works for Iraqi transformation. But Iraq was not Germany. Germany was a highly industrialised, developed nation. Its economic strength underpinned the threat it posed to the balance of power in Europe which precipitated the two world wars of the 20th century. Thirteen years of Nazi rule, begun through the ballot box, their military defeat and Germany's total surrender, had not obliterated democratic capacity or free-market inclinations. The need was for investment to rebuild after the ravages of war. Iraq had never been permitted to develop its own democratic tradition, first by colonialism and then by the authoritarian regimes that followed. Its developmental gains had been eroded from the inside out by under-investment and the sanctions regime. Its greatest problem was under-employment – teachers and professionals working as taxi drivers, for example – and wholesale unemployment that crippled the local economy as it diminished living standards. And yet, ten days before it launched its invasion in March 2003, the White House issued a press release stating:

> Iraq is a country rich with an educated populace, abundant and valuable natural resources like oil and natural gas and a modern infrastructure system. The United States is committed to helping Iraq recover from this conflict, but Iraq will not require substantial aid.

In post-war Germany, de-Nazification was a necessary quid pro quo for massive investment. In Iraq, which would not require substantial aid, de-Ba'athification turned out to be the road to further ruin because for more than a generation the Ba'ath had become the convention of all Iraqis' lives, not an ideological structure but an organisational one by which almost everyone was compromised and to which everyone was beholden. At a stroke of Paul Bremer's pen, the US rendered all Iraqis 'uncertain about [the invasion's] implications for their future', just as Britain had in an earlier age. And for just such reasons, it laid the foundations for a locally generated and sustained insurgency.

The official website of USAID (www.usaid.gov) credits the publication of *The Ugly American* with expressing a general dissatisfaction with America's handling of foreign assistance as the Marshall Plan came to an end. According to the website, this prompted a debate about the objectives of America's aid policy in the 1960 presidential election. *The Ugly American*'s critique is presented through a cast of characters who concentrate on improving the real lives of ordinary people with simple, appropriate solutions attuned to their culture and circumstances. It is a bold prospectus; and in the novel it is doomed to failure. Each and every character that follows this alternative route and thereby succeeds in winning hearts and minds is opposed by the foreign policy establishment of the United States. For example, instead of being granted a couple of thousand dollars to develop a machine for making locally grown chicken feed, Tom Knox has to listen to a proposal for a new canal, costing two and a half million dollars, which will replace eighteen square miles of mangrove swamp with a mechanised farm requiring the import of 200,000 tons of commercial fertiliser a year for four years. 'What our two governments want is something big that really helps people fast', he is told.[42]

When it came to Iraq, 'the policy of the United States did not change'. USAID and the US Treasury agreed to collaborate on a plan set out in the 101-page document 'Moving the Iraqi Economy From Recovery to Sustainable Growth'. It proposed promoting aggressive free-market reforms. They would 'lay the groundwork for a market oriented private sector recovery' in what had been a centralised command economy with a welfare state on which all Iraqis had come to depend. There would be a 'broad based mass privatisation programme', a 'comprehensive tax system consistent with current international practice', and investment laws 'blind as to whether the investor is from the country or elsewhere', all of which would promote 'private sector involvement ... especially in the oil and supporting sectors'. The one thing seldom mentioned in this sweeping vista was employment. Nor did it consider how highly questionable its proposals were in light of Article 43 of the Hague Convention of 1899, the basis of the customary international law of war, which requires occupying powers to respect the law of the occupied country, except where necessary to promote public order and safety. Nor did this vision for the Iraqi future consider how consistent it was with UN Security Council Resolution no. 1483, which spoke of working to promote 'economic reconstruction and the conditions for sustainable development'. But things did not quite work out as planned. The cancellation of intergovernmental debts between state-owned companies in practice rewarded the bad and penalised good companies, by wiping out exactly the financial resources that viable enterprises needed to resume production. The elimination of import duties sucked in truckloads of imported goods which flooded street markets, undercutting demand for locally-produced goods, and hence jobs and wages for Iraqis. And as for employment creation, the disbanding of the Iraqi army released hundreds of thousands of trained and armed men into the swelling ranks of the jobless. When this order was issued, the adult unemployment rate already stood at 40 per cent. Harsh economic reality could only undermine the other element of the grand strategy: establishing an exemplary democracy. As one unemployed Iraqi oil engineer observed: 'Now we wish we had the old times back. Saddam was a ruthless man, but at least we had the basics of life. How can we care about democracy now when we don't even get electricity?'[43]

Investment and employment creation certainly took place, but it was more in keeping with the message that appeared on an earlier version of the USAID website, circa 2001, which assured Americans that 80 per cent of their foreign assistance was actually spent in America! Contracts to support and supply the US occupation force went to American corporations, awarded without competitive tender. So Halliburton, the company for which Vice President Dick Cheney had worked, provided catering in the Green Zone. It employed imported Indian and Pakistani staff – Iraqis, it was feared, might poison the food. Halliburton's subsidiary, Kellogg Brown Root, was in charge of laundry for the Green Zone – and sent it to Kuwait. The rebuilding of infrastructure was parcelled out to American corporations who again imported American and non-Iraqi staff, earning premium salaries, who had to be protected by employees of private security firms, also earning premium salaries. The private security firms became notorious. They recruited ex-soldiers, for whom they increasingly provided an attractive high-paying alternative to re-enlistment; devised their own rules of engagement – shoot first and don't ask questions – while they operated beyond the reach of the law of Iraq, the United States or Great Britain. The entire reconstruction process was riddled with corruption which congressional authorities are still attempting to unravel. But one thing is certain: it was a monumental mistake of information that vastly underestimated the real needs and costs, even without considering the additional outlay taken up by corruption, waste, maladministration and sheer, incompetent idiocy.

The Iraqi stock exchange, such as it was, could have been revitalised by provision of a blackboard. Instead the plan was to create the most modern stock market in the Arab world, with a fully computerised trading settlement system, independent of the Ministry of Finance, supported by a new securities law, its own by-laws, and a securities and exchange commission to oversee the market, list companies, license brokers and ensure financial disclosure. And all this in a country where electricity output, during the entire remit of the CPA, failed to achieve the performance it had done during the last days of Saddam, and where clean water supplies and sewage treatment were virtually nonexistent. And as so many observers have reported, while Iraqis regarded Saddam as a brutal tyrant who had to go, there was no such consensus for a wholesale transformation of the economy. As the manager of a local vegetable oil factory is quoted as commenting: 'You can't solve a problem by creating a new problem. You have to prepare the people for the decision.'[44]

Not all grandiose schemes were equally welcome to the CPA. Education had been the bedrock of Iraq's developmental capacity, but the man put in charge of planning a liberal education transformation for its 22 university campuses with 375,000 students found he was working with an entirely ravaged system. As Dilip Hiro had seen in the last years of Saddam, most Iraqis could not afford pencils and notebooks and were reduced to writing on any scrap of paper they could find. The estimated cost of revitalising the universities was $1 billion. The allocation made was $8 million. When a request was made for 130,000 classroom desks just to get things started, USAID gave 8,000.

America was not only uninformed about the attitude of the Iraqi people to foreign invasion, occupation, and economic and democratic transformation; it was also unprepared for the popular response to liberation. Anyone who read with care Dilip Hiro's account of life under sanctions could have anticipated the possibility of the stuff that happened once Saddam's regime evaporated. The extravaganza of looting was independent recycling of everything on a grand scale. It was an epic continuation of how Iraqis had learned to survive under the sanctions regime, personal initiative taken to the highest power. In a country where everything had for so long been in short supply, anything that was not nailed down, secured and guarded became fair game for anyone bold enough to lay claim. What you could not use you might conceivably be able to sell. Plans for securing major institutions had been prepared, but the confusion of lines of authority within the US government meant that the orders to American troops on the ground included only one priority: securing the oil ministry. This is not to discount the probable presence of criminal elements among the looters, but criminals exist everywhere and only people wilfully ignorant that Baghdad contained one of the world's finest museums of the world's most ancient antiquities could be taken unawares that it would be a prime target for looting should a security vacuum occur. American laxity was a boon to the underground trade in antiquities, as evidenced by the hundreds of items smuggled across the border to Syria whose return has been negotiated.[45] An even greater indifference to the patrimony of human history is detailed in the report by John Curtis, keeper of the British Museum's Middle East department, that will be the final part of their special exhibition on Iraq's ancient heritage.[46] A US military encampment was located on the site of ancient Babylon, where significant archaeological deposits were used to fill sandbags while gravel and fuel was poured over swathes of the site, damaging the remains beneath, which also had to bear the effects of heavy military vehicles driven over them. Babylon was the place where the world's first known legal code and written language were employed; its significance ought to have been obvious, as should the legal obligation to protect such an international treasure. Babylon is only one of at least 10,000 other archaeological sites of importance known to exist in Iraq.

Open armed resistance to the American-led occupation quickly developed. America 'mistakenly insisted, however, that Sunnis were upset by what the occupation had done (i.e. removed them from power) rather than by what the occupation was (i.e. an insult to Islam and a stain on the nation's honour)'.[47] What America seemed to know about Iraq was the existence of three distinct communities: Sunni, Shia and Kurds. Just as the British had rebuilt Iraq's social order according to their own interpretation, so America proceeded to administer the country proportionately along these sectarian and ethnic lines. Not only did this invest significance in these identities that they had never previously enjoyed, it created real communal tensions contending for power and access to much-needed opportunities and resources. America not only laid the groundwork for resistance to its occupation but also planted the seeds for civil war.

The Americans were just as much at a loss to understand the workings of the Shia community in Iraq as they had been a generation earlier in Iran. Anyone interested can read a detailed discussion of the structure, functioning, organisation and personal history of the main characters in Ali A. Allawi's account, *The Occupation of Iraq*.[48] The obvious point being that Allawi, a former exile, informed, urbane and fluent in English, held ministerial office in the Governing Council, was elected to the Transitional National Assembly and served as minister of finance in Ibrahim al Jaffari's cabinet of the Transitional National Government – so his expertise was not exactly hard to find. Nevertheless, the Americans found it incomprehensible that one old man living as he had for years in modest seclusion could confound their plans for directed democracy-building by the simple expedient of insisting that writing a constitution should follow, not precede elections. Grand Ayatollah Sayyid Ali al-Sistani had been the acknowledged religious leader of Iraq's Shia for over a decade. Like the majority of the Shia *maraji*, religious authorities, he took a quietist position, standing apart from politics, which explains why he would have no direct dealings with the Americans. The rationale for political quietism derives from Shia theology, in particular the belief that the community must await the return of the Hidden Imam. But, despite this, the religious organisation and workings of Shia Islam are inherently political, with a small 'p'. An ayatollah is not merely someone learned in Islamic theology and law, though that is a pre-requisite; an ayatollah emerges by gaining the acknowledgement of the learned and attracting a loyal following among the people. To be an ayatollah, and especially a Grand Ayatollah, is an accolade bestowed and adhered to by the community. No one becomes an ayatollah without a subtle understanding of public mood and attitudes, considerable diplomatic and political skills, and a strong grasp of strategy. Quietism meant that the Shia *maraji* concerned themselves principally with matters of personal and family law. But this did not mean they escaped Saddam's repressive and murderous attentions as he sought to control every aspect of life in Iraq. Many were martyred and others exiled themselves in Iran, the only Muslim country where Shiism is the official religion. While Shiism appears more hierarchical and formally institutionalised than Sunni Islam, its acceptance of *ijtihad*, independent reasoning by religious scholars, has historically made it more flexible and adaptive than Sunnism, which literally means 'the orthodox'. A significant break from the quietist mainstream in Iraq was made by the Sadrist movement, founded by Ayatollah Muhammad Sadiq al-Sadr, murdered by Saddam in 1999. He built a massive following, particularly among poor urban Shia. The Americans soon found to their discomfort that his following had continued to strengthen after his death. After the invasion it quickly morphed into an anti-occupation movement under the auspices of his son, Moqtada al-Sadr. Sadrists were nationalists, wary of those religious scholars who had exiled themselves in Iran, and activist in serving their social base among the poorest by providing vital social services and protecting neighbourhoods amid chaos. As nationalists, al-Sadr and his followers emphasised Iraqi unity among Shia, Sunni and Kurd. Without investigating the basis of Moqtada al-Sadr's loyal following, or asking why he was so popular, the Americans responded solely to his rhetoric and immediately dubbed him a nightmare, either a 'Bolshevik' or 'fascist' one, but definitely a thug. By demonising al-Sadr, who eventually emerged as an essential political prop of Nuri al Maliki's government, America aligned itself with those Shia factions closest to Iran, which presumably was not the prime directive. Shia Islam is complex but not incomprehensible, diverse but not indecipherable. It is the religion of the majority of Iraqis and was bound to be a potent influence on how democracy would operate once Saddam was removed. The Ba'ath was a secular socialist movement, though Saddam toyed with Islamic imagery and courted Muslim support, especially among the purchasable and stupid around the world, when it suited his needs. The expectation that Iraq would remain a secular domain with Saddam gone was a triumph of aspiration over experience, an easily avoidable error. To insist on seeing Iraq through the prism of sectarian affiliation and then to fail to master the intricacies of those affiliations is a major mistake of judgement and information. It is just the kind of response summed up by Joe Bing in *The Ugly American*, who blithely deems the happenings reported in the local papers to be 'native matters' and turns a deaf ear to local politics conducted in a language he cannot understand.

In Vietnam, America sought to defuse support for the communist insurgency by following Britain's strategy, employed in Malaysia and Kenya, of resettling the population in model villages which were virtual open prisons. In Iraq, America responded to the insurgency and civil strife by following Britain's policy in Northern Ireland of building walls to separate communities on sectarian lines, thus concreting a problem it had created. The increasing violence not only led to separate communities defined along sectarian lines, it produced a vast displaced population, numbering some one and a half million, within Iraq. This displaced population became the humanitarian disaster that the coalition had expected to find and had planned for on their arrival. In practice it materialised only through acts of omission and commission associated with their decision to remain in Iraq.

A country oppressed by a tyrannical dictatorship is not a country devoid of politics or the means of civic organisation. The evaporation of Saddam and his Ba'athist regime was quickly followed in Fallujah, for example, by the community establishing its own new municipal council. The Americans, however, had different ideas and stationed a much-resented contingent of soldiers in the town. They set up headquarters in the local school, which therefore could not be reopened. The independent-minded citizens of Fallujah had clear memories of occupation, courtesy of Britain's stay in the region, and of how to resist. The town quickly became a flashpoint, first of protest then open revolt. 'We had no idea we weren't wanted', was the response of Lt. Col. Nantz, whose troops were occupying Fallujah.[49] The insurgency in Fallujah, as elsewhere in Iraq, was the work of Iraqis. Every test of Iraqi public opinion showed a rapid increase in resentment of American and British presence and support for armed resistance. The more coalition forces struggled to contend with the armed resistance they encountered, the more they fuelled the insurgency and made it a *cause célèbre* for the entire Arab and Muslim world. This too could have been foreseen. The warnings were voiced on the Arab street and written about and relayed to Western journalists by politicians, academics, pundits and authors from across the region and around the Muslim world. Adnan Abu Odeh, a Palestinian-Jordanian and a former ambassador to the UN, expressed a general attitude to American foreign policy and the effect that its determination to pursue regime change in Iraq would have:

> The Americans are masters at making other people hate them. People used to be ambivalent about America. They admired American education, technology, freedom of expression. Until this war they only hated one thing about America, its Middle East policy. This war will take the scales of hatred and add new degrees to them.[50]

He likened the invasion of Iraq to 1258, when the Mongols overran Baghdad. 'It's also like the British arrival in Baghdad in 1918 ... Now it's being colonised for a second time ... The fall of Baghdad will create an extra level of suppression ... There will be more frustration, anger, uncertainty about the future and hopelessness ... Humiliation is being fuelled not just by the external impact of defeat but by the internal sense of impotence.'[51] As the violence grew in Iraq it is undoubtedly true that fighters were drawn in from many countries across the region. But Jonathan Steele is surely right to liken this to 'an Arab version of the International Brigade made up of young European and American radicals who rushed to support the republican side during the Spanish Civil War in the 1930s.' However, that was not what America saw or understood.

There are systemic mistakes ingrained in the worldview of the lone hyperpower; they are the 'perils of dominance': the ability to project power according to purely self-serving criteria. But going to war requires something more – it needs a rationale that can be sold to and supported by elected representatives and the American public, and potentially endorsed by world opinion. It needs a *casus belli*, an incident, a trigger mechanism to legitimate the unleashing of the dogs of war. How America goes to war provides the greatest parallel between the Vietnam era and the Iraq invasion.

In 1964 the Tonkin Gulf incident, the highly dubious alleged attack on an American naval vessel in waters off North Vietnam which was claimed, then denied and never fully authenticated, nevertheless prompted Congress to authorise the deployment of US forces. There were already some 12,000 American military 'advisors' in South Vietnam, maintained at a cost of $400 million a year. Fifty had already died in action, though officially they were not participants in the fighting. However, the Tonkin Gulf Resolution was not based on careful scrutiny of either the alleged incident or of the wider context of involvement in Vietnam and the profound consequences of committing troops to the conflict. The Tonkin incident had all the finesse of 'Remember the *Maine*', another alleged attack on a US naval vessel which had blown up in the harbour of Havana, Cuba in 1898 and was used to precipitate the Spanish-American war, the conflict which launched America's overseas imperial career. Warmongered in the pages of W. R. Hearst's newspapers as an outrage against the pride of the nation, the fate of the *Maine* became an irresistible *casus belli*. In 1963 a survey of public opinion showed that 63 per cent of Americans were paying 'little or no attention' to events in South-East Asia. A reported attack on an American ship was a wake-up call. When the Tonkin Gulf Resolution reached Congress there were only two dissenting votes.

Invading Iraq was the culmination of more than a decade of American focus on and demonisation of Saddam Hussein in the wake of the Persian Gulf war. Contained by the no-fly zones and the sanctions regime, nevertheless Saddam was a continuing affront and an enduring problem, not least because of the growing international outcry against the impact of sanctions on the civilian population. Since the end of the 1990 war, the US had continued to maintain a considerable military presence in the Gulf. Supported by Britain, and on occasion by France, it had repeatedly launched further aerial assaults on Iraqi targets. In the aftermath of 9-11, the American Congress swiftly wrote a blank cheque conferring war powers on President George W. Bush, with only one dissenting vote in the Senate. What was lacking was a *casus belli*, a direct rationale for a war long anticipated by the neo-conservatives now in key positions in the Bush administration. This was manufactured from the inspection regime, established by UN Security Council resolutions to oversee the dismantling of Saddam's chemical, biological and nuclear weapons capacity and arsenal of missiles. Immediately after the Gulf war, the United Nations Special Commission (UNSCOM) reported the destruction of considerable quantities of WMD and disabling of production capability. But the inspection regime had been suspended since Saddam threw out the inspectors. Having already taken the decision to remove Saddam, America, with the willing assistance of the British government, launched an international campaign claiming that

Saddam not only retained banned WMD but was actively engaged in the acquisition and production of a new arsenal of the banned weaponry. Their offensive was designed to convince domestic and international opinion that Saddam was an imminent threat that had to be confronted by military means. The onslaught was intelligence-driven, and presented with theatrical panache to the UN Security Council by secretary of state Colin Powell.

By its very nature, intelligence obtained by covert means is a matter of judgement, even for the specialists; it is even more difficult for lawmakers and the general public – who are never privy to its source – to assess. Without full disclosure, intelligence becomes a test of public trust in authority. But that does not mean that it should not be carefully scrutinised and questioned in the context of what is known; it should not inevitably trump publicly available information, expertise and opinion to the contrary. In the case made for the invasion of Iraq, 'intelligence' turned out to be a misnomer for flimsy wishful thinking massaged, sexed up and hyped to support a policy that had already been decided. The German publication *Der Spiegel* investigated one aspect of the case made by Colin Powell. It reported on the source of Powell's claim, complete with illustrations and schematics, that Saddam was operating mobile biological weapons labs to evade the inspection regime. The information was provided by an 'asset', an informant of German intelligence known as 'Curveball', and passed on to the Americans. Doubts about the honesty and reliability of this source were raised by, among others, Tyler Durmheller, former chief of the CIA's European Division (interviewed on *Newsnight*, BBC TV, 25 March 2008). There was suspicion that Curveball was feeding his minders what they wanted to hear for financial reasons and to bolster his case to remain in Germany. But what astounded former weapons inspector David Kay was that no American agent ever interviewed this source directly, on the topic of biological labs or anything else.[53] The mobile labs turned out to be a fiction. Yet, despite the paucity of evidence, they were included in the presentation to the UN Security Council. Colin Powell has apologised for misleading the global public. Interviewed on BBC TV as part of a report on the *Der Spiegel* investigation, Powell's Chief of Staff, Col. Lawrence Wilkerson, said:

> I will tell you this. There was far more serious error in that presentation than mobile biological labs, there was assertion that there was an active nuclear programme based on aluminium tubes, there was an assertion that there was active contact between al-Qaeda and the Mukhabarat in Baghdad given from testimony rendered under torture. These were far more damaging than mobile biological labs. If you want me to condemn the presentation I will sit here and do it. It was a horrible hoax on the American people, on the international community and the UN Security Council. No question about it. And the biological labs were just a component of that hoax.[54]

In the entire farrago of justifying the decision to invade Iraq, the only person who consistently told the unblemished truth was Saddam Hussein, the one person whom no one was likely to believe.

When Saddam's assertion that he had no weapons of mass destruction was proved by the inability of exhaustive searches by large teams of investigators to find any, the argument made by President Bush and Prime Minister Blair subtly changed. They had acted on the information held in common and believed by many governments, they asserted. This was sophistry dancing on the smallest of pinheads. Many possessed the same intelligence, but only the US and Britain believed that it justified invasion, especially in the absence of specific authorisation from the UN Security Council, the only authority that can legitimate war. The unconvinced included the late Robin Cook MP, the former

British foreign secretary, who resigned his cabinet post and in his resignation speech denounced the intelligence information before voting against going to war. The mistake of information was secondary to the mistake of judgement. It was the judgement of Bush, Blair and all the elected representatives supporting them in default of careful weighing of the evidence that was at fault. It was a mistake of judgement not made or endorsed by other governments, nor numerous experts, academics, pundits or large sections of the general public around the world. It is the dissenting opinion that has been vindicated. The mistake of judgement and information is responsible for hundreds of thousands of deaths and has caused a continuing humanitarian crisis, considered by relief agencies to be among the worst in the world, as well as the displacement of millions of Iraqis.

What made the mistake of judgement so seductive that it could not be questioned by so many elected politicians in the US and Britain? Why was the case for war not more critically challenged in America's mainstream media? What led a majority of the American public to support the war as a necessary, inevitable step to secure the safety of the American people? The answer is to be found by reading strategic and cultural histories together. The battle to inform public memory, as Tarik Barkawi argues, is crucial in gaining support for and advancing strategic policy.[55] On the second anniversary of the invasion of Iraq, CBS News examined public attitudes in the wake of the failure to find WMD, an increasingly violent insurgency, and growing suspicion that the war might be unwinnable. They interviewed mothers whose sons had been killed while serving with the American forces in Iraq. One mother felt the war was a mistake. Another, from Essex County in California, argued that the war had been essential: 'If we hadn't gone to war I'd be wearing a burka by now', she asserted. This was something more than a mother seeking some desperate consolation for the loss of a child. This was an authentic voice of the coalescing of strategic and cultural rationales for the war on terror, a wholehearted belief in the concept of an apocalyptic battle with a global, civilisational enemy bent on the destruction of the American way of life that has to be opposed everywhere by any means necessary. It is this narrative, the fears it engenders and the fears on which it relies, which is the greatest mistake of judgement and information. The global communist conspiracy that urged America to war in Vietnam has been succeeded by the global war on terror as the ideological underpinning for American foreign policy and legitimation for the projection of American military power around the globe.

It is impossible not to have sympathy for a mother who has lost a child. But sympathy must not preclude examination of the reasonableness of the policy, the proportionality of the fear and the imminence of the threat which, in her mind, justifies the sacrifice. The willingness of Americans to believe in an axis of evil is the fulcrum of American fear. The public willingness to accept this argument proves that 'the domain of the popular is a key battleground in wars waged by the United States'.[56] The perceived weight of public opinion structures and constrains the critical stance, or rather supine acquiescence, of politicians and media. Winning the battle of popular endorsement for a reductive view of all the diversity of grievances, causes and animosities, as well as the substantive issues between America and Muslim countries, empowers not only the rhetoric but also the prosecution of the war on terror. America's addiction to viewing the world in Manichean terms, as a battle between good and evil, darkness and light, is maintained. The simplistic 'with us or against us' outlook it produces empowers militarism and the use of military force as the appropriate responses. The policy of the United States does not change.

Before America can change, its addiction to grand strategic narrative has to change. America will change only when it examines its fears and can acknowledge that there are other ways to understand and think about its supposed enemies and the challenges it faces.

CHAPTER THREE

Rules of Engagement

On the morning of 9-11, as the world watched in horror, there was no doubt about the identity of the people responsible for the atrocity. The first thought in everyone's mind was simple: the terrorists were Muslim/Arab/Islamic/extremists/fundamentalists. The conclusion preceded investigation or evidence because it is generic, a cultural cliché. The terrorists' actions challenged our credulity in only one sense – this was real and not a Hollywood screenplay. At the movies, when the blockbuster *Independence Day* (1996) featured aliens destroying the Empire State building and blowing up the White House, audiences cheered. Nothing in the Hollywood archives desensitised anyone to the shock and horror of 9-11. But in response to those events, public attitudes and debate have been shaped by make-believe pictures, the movies we have seen.

When it comes to Muslim terrorists the key battleground, the domain of the popular, is already a done deal. Political rhetoric and strategic plans reference and rely on popular memory informed by innumerable movies. And those movies recycle a welter of ideas embedded in the popular imagination through a thousand years of Western civilisation. The war on terror combats what the US department of defence defines as 'the unlawful use of – or threatened use of – force or violence against individuals or property to coerce or intimidate governments and societies, often to achieve political, religious or ideological objectives'.

The more emotive language of an axis of evil, President Bush's insistence on the existential nature of the threat posed by people who hate the freedoms and liberties of the American way of life, or John McCain's insistence that America is dealing with 'a transcendent evil', a 'mirror reversal' of itself[1] reach deeper into the recesses of popular memory. What is rekindled is the imagery of 'the natural candidates for the role of metaphysical enemies': Muslims and the set of ideas which describe them that have been familiar, and enduringly frightening, in the collective imagination of the West for centuries.[2]

From the 1960s onwards, movies have been conditioning the expectations of cinema audiences, defining cultural literacy on the issue of terrorism long before it became the context of real events. Muslim terrorists seeking to acquire or using weapons of mass destruction is a standard Hollywood plot. The scenario got its first general release in *Trunk to Cairo* (1966), a product of the Menachem Golan oeuvre. Starring Audie Murphy and George Sanders, *Trunk to Cairo* is a sequel on the same theme as Golan's Israeli-made and -released *Cairo Operation* (1965). In both films, German scientists work to provide backward Arabs with nuclear weapons to target Israel. The identity of the culprits provides a mutually reinforcing definition of evil: their compatibility and guilt by association condemns, it provides contextual detail and meaning without the need for elaborate argument, never a significant feature of action pictures. Audie Murphy plays the US secret agent who helps the Israelis to foil the plot. It is clear that these terrorists are also an imminent danger to the US. In one scene, an imam who prays in a mosque which conceals a weapons cache tells Murphy: 'We hate Americans above all!' A similar nexus of characters and plot features in the Golan-Globus 'Delta Force' series of films of 1986, 1990 and 1993. The tagline for *Delta Force* (1986) could not be clearer on how to respond to this threat: 'They don't negotiate with terrorists ... they blow them away!'

Muslim terrorists seeking to bring mass murder to the

American homeland is the theme of *Black Sunday* (1977). They plan to bomb the Super Bowl with the president in attendance to strike at Americans 'where it hurts, where they feel most safe'. In *Wanted Dead or Alive* (1987) the terrorists aim to release poison gas to exterminate Los Angeles and in this film are assisted by Arab-American students at UCLA who help run a bomb factory. In the Arnold Schwarzenegger blockbuster *True Lies* (1994) the terrorists' objective is to set off a nuclear device in Florida. 'They can go anywhere in the United States. There's nothing, no one to stop them', a TV newscaster reports in one scene. At the movies the audience can relish the fact that this is untrue: they have come to watch the indestructible Arnie do just that. *True Lies* spares nothing in representing the terrorists as truly demonic, their leader a portrait of malevolent obsession played to the hilt by Art Malik. The film underscores the association of fanatical terrorism with religion, since at every opportunity they intone 'Allahu Akbar'. The dynamics of the genre are so established in cinema literacy that *True Lies* can use them as pastiche, parody and even slapstick comedy alongside spectacular high-budget fight scenes and special effects with hi-tech gadgetry, including flying a plane through a skyscraper.

Executive Decision (1996) is another high-octane thriller in which Muslim terrorists are determined to explode a device filled with lethal nerve gas over the American homeland. The film testifies to its sophistication by literally blowing away Steven Seagal, martial arts action hero, before the main action gets under way. The cold-blooded, always calm and thus truly fanatical leader of the plot, played by David Suchet, reads his Qur'an as the passenger plane they have hijacked makes its way to New York. The executive decision of the title is the order to sacrifice the civilian passengers by shooting down the plane before it can reach its destination and kill millions. Unless, that is, the intrepid elite force smuggled aboard in mid-air, the manoeuvre which dispensed with Seagal, can succeed in defusing the device under the very feet of the terrorists. In the end all that stands between

America and disaster is a cocktail stick and a band of heroes.

Audiences are so familiar with the unbridled desire of Muslim terrorists and nations to acquire nuclear weapons that it can be used as a McGuffin, the incidental plot device that sets the story in motion. In *The Peacemaker* (1997) the opening scene establishes the collapse of the Soviet Union. That 'evil empire' no longer exists, but its nuclear arsenal could empower a much older 'evil empire' waiting in the wings. A Russian general diverts nuclear devices destined for the scrap-heap of history to sell them to Iran. The Muslim threat is so understood that it is a mere script point. After this set-up, the actual film can begin dealing with the lone actions of a demented Serbian who diverts one of the nuclear devices to avenge himself on the United Nations for all the suffering his family and community has endured.

Action films with their special brand of hero are a global box office staple. Film historian Eric Lichtenfeld has described the elements of the genre as 'a celebration of empire and conquest'. The conventions of action films were assembled to answer a problem in the American zeitgeist. The problem was not the nature of villainy and evil. The problem was the crisis of heroism, patriotism and militarism. The genre responds to doubts about America's role and place in the world raised by war and defeat. The crisis of the American self-image induced by the Vietnam war prompted a major reconfiguration of the movie hero. At a time when America had lost its innocence and found itself entangled in corruption, bureaucracy, and the complications of idealised ethical standards that tie the hands and make hidebound the conscience of society at large, the persistence of evil licensed the action hero. He is set loose to glory in the unbridled use of force and violence to obliterate the enemy. From 'Do we get to win this time?' (John Rambo in *First Blood Part Two*) to 'Yippee-ki-yey motherfucker' (John McClane in *Die Hard*), the action hero gives the audience reassurance that the willingness to use unrestrained power will keep Americans safe and eradicate evil.

The action hero's legitimacy is derived from his enemy. Without a truly monstrous adversary the action hero is merely a brutal thug. Indeed there is an ambiguous compatibility between hero and villain in this genre. Both are masters of dealing death and causing pain, of being remorseless and unyielding. Tactically, hero and villain are well matched – except for the dictum of Hollywood which states that the hero must prevail to deliver the happy ending and reassurance that audiences require. The distinction between them is the hero's unquestionable commitment to justice and right because of what he seeks to defend, while the enemy is irredeemably evil because of what he seeks to destroy. However, since the hero so often has to act extra-judicially, to go beyond the law and proper protocols to eradicate imminent threats, the genre calls into question the very values of civilised society it supposedly upholds: can America really defend itself by sticking to its own highest principles? The hero is always fighting against the rules as much as he is fighting against time. All that matters is to achieve total victory, the outcome the audience is emotionally invested in – and that is what the hero delivers. It is catharsis, wish-fulfilment and reassurance. The hero can coerce and intimidate by the use of force and violence, but in his case it is not 'unlawful' because his cause is just and his intentions righteous, and that makes everything alright.

In a genre that is short on talk, the villains who work best are those whose evil is self-explanatory. They are sociopaths, psychopaths, megalomaniacs; they can represent strategic threats which are inherently evil, such as the Nazis or Russians once did. But time after time in the movies they are Muslim terrorists. Long before anyone heard or conceived of al-Qaeda and militant jihadists, before a global war on undifferentiated terrorism, the cinema paraded an undifferentiated set of identikit, plasterboard Muslim villains, indeterminate of origin, needing no special explanation of motivation because the audience, the domain of the popular, could be expected to supply the necessary background detail. What are the origins of this stereotype?

The history of these villains can be traced back through the century of film. From its early days Hollywood developed two modes of representation for the Muslim world: the exotic Orient of the *Thousand and One Nights* kind, and the desert where the battle for empire and conquest confronted barbaric Muslim hordes. Both modes were established in the public mind by the ultimate in Hollywood star power. The first 'king of Hollywood', Douglas Fairbanks Snr, established the exotic cities of the ancient East with all their marvels in *The Thief of Bagdad* (1924), 'the most expensive film ever made' in its day. This swashbuckle through the fabulous world of Aladdin, Ali Baba and Sinbad established a location and cast of stock characters which has played host to everyone from Abbott and Costello to Mickey Mouse and the entire family of Donald Duck to Elvis Presley. The locations and stock characters have made regular reappearances in each decade of the century of film. *The Thief of Bagdad* followed the sensation that was *The Sheik* (1921), starring Rudolph Valentino. Women literally shrieked for the Sheikh and in his case were not entirely put off by the film's tagline: 'When an Arab sees a woman he wants he takes her.' Hollywood got around its strict rules on not showing miscegenation by revealing in the last reel that Valentino's Sheikh, who had captured and vainly yet so seductively courted a white woman, Lady Diana, was in fact Viscount Caryll, Earl of Glen Caryll, a lordly foundling raised by desert Arabs. But by then the Sheikh had been admonished for the error of his ways in his treatment of Lady Diana and had rescued her from the clutches of another truly villainous, fully Arab desert sheikh and his band of barbaric warriors.

The plots played out in these locations depended upon the persistent presence of evil viziers, caliphs and their hordes of murderous warriors. These barbaric and cruel men were not only implacably opposed to Western civilisation but lusted after white women as much as they made playthings of their own women, confined to harems – always dressed in the diaphanous garb of a belly dancer – existing only for the pleasure of men. The movie locations established ancient, unchanging cities as places of intrigue, corruption and lurking threat where barbaric cruelty found delight in the arts of torture. Those who ruled in this environment were the incarnation of despotism: arbitrary, absolute power wielded according to personal whim and commanding the total obedience of the whole society on pain of unspeakable punishment. So established was this concept of place that the names of cities were used as film titles to signal the kind of thrills audiences could expect. The ultimate example is Hollywood's remake of the French classic *Pépé Le Moko* (1937) which appeared a year later as *Algiers*, starring Charles Boyer, who, incidentally, did not say 'come with me to the casbah'. The dark network of winding streets of the ancient casbah, the medina or old city, serves as a metaphor for the uncivilised world of corruption in which Pépé (Boyer) is trapped. In the last scene he is shot as he tries to board a ship bound for his dream of civilisation: France. The police inspector he helped tends to him, and says: 'I'm sorry, Pépé, they thought you were trying to escape.' To which, with his dying breath, Pépé relies: 'And so I have, my friend.' The association of place with intrigue made Muslim cities perfect locations for spy films: *Tangiers* (1946), where the opponents are Nazis; and *Tangiers Incident* (1953), in which the opponents are Russians. Time and villainy may move on, but the Muslim city endures as a marker of lurking danger to the West, the 'festering sink' as it is described in *Algiers/Pépé Le Moko*.

The desert provided Hollywood with another way of replaying its most basic storyline. The Sahara became 'a mythical landscape of the heart, like the American West'.[3] In westerns, America was offered its own history of national empire and conquest achieved by the use of military force to defeat and eradicate the wild, savage Indian and thus make the land secure for liberty and democracy. In the Sahara, the movies could appropriate the global history of the West's imperial colonising crusade. In place of the US cavalry, the Sahara offered the equally romanticised French Foreign Legion. In place of the Indians it teemed with robed and turbaned Riff. In place of Fort Apache enter Fort Zinderneuf, the lone and beleaguered outpost of a fragile and imperilled civilisation that must fight for its very existence against the barbaric hordes. Fort Zinderneuf is where Beau Geste rises to the challenge of heroism in the film of the same name (1926, 1931, 1939 and variously thereafter). As in westerns, the enemy exists merely to oppose, and there is scant attention to their motivation; it is their function to be fiendish and be slaughtered in numbers uncounted – the inevitable punishment for opposing the march of Western civilisation.

The only thing which stopped Hollywood making more use of the *Beau Geste* setting was French objection to the portrayal not of their North African Arab and Berber citizens, but of the Foreign Legion. In the days when cinema was king, the possibility of France banning films and restricting Hollywood's access to its market urged caution. But there was another location where the same scenarios could be played out: the north-west frontier of India, where barbaric Afghan warriors lurked behind every rock and in every crevice and the romantic regiments of Britain's Indian Army, the Guides and the Bengal Lancers, could carry forth the mantle of civilisation. Gary Cooper, a quintessential western hero, graduated to being Beau Geste (1939) after service as Beau Sabreur (1928) and a stint as a Bengal Lancer (1935). *Lives of a Bengal Lancer* is the origin of the immortal line 'We have ways of making you talk', though in the film the Afghan arch-villain Mohammad Khan (played by Douglas Dumbrille), who delights in inflicting pain and specialises in torture, actually says: 'We have ways of making men talk.'

Do old films and their stereotypes matter? Is it anything more than an interesting curiosity to come across a film such as *Dream Wife* (1953), one of the succession of comedy-of-manners movies starring Cary Grant and Deborah Kerr? Kerr plays the modern professional woman who will negotiate a deal with the ruler of Bakistan. This imagined country is literally on the other side of the globe: 'We have just one thing in common,' a state department official tells Kerr, 'oil.' Grant plays Kerr's fiancé, who suspects she cares more about the oil deal than him and finds himself entranced with Bakistan, a land where women are brought up 'to make men happy. Women as wives and mothers as Allah intended them to be. They are not taxi-drivers and wrestlers.' The comedy ensues when Grant finds that he has unwittingly become engaged to Princess Tarji, a woman trained from birth to be a dream wife. By the end of the film the ruler of Bakistan who considered America 'foolish to allow women in government' is won over by Kerr and concludes the oil deal. Grant discovers that a dream wife is too much of a headache and returns to his fiancée. It only remains for Kerr to instruct Tarji in modernity. She learns 'a new word: freedom'. Though whether she entirely grasps the theory of women's liberation is moot, since she delivers the moral in its Hollywood variant as: 'Woman not have to obey man she not love.' So here on film is a fair approximation of the political agenda of the noughties – secure the oil, instruct in freedom and liberate the women – presented as smart and witty divertissement half a century earlier! Did the movies invent the policy, or has the policy just not changed? Most definitely the cultural stereotypes essential to the storyline have not changed.

As action, historical adventure, comedy or tragedy, the character notes for Muslim roles do not change. They need little elaboration because they were familiar long before cinema was invented. They derive from the eclectic spirals of the Western imagination,[4] they are to be found in art and literature, learned works, travellers' tales and religious polemics dating back to the first encounter of Islam and the West. The movies recycle the stereotypes employed in the action genre of the medieval period: the *chanson de geste*, songs of deeds. *The Song of Roland*, written circa 1100, retells the battle of Roncesvalles, a rearguard action in the mountain passes of north-east Spain by an elite force, the Paladins, in the service of the Emperor Charlemagne, standard-bearer of the values of Western civilisation. The Paladins are overwhelmed by Muslim forces. With his last breath, their leader, Roland, summons Charlemagne to avenge their death. This 'band of brothers', symbolic of the sacrifice of a 'finest generation' in Europe's past – Roncesvalles occurred in 778 – are carried off to heaven by angels. Just as Tarik Barkawi argues that action movies of the 1970s and 80s gradually rehabilitated the American military in the domain of the popular and spread the conviction that they had won the Vietnam war,[5] so *The Song of Roland* assures Europe that Charlemagne reconquered Muslim Spain in the 8th century, which he did not. Indeed, by the 14th century the domain of the popular was crediting Charlemagne with liberating the Holy Land as well, a feat also accomplished by King Arthur in the other literary cycle that popularised the chivalric ideal of the military as a moral force in the service of good. In representing the Muslim enemy, *The Song of Roland* uses time-honoured character notes. Their leaders' names all imply some connection with magic or the devil; their society is presented as the moral reverse or inversion of Christian society, especially in their dedication to carnal pleasures and violence. And the heroic deeds of the Paladins 'confers an apocalyptic character' on the conflict: 'We are in the sphere foreshadowing the final battle between the forces of Light and the forces of Darkness.'[6] And, as Cardini points out, throughout the medieval epics the Muslim adversaries 'are rarely depicted as mere human beings, but endowed with a ferocious, contorted kind of humanity: in general they are either superhuman, inhuman or anti-human.'[7]

The domain of the popular was the key battleground that sustained the ethos of the military, economic, political and cultural endeavour we know as the Crusades as a central motif of European life over a period of centuries. *The Song of Roland* and the whole gamut of popular entertainment concerning knightly chivalry looked to the past both to explain why this conflict with the forces of Islam was necessary and for the detail to portray the nature of this enemy. 'The Crusades are the opening chapter of European expansion and foreshadow all later colonial movements.'[8] They were celebrated in all the literary and learned products of the whole of Europe. Black propaganda, polemic and scholarly inquiry as well as popular entertainment all made a contribution to how the Muslim world was understood and portrayed. The attitudes and ideas of this era were elaborated to explain the project of empire and conquest. They are so subtly interwoven in the mindset of Western civilisation as to be invisible, in the sense of being the normality of common-or-garden everyday ideas, things everyone just knows. The project of empire, from 'repossessing' the Holy Land onwards, was the march of progress to liberate lands and peoples and bring them into the light of Western tutelage from the darkness of ignorance and barbarism. Islam, on the other hand, was 'spread by the sword' to oppress and trap people in the darkness of dehumanising tradition. The grand strategic narrative has been reworked many times without unseating the potency of the original version in popular memory.

The idea of the crusade endured long after the Fall of Acre in 1291, the last outpost of the Latin presence in the Middle East. In that year the Italian traveller Ricaldo de Montecroce visited Baghdad and found its people to be confused, mendacious, irrational, violent and obscure, a fair paraphrase of the general and enduring consensus. The legacy of the attitudes and ideas of this era is perhaps best summed up in the words of the French monk, Guibert of Nogent (1053–1124), who produced a chronicle of the First Crusade and is one of the most important writers of the medieval period: 'it is safe to speak evil of one whose malignity exceeds whatever ill can be spoken.' It is a convention that finds and has found a ready place at the movies.

El Cid is the medieval national epic of Spanish literature, and its hero, Rodrigo Diaz de Viver, is immortalised as the quintessential hero. While his character has all the nobility, virtue and inherent goodness that can be conveyed by being played by Charlton Heston, the film *El Cid* (1961) struggles to accommodate the complexities of the cross-cutting relationships and shifting alliances between Christians, Muslims and Jews that is the history of medieval Spain. But in contrasting the hero with the movie's villain it had no such problems. This big-screen version is faithful to the stereotypes of its medieval forerunners in portraying the Moorish leader Ben Yusef, played with consummate malice by Herbert Lom. Always swathed in black robes, Ben Yusef is incarnated, in anticipation of future villains, as the essential religious fanatic. He intrigues, he is craven and cowardly, but his dream of domination will become the lurking fear of future decades. He exhorts his followers:

The Prophet has commanded us to rule the world ... Let your doctors invent new poisons for arrows. Let your scientists invent new war machines and then, kill, burn ... I will sweep up from Africa and let the empire of the one God, the true God, Allah, first spread across Spain, then across Europe, then the whole world.

After Ben Yusef, the Muslim terrorist marches onto the screen as a logical consequence of history. The religious fanatic as terrorist becomes an ideal enemy to drive the plots of movies set in contemporary times.

The domain of the popular has always reworked history to suit the ideological purpose and the circumstances of its time. Hollywood's most recent epic of the Crusades, Ridley Scott's *Kingdom of Heaven* (2005), is no exception. It offers audiences the Crusades as vindication of the American Dream and thereby provides a rationale for pre-emptive democracy-building. The plot is a very particular kind of fairy tale. The central character, Balian (Orlando Bloom), is a not-so-simple blacksmith living in a scruffy village in France. At a moment of crisis in his life he discovers that he has a (fairy, god) father, a Crusader knight. Balian is offered the prospect of the greatest adventure: to set off for Jerusalem where he can erase his sins and gain his inheritance. It is his long-lost father, Godfrey (Liam Neeson), appropriately the only completely invented character in the film, who explains what awaits Balian. He goes to make a new world, a better world than there has ever been, where a man is not what he is born but what he has it in himself to be. It will be a society where Christian and Muslim live side by side; a kingdom of conscience; of peace instead of war, love instead of hate. 'That is what lies at the end of crusade.' We did say it was a fairy story!

To attain this vision, Balian is schooled in the use of arms in a reprise of the stern drill sergeant and boot camp sequence familiar from all war movies. But Balian must also absorb the moral code of a knight crusader: 'Be without fear in the face of your enemies; be brave and upright that God may love thee. Speak the truth always even if it leads to your death. Safeguard the helpless and do no wrong. That is your oath.' It comes down to the proposition that 'holiness is right action and courage on behalf of those who cannot defend themselves', which is a neat paraphrase of how America thinks of its role in the world. Generations of politicians have convinced Americans that they are the indispensable nation because they use military force only under duress and to protect those who cannot defend themselves. This familiar idea was effortlessly extended to accommodate the Bush doctrine of pre-emptive war and regime change in Iraq.

In the role of implacable enemy, Balian must face Salah ed Din al Ayyubi, leader of the Muslim forces, more commonly known as Saladin. The most that can be said for his portrayal is that for once everyone uses his proper name and pronounces it correctly. Beyond that he is merely another in the long line of noble savages who so often serve as principled adversaries in various tales of empire and conquest. The Muslim world has no role in the film, it is merely the horde, the huge army massing off screen waiting to burst on Jerusalem in scenes reminiscent of the shock and awe footage of America's assault on Baghdad. The inhabitants of the Holy Land are invisible, displaced and irrelevant. There is no indication that at the time of the Crusades the Middle East was the centre of a global culture, the height of civilisation in arts, science, technology, medicine, philosophy and much else which Europe was busy appropriating wholesale. Indeed, what Europe acquired and learned from Muslim civilisation during these centuries was the foundation from which it crafted what we call modernity.

In *Kingdom of Heaven* the purpose of the great adventure will be to settle a new land and there transcend the failures of old Europe. The Crusades were the first European colonial experiment, America the second. America, the city on a hill, the newer new Jerusalem, then becomes the only nation capable of achieving the real meaning of crusade. The hero is an enlightened common man whose skills make the desert bloom, digging a well that instantly produces green, flourishing crops. He is a master of technology, using it to devise the means for the final defence of Jerusalem. And for the last defence of the city he outrages the Church by abolishing the last vestiges of the old social order. He extends the promise of crusading to include all the men of the city, making them all knights, arguing that it will make them better fighters. Pursued with the ideals of the American Dream, it seems, the Crusades would be no bad idea. And that's a dangerous moral to set before audiences with little grasp of history. The story ends in classic 'western' convention: Balian rides off into the sunset with the 'exotic and forbidden queen' who abandons her kingdom to be his woman.

The most interesting question is why this subject was considered worthy of a mega-budget epic at a time when America was engaged in invading Iraq. The film is set in 1187, at which time Baghdad was the capital of the Abbassid Caliphate, the centre of the Muslim world. We are presented with an epic story that celebrates an endeavour of empire and conquest unfulfilled in history, perhaps the better to imagine the mission that remains to be accomplished today.

If, as Barkawi insists, 'cultural and strategic histories must be written together', then the cinema stereotype of Muslims prepares the ground for strategic verities, planning and operations. It provides what might be called the 'known known' of the Western imagination that delivers public support for foreign policy. ('There are known knowns; there are things we know we know. We also know there are known unknowns; that is to say we know there are some things we do not know. But there are also unknown unknowns – the ones we don't know we don't know.'[10]) Muslim society is represented as barbaric, despotic, backward, inferior, weak, irrational, and all of its deficiencies are explained by the tradition which shapes its character: Islam. What is known explains Muslim society's hostility to the West and the nature of its strategic threat: terrorism is the weapon of the weak, a tactic suited to a chaotic social order steeped in intrigue. Terrorism neatly fits the urge for vengeance sought with the violence and brutality that, it is claimed, are licensed by its core tradition.

There is, however, a third arena which provides the explanatory link between popular culture and the strategic: academic orthodoxy. Academic study directly and indirectly services government and all its strategic agencies which feed on the fruits of its work. The academy also reaches out to the public through the strategic services it provides to journalism by way of punditry and expert opinion. Academic study of Islam and Muslim civilisation developed from the same sources as the popular cultural stereotypes. Indeed it was the learned, the monastic clerics who were the scholars and writers of the medieval period, that first manufactured and disseminated the black propaganda, the knowledgeable ignorance, that constitutes popular memory. The worldview of the known knowns developed over time to support a hierarchical vision of human history in which Muslim civilisation, along with those of China and India, were seen as stalled stages, remnants of conditions the West had transcended, through which it had progressed by nurturing the seeds of modernity which became liberal democracy. The academic schema places Muslim civilisation in the predicament of having been surpassed, and thus provides another rationale for its resentment of and animosity to the West. Academic questions structure journalistic questions and link with the ideas contained in popular memory until the vital question, the question of the unknown unknown, is impossible to ask: What if it is not like that at all?

The known knowns create the context in which political debate and judgement calls occur. It is not the case that everyone thinks only in terms of stereotypes, in America or anywhere else. Not everyone is unquestioningly convinced that a lurking menace unites Muslim nations and terrorist organisations in one vast conspiracy against America. But it does not take unanimity to push forward even contentious policies. It does require a climate of opinion where serious questions about the basis of strategic, political and intellectual judgements are not asked. And academic orthodoxy plays a crucial role in legitimating and justifying the failure to ask pertinent questions.

For some decades, academic orthodoxy on Islamic history and contemporary Muslim society has been personified by Bernard Lewis, 'the doyen of Middle Eastern Studies' according to the *New York Times Book Review*, and a professor at Princeton University. Through his numerous books, articles, opinion pieces and punditry, Lewis has acquired the ear of US administrations and, more strategically, over the years has trained many who served in the ranks of various administrations. Lewis's specialism is Ottoman Turkey but his predilection is Kemalist Turkey, the modern state founded after World War I by Kemal Ataturk, who had, he wrote, 'taken the first decisive steps in the acceptance of Western civilisation'.[11] The phraseology is crucial, since Lewis originated the concept of the clash of civilisations, a term he coined in a 1990 essay, 'The Roots of

Muslim Rage', that was subsequently taken up and popularised by Samuel Huntington. Central to this view is the fact that Islam and hence Muslim society is incapable of nurturing democracy. Therefore its only route to modernity is to embrace secular westernisation, just as Ataturk engineered the transformation of Turkey. From this much follows. All who persist in adherence to and reflection on Islam are by definition un- and/or anti-modern, not only backward-looking but either futile idealists or potentially demonic opponents of the West, out of step with the real needs of their own societies. The only acceptable voices from within Muslim society are those who can be co-opted to do the bidding of Western powers and promote westernisation, or those who are secularist critics of Islam. By definition this makes the majority of Muslim opinion and debate irrelevant both to its own future and to the interests of the West – even when it is not the latent antipathy in which terrorism is fostered and supported. Clearly it is an analysis that prepares the way for pre-emptive democracy-building in the Middle East.

This is exactly the case made by Michael Hirsh in an article for *Washington Monthly*. Hirsh reports that Lewis not only supplied op-ed pieces but was a behind-the-scenes enthusiast, stiffening the resolve of the Bush administration and urging on its commitment to the invasion of Iraq. Hirsh explores the academic career of Bernard Lewis to raise the 'What if it is wrong?' question. The orthodoxy represented by Lewis, as well as Lewis's work itself, has its critics in Western academic circles – and many more among Muslim intellectuals. Hirsh cites the alternative perspective put forward by Richard W. Bulliet for Islamo-Christian civilisation.[12] Bulliet, professor of history at Columbia University and a former director of the Middle East Institute, argues that instead of anticipating an inevitable clash of civilisations we should recognise that Islam and Christianity share the same roots – in the tradition of Abrahamic mono-theism – and grew out of the same cultural formation in the Hellenised Middle East. This common origin, as well as shared principles, enabled an ongoing exchange of mutual influence over the course of centuries despite the history of conflict. Furthermore, Lewis makes light of the impact of colonisation in the Middle East. In particular he overlooks the phase that followed World War I when the contemporary nation states of the region were formed, preferring to read his view of history into contemporary times. In contrast, Bulliet gives careful consideration to the socio-cultural and political consequences of this colonisation. He traces the connections between the legacy of colonisation and the flawed and faulty policy interventions complicit in the region's contemporary problems. Bulliet then argues that far from being a retrograde force inevitably plunging the Middle East into violence and obscurantism, turning to Islam, the source of the cherished values and moral principles of the region's people, may be a necessary part of developing coherent and autonomous democratic transformations. The transition may be complex and messy – but an Islamic orientation is not simply going backwards, nor merely turning against the West. It can be and is simultaneously about creating a different and better future. Hirsh is surely correct to point out that privileging only one academic viewpoint prejudices policy-making as much as it does public opinion.

Edward Said's *Orientalism*, published in 1978, pioneered the study of the consistent motifs used by Western literary and academic works to (mis)represent Muslim culture, history and society. Said drew upon the argument that knowledge is power, and that the ultimate power is dominance of ways of knowing – that is, framing the disciplines by which information is categorised, accumulated and interpreted, the process in which the Western academy rules. Orientalism refers to that range of interdisciplinary studies specialising in knowledge of the East in general and Islamic civilisation and Muslim society in particular. The knowledge created by the Orientalist way of knowing, Said argued, has been and is a self-serving misrepresentation generated and employed as a means to control, contain and make the Muslim world compliant with the interests of the West. In 1997 the Runnymede Trust, a British think tank, published its report *Islamophobia: A Challenge For Us All*. Islamophobia, they argued, is an irrational fear and hatred of Islam and Muslims, a product of the persistence of the Orientalist mindset with pernicious consequences for representation, reporting and dialogue, especially with Muslim communities living in the West. Both studies pinpointed the media, the arena of cultural production, as the prime location for the maintenance and transmission of what is ultimately a problem of knowledge.

As diagnoses with pithy labels, Orientalism and Islamophobia stimulated debate and backlash. They raised awareness of and sensitivity to Orientalism and Islamophobia in the media and more generally in society. But their greatest impact was among Muslim communities in Europe, North America and Australasia. Armed with these expert diagnoses, Muslim communities in the West became fixated on the problem of the media and focused a great deal of activity on demanding change through constant complaint.

There is precedent for such activism. From its inception as the medium of mass entertainment, community guardians everywhere worried about the influence of cinema on impressionable children, public morals and attitudes. The evidence for the immediacy and potency of its effect on the audience was not hard to find. People wanted the goods they saw up on the silver screen, which stimulated American manufacturing and exports and ultimately spawned consumerism. People wanted to know more about the stars who illuminated the screen, incubating whole new media industries based on fan magazines and celebrity lifestyles, phenomena germinated over the course of a century rather than new-minted in recent decades. Through cinema, people everywhere got to see the material abundance of American lifestyles which became global aspirational dreams. If cinema was so effective as a commercial vehicle, how could it not influence social mores, attitudes and ideas? Guardians of public morals quickly moved to establish censorship boards to regulate the content of movies. In America, Catholics played a prominent role in this organised complaint. Hollywood studios quickly learnt that complaint and censorship could influence their bottom line by enforcing expensive post-production changes or barring a film from lucrative markets. Complaint was not only domestic. By the 1920s, Hollywood was approaching an 80 per cent share of the global cinema market, a dominance it has never relinquished. Access to foreign markets and their sensitivities was factored into the studios' response to complaint: self-regulation. Catholics came to play prominent roles in the operation of the Production Code Administration, or Hays Office, by which Hollywood institutionalised its self-censoring guidelines to mollify complaint.

In the preamble to the Motion Picture Production Code of 1930 the movie-makers seemed to endorse the perception of their influence, with typical hyperbole: 'If motion pictures present stories that will affect lives for the better, they can become the most powerful force for the improvement of mankind.' It went on to mix equivocation with exaggeration:

Motion picture producers recognize the high trust and confidence which have been placed in them by the people of the world and which have made motion pictures a universal form of entertainment.

They recognise their responsibility to the public because of this trust and because entertainment and art are important influences in the life of a nation.

Hence, though regarding motion pictures primarily as entertainment without any explicit purpose of teaching or propaganda, they know that the motion picture within its own field of entertainment may be directly responsible for spiritual and moral progress, for higher types of social life, and for much correct thinking.

Among the items in the 1930 Code, as in all preceding guide-lines, to ensure 'a still higher level of wholesome entertainment for all the people', were the stipulations that 'no film may throw ridicule on any religious faith' and that 'the history, institutions, prominent people and citizenry of other nations shall be represented fairly'. The citizenry of other nations would suggest that 'correct thinking' on this last rule was honoured more in the breach than the observance. In the early years of silent cinema, Mexico created a diplomatic incident over the stereotypes of its representation. But have the stock characters of the comic peon – the quintessential lazy native – the bandoliered revolutionary or the bad bandito actually changed in a century of film?

However, the bulk of the provisions of the Production Code, which lasted until the 1950s, concerned social mores: crime, sex, scenes of passion, vulgarity, obscenity, profanity and a list of repellent subjects which included 'the sale of women or a woman selling her virtue', 'third degree methods' and 'brutality and possible gruesomeness'. These sensitivities determined the language of film in the golden age of movies: the 1930s and 40s. They also determined how stories were told, or mangled, re-imagined and recast in the telling to make them acceptable to the sensitivities of the American audience, and what it would tolerate being told. An entire institutional framework existed to vet scripts and view production footage. However, the system worked most effectively as self-censorship, the internalisation by writers, directors and producers of the conventions that would meet the requirements of the American public. Where there was self-censorship there was also adventurous subversion by film-makers who devised creative ways to intimate and allude to more risqué behaviour, ideas and meaning, to reach beyond polite society and speak elliptically to the more broad-minded. In the observance and the breach, the Code worked because movie-makers and audience shared a common framework of cultural understanding. As American society changed, so the interpretation and application of the Code changed and eventually ended.

But for precisely these reasons the representation of 'other nations' remained stuck in the domain of popular memory, the perspectives of the known knowns. American Muslim organisations would arrive to protest and complain, but the diagnosis they advanced required a drastic cure. To succeed they had to secure a mutual recognition that necessitated dismantling the very conventions and stock characters that made story-telling possible. What writers, directors, producers and audiences did not know they did not know, the unknown unknowns, could not be internalised to effect change. There simply was no coverage to make visible the diversity of ideas, practice or debate, to distinguish and explain the differences between the ideal and actual or to reveal the different contexts, experiences and histories of Muslim life around the world. There was little or nothing to lift the veil on the unknown unknowns.

And then along came Osama bin Laden. In word and action as well as look, bin Laden embodies every negative stereotype in the lexicon of Orientalism and Islamophobia, he is the fulfilment of every worst nightmare of the Western imagining. And his is a waking nightmare wreaking horrific devastation. A self-proclaimed authentic voice of Islam, bin Laden is a self-appointed leader of a loose assemblage of shadowy forces. He appropriates contentious and extreme interpretations of Islam – though he is no Islamic scholar – with the same scrupulous disregard as he assimilates every grievance around the Muslim world to bolster his own aim of unending jihad. Bin Laden represents only himself as he represents everything popular memory has ever claimed about Islam and Muslims. His politics of oppositional destruction – which is not the definition of the term *jihad* but its perversion – is no age-old tradition but rather an entirely new development, a creation of globalisation, not history, and not rooted in specific place or actual politics. It appeals to the generalities of disaffection of global Muslim dissent. But it is not, nor is it capable of being, an answer to any specific dilemma of any actual Muslim community. It seduces the emotive sense of impotence that many Muslims in many places feel at being unable to alter the realities of their lives for the better, confronted as they are with the various conundrums of the historic legacy of particular kinds of democracy deficits. It deploys the subtle seduction of the gun, the populist urge to fight the multiple injustices apparent around the Muslim world, and turns it outward by blaming the lone hyperpower adjudged complicit in perpetuating the woes of Muslims everywhere. Though as ideology, strategy and tactics it is rejected by and abhorrent to the vast majority of Muslims, in an instant bin Laden succeeded in making the scenarios of innumerable movies manifestly plausible by the enormity of suffering he inspired. The fear unleashed by this onslaught found expression where the concerns of American life eventually go to be mediated, not on the big screen but in the security of people's living rooms on television.

Television is the principal domain of the popular, the forum that hosts the national conversation. Television responds to, reflects, comments and speculates on the news as well as making news in the sense of setting the fashion, creating the buzzwords and punchlines that set the mood of the times. Television appropriates the techniques, conventions, storylines, plots and stock characters initially created for the movies. It domesticates cinematic themes to the dictates of being resident in people's homes as part of family life. Television feeds off what is reported, recycles what is known. Familiarity and accessibility are the most basic definitions of television and its success.

A national trauma as dramatic as 9-11 inevitably found expression across the entire gamut of American television output. Previously, American television had not been lacking in occasional reference to terrorism or recourse to the familiar stereotypes of Islam and the Muslim world, but after 9-11 these became central motifs and references in series drama. *La Femme Nikita* (1997–March 2001) sums up the high-concept series that preceded the trauma. Its heroine personified a perplexed and conflicted America. She might be a trained assassin but she had questions about the use of her powers in the less certain complications of a new world order. 9-11 reunited and clarified the writing of cultural and strategic histories; the dynamics of television drama were reconfigured accordingly. The reconfiguration was not something new: it mirrored the transformation of action movies in the 1970s and 80s.

Within three weeks of 9-11, *The West Wing*, as we have seen, held its civics lesson on the problem. The special edition stood outside the ongoing series, which continued for five more seasons to run its own discreet and distinct foreign policy subtly at odds with that of the actual White House. But the parallel presidency of Jed Bartlet returned continually to the persistent presence of Muslim terrorism. *The Agency*, a series based on the workings of the CIA and made with its cooperation, had the misfortune of an intended debut in September 2001, at exactly the time the real CIA was being blamed for one of the worst intelligence failures in American history. The series launch was delayed, the show's focus rapidly sharpened, its central characters recast, its storylines reworked. It could then set about showing how the expertise and workings of the Agency could win the war on terror. *Sue Thomas: F.B. Eye* (2002–05) came along to demonstrate how the domestic agency, the FBI, was tackling the war on terror and did so with a strong emphasis on family and religious values designed to appeal to the American heartlands. The deaf federal agent, Sue Thomas, and her associates only ever encountered and always foiled Muslim terrorists. An already established series, *JAG* (1995–2005), about the workings of the Judge Advocate General department, mixed character themes lifted from the film *Top Gun* with the courtroom format of *Law and Order*. After 9-11 it suddenly leapt into the top ten of television ratings. It consistently employed storylines reflecting the wars in Afghanistan and then Iraq as well as the war on terror. In 2003 it gave birth to a spin-off series, *NCIS*, about the Naval Criminal Investigation Service, where again terrorist threats were a recurring theme. *Law and Order* is a long-running institution of

American series television. For nearly two decades it has mined the news for storylines that can be reworked into scenarios of crime detection and courtroom resolution that allow the moral dilemmas of American life to be debated, along with extremely sharp dialogue between its central characters. In recent years it has tackled the issue of Muslim female circumcision or genital mutilation. In homage to John Walker Lindh, the American Muslim convert captured in Afghanistan, it featured the case of a convert to Islamic fundamentalism – apparently his parents' infidelities meant they did not love him enough. The action end of the spectrum produced *Alias* (2001–06) and its confused and confusing world of nefarious but insistent threats with terrorism at its heart. *E Ring* (2005–06), named after the outer circuit of the Pentagon, is a political drama directly concerned with the worldwide threat of terrorism and covert military response. *The Unit* (2007–) is about a covert military unit, modelled on Delta Force, which officially does not exist but which is despatched to do what is necessary to combat the realities of the war on terror. But most of all there is the high-octane action of the award-winning series *24* (2001–) and the very bad days endured by Jack 'I'm going to need a hacksaw' Bauer.

In the recurrent storylines of such programming, American television has domesticated a sustained climate of fear. Terrorism has become a nightly reality of American life, an ever-present and all-pervasive threat. But the reconfiguration of series television has done more than appropriate elements of the action movie genre. It has domesticated a popular understanding of the rules of engagement by which terrorism operates and how the war on terror should be waged. The audience's familiarity with these rules of engagement demonstrates how compatibly America's cultural and strategic histories coalesce.

The first rule of engagement concerns the character notes of the Muslim terrorist. This stock character remains consistent: fanatical, relentless, brutal, barbaric and so driven by hatred of America as to seek its demise through indiscriminate mass slaughter of innocents. The terrorists continue to be indeterminate of origin and shorn of actual and specific cultural and political histories. The more television reflects America's increased direct involvement in the Middle East, the less the domain of the popular deals with the complex realities of the region's culture or history, the more the unknown remains unknown. And television highlights a chilling addition: the threat is not only 'over there' but is also lurking next door in the form of a suburban neighbour harbouring the malice and willing to advance the plans of terrorists. As the set-up of an episode of *Sue Thomas: F.B. Eye* once commented: 'It was only a matter of time ... Before they sent people with our face.' This referred to the possibility of a plot involving an Albanian Muslim terrorist and the fraught question of how America would cope if it could not recognise potential enemies by the simple expedient of racial profiling.

The second premise of the rules of engagement of terror is that all terrorists seek to acquire and deploy weapons of mass destruction: nuclear, chemical and biological. In this television is doing no more than mirroring the basic premise of the thinking and planning of the department of homeland security. Sources within the department are unequivocal that these threats are the bottom line. It may seem logical for government to plan for worst-case scenarios, just in case. But the authors have listened to some working within the security establishment who question how it is possible to make a sensible risk assessment of such a premise. So far, terrorist atrocities have been caused by resort to box-cutters and home-made explosive devices that are entirely conventional. We have also heard some in the security community who are prepared to whisper a heretical thought: given the incestuous world of listening to the chatter of terrorists while the terrorists listen to the chatter of American discourse – popular, learned and political – are the terrorists being given ideas of what they should aspire to do? Or are Western agencies hearing what they expect to hear rather than what is actually being said?

The nature of the threat assessment has more than speculative consequences. It determines the allocation of real resources, the funding of research programmes, the development of detection devices, security infrastructure, procedures and systems, the nature of surveillance and the monitoring of populations and people's movements. The premise becomes the basis for investment in careers and generates new industries. Once established, as history demonstrates, the entire panoply becomes a status quo, an establishment of vested interests that cannot easily contemplate the unknown unknown, the 'What if we are wrong?' question, that would mean its own demise. It was just such a mindset of institutionalised fear of a global communist conspiracy that underwrote the development of America's military-industrial complex. It was this institutionalised politics of fear that delivered electoral support for the greatest peacetime expansion of America's military-defence budget under Ronald Reagan, at the cost of burgeoning debt that transformed America into the world's principal debtor nation. But as the former head of the Iraq Survey Group, Dr David Kay, told the Senate Armed Services Committee, the end of the Cold War revealed that all the strategic planning and enormous financial outlay to counter 'what had looked like a 10 foot power' was expended against an over-estimate of Soviet military capacity. What Russia actually possessed was a rusting and degraded arsenal as badly maintained as the fabric of its society.[13] Such concerns have no place in the certainties of series television.

And this leads to the third of the rules of engagement. David Kay was not only making the point that threat assessments taken as strategic verity historically have turned out to be wrong. His argument was far more profound. The failure he identified was a failure to invest in 'our human intelligence capability', the problem of knowledge in 'understanding the other'. Reliance on remote surveillance, a technological industry that observed and gathered information at a distance, along with the withering of actual human intelligence agents operating on the ground in foreign countries, had been substituted for listening to and learning about the ideas and attitudes of other people. It was reliance on the wrong kind of intelligence which led to the debacle of a war premised on the existence of Iraqi weapons of mass destruction which had already been destroyed. Agencies listened to what they wanted to hear and did not question sources that told them what they expected to hear. They saw from space and by over-flying what they expected and wanted to see – not what actually existed.

But such sage opinion makes for awful television drama. Despite the failure of intelligence and federal investigation agencies to foil 9-11 or prevent an illegal war on false pretences, television, since 9-11, has been doing for these services what action films once did for the military: redeeming their reputation and convincing Americans that their capabilities are essential to national security and survival. In series after series, intelligence-gathering dependent on computer and satellite technology is central to the plot, unfailing in alerting all relevant agencies to imminent threats and dangerous individuals and crucial to keeping Americans safe. Government and its intelligence agencies know the threat which is out there. They will develop the threads and by covert action eradicate the evil-doers – this is the promise that television plays repeatedly to the American audience without ever questioning the deficiencies of 'human intelligence capacity' or problems in 'understanding the other'.

The fourth of the rules of engagement concerns how America contends with terrorists. The answer given repeatedly on television is by any means necessary. When government contends that 'enemy combatants' have no legal status under the Geneva Conventions, and that torture is not torture but extreme interrogation and hence acceptable, nightly television repeatedly makes such practices familiar and dramatically justified. The necessity of American safety becomes the mother of inventive abrogation of national and international law. It is a scenario pursued through overt and covert action that any television series could have mined from the news:

> The present war is no bloodless, fake, opera bouffe engagement. Our men have been relentless; have killed to exterminate men, women, children, prisoners and captives, active insurgents and suspected people from lads of ten and up ... Our soldiers have pumped salt water into men to 'make them talk', have taken prisoner people who ... peacefully surrendered, and an hour later, without an atom of evidence to show that they were insurrectos, stood them on a bridge and shot them down one by one ... It is not civilized warfare, but we are not dealing with civilized people. The only thing they know and fear is force, violence, and brutality, and we give it to them.[14]

It is unlikely that today's television script writers refer to the *Philadelphia Ledger* of 1899, where this report appeared on America's first overseas intervention as an imperial exercise of democracy-building by military occupation. It tells us something about the unchanging response of power to the challenge of insurgent opposition, but it's not the kind of scenario that feeds nightly television drama. The article concerned American forces operating in the Philippines. The initial explanation for the Spanish-American war of 1898 was to support those struggling for independence from corrupt and overbearing Spanish colonial rule. But in the Philippines this promise soon turned into open insurrection against American forces. Two weeks after defeating the Spanish in Manila harbour, America returned the leaders of the independence struggle, headed by Emilio Aguinaldo, from exile. Aguinaldo declared Filipino independence in June 1898. Despite earlier assurances, on reflection the US found the country unready for self-government, and worse, that the removal of its troops would usher in chaos and leave the country to the untender mercy of outside forces. A peace treaty was signed by which Spain ceded the Philippines to the US. President McKinley declared a policy of 'benevolent assimilation', assuring the Filipinos that 'we come not as invaders or conquerors but as friends'. There was little that was friendly about US response to the insurrection that followed, as reported by the *Ledger*. The 'little brown brother' characterisation of Filipinos morphed into the demonisation of *insurrectos*, indistinguishable from the terrorists of today. President Theodore Roosevelt issued a Peace Proclamation on 4 July 1902, but independence did not come to the Philippines for another 42 years.

Without looking that far back in its history for themes and images of the rules of engagement, American television drama nevertheless anticipated rather than followed the revelations of Guantánamo Bay and Abu Ghraib. Television picked up where action movies had led. *GI Jane* (1997) showed Demi Moore's would-be Navy Seal being waterboarded. In that case it was part of her tough-love military training: 'It's an exercise in controlling your panic', her instructor says as water is poured over the rags covering her face. Surely what is good enough for American military training cannot be torture when applied to an enemy – just as the Bush administration has been so anxious to argue.

There is another reason why questionable, not to say unlawful, issues of military practice are mediated as justifiable action by television drama: the cosy relationship maintained between the Pentagon and Hollywood. The relationship is not new – it stretches back to World War II. During the mass mobilisation of that global conflict, Hollywood went to war in earnest. Apart from the stars who actually enlisted and saw service, Ronald Reagan spent the duration making military training films. John Ford led a naval film team that recorded the battle of the Pacific, and Frank Capra made the consciousness-raising film series *Why We Fight*, seen by every enlisted man. After the war, relations between Hollywood and the Pentagon matured, an entire department now being devoted to facilitating film and television productions. The quid pro quo for saving producers huge sums by making available filming locations and military equipment – from aircraft carriers to helicopters and stealth bombers – is oversight of scripts and the provision of military advisors to suggest what should and should not be shown.

A series such as *JAG* is a prime beneficiary of this cosy relationship. 'As such, it has become a tool of wartime public policy', according to an article in the *New York Times*.[15] By marrying themes from the action movies of the 1980s with contemporary conflicts, it also acts as a bridge in the transmission of the reconfiguration of the rules of engagement from one era to another, as much as from one medium to another. The central character in *JAG*, Harmon Rabb Jr, is a naval fighter pilot, qua the zeitgeist movie *Top Gun* (1986). A night vision problem diverts him from carrier duty to becoming a top-flight JAG lawyer, though he regularly gets to strut his stuff as an ace pilot to solve cases and provide the series with action adventure scenarios. But there is another recurring storyline of the early seasons of *JAG* that provides connective links between past and present. Rabb is the son of a naval pilot who went missing in action (MIA) over Vietnam. *JAG*, a series which ran from 1995 to 2005, thus domesticated a signature issue of the action movie genre of the 80s. In action movies, MIAs symbolically represent the humiliation brought upon America by its defeat, the fact which had to be redeemed by the renewed projection of military might in new rules of engagement. Stanley Karnow points out that in World War II, more than 20 per cent of American soldiers who died in the conflict were listed as missing in action. The proportion was roughly the same in the Korean War. But in Vietnam the bodies of only 4 per cent of the 58,000 killed were not recovered, the combination of tropical conditions and inhospitable terrain making finding all the fallen unlikely. Yet the MIA issue became both a cinematic and political cause célèbre. The movies provided audiences with visual images of Americans held against their will, still being tortured in inhuman conditions in Vietnam long after the war had ended. A *Time* survey published in 1990 found that '62% of Americans – 84% of veterans – maintained that the Vietnamese were holding US captives'. Karnow argues that not a single American political figure, including presidents, would admit openly what most of them believed privately: that no such American captives existed.[16]

The myth that American leaders would not lay to rest provided *JAG* with the recurring storyline of Rabb Jr's relentless search for information about his father. One episode reprises Rabb's teenage mission to Vietnam to search for his father, the enterprise which makes him the fighting man he is. Other episodes follow the trail and suggest that his father, for reasons that forever remain unclear, became a prisoner first of the Chinese and then the Russians, before being lost in the Siberian wastes of the gulag where he eventually died, but not before giving Rabb a Russian half-brother. By thus linking Vietnam to the opposing powers in the Cold War, *JAG* continues not just the myth of the MIAs but also the mindset which 'underlined the ignorance behind America's involvement in Southeast Asia'.[17] And this ignorance sets the context of attitudes and ideas with which the series addresses the contemporary conflicts in which Rabb becomes involved.

The episode that brought *JAG* to the attention of the *New York Times* as 'a tool of wartime public policy' was 'Tribunal', shown on 30 April 2002, in which an alleged architect of 9-11 is captured in Afghanistan. He confesses his part in the atrocity after being grilled under hot lights for thirteen days and subjected to interrogation with truth serum. It then falls to the familiar cast of JAG lawyers to debate the rules of evidence and enact the details of the military tribunal which will administer justice. The scriptwriter of this episode admitted to being given details of the proposed rules governing these military tribunals two weeks before secretary of defence Donald Rumsfeld made them public at a news conference. 'News used to be the first rough draft of history. Now it's the first draft of a Hollywood screenplay', Robert Lichter, president of the Center for Media and Public Policy, a non-partisan Washington research group, is quoted as saying.[18] On television, the 'full and fair' tribunals that Rumsfeld promised were instantly up and running. As the *New York Times* concluded:

> In real life, no such luck, Osama bin Laden and his top lieutenants have proved elusive. Pentagon officials paint a frustrating picture of interrogations yielding little evidence on which to build a case against anyone in captivity. They say putting together cases will be so painstaking that real tribunals may not be held for months, if ever.

In fact, it was another six years before the first tribunal verdict. In August 2008 Salim Hamdan was found guilty of providing material support to terrorists, by virtue of being employed as Osama bin Laden's driver. He was acquited of conspiring with al-Qaeda. However, the outcome was far from 'full' or 'fair'. In 2006 the Supreme Court ruled that the President did not have authority to institute such military tribunals. The Military Commissions Act was quickly passed into law. In June 2008, the Supreme Court ruled that under habeas corpus Guantánamo detainees had the right to full judicial review in US civilian courts. And after all that, the US had to admit the entire exercise was futile. Guilty or innocent, Hamdan was condemned to Guantánamo because no country would accept him. Hardly justice, but a signal tribute to the power of demonisation.

But what effect did the vicarious experience provided by television have on the climate of public opinion? The public had already received the reassurance of dramatic catharsis that justice is being done. Viewers could recall images of principled and honourable characters they had come to know and trust actually doing the right thing: upholding the rule of law, albeit by unconventional means in the most extreme of circumstances. Does planting that idea in the public domain induce a sufficiently complacent and compliant public in support of government policy? Incarceration at Guantánamo is a continuing story. Over the years, more than half of Guantánamo's inmates have been quietly released without ever having been charged with any offence, never having had the faintest suspicion of a day in court. Reality never caught up with its fictional representation. But when the majority of people admit to getting their news from entertainment and the line between entertainment and news continues to blur, the fictional fairy tale told them there was no problem to be concerned about. Can the same be said for all the other issues where scriptwriters 'felt obliged to inject heroism into the story to raise the morale of viewers and troops',[19] as the JAG lawyers resolved cases involving friendly fire or collateral damage, otherwise known as the bombing of civilians? JAG's lawyers even vindicated America's entire case for the invasion of Iraq before the International Criminal Court! So, surely, there is no cause for concern.

The ability to be shocked is a basic stimulus to dissent and protest. But what impetus does a culturally aware public have to be taken aback by reports of what happened in Guantánamo, Abu Ghraib, Falluja or Haditha when the underlying issues and even the images have been prefigured, already defused through dramatic justification by television? In 2003 a two-part episode of *JAG* introduced the characters of what became the spin-off series *NCIS*. While Harmon Rabb is being tried for a murder that he, of course, did not commit, the members of NCIS are preoccupied with getting information from a captured terrorist. So, lodged in the visual memory of the audience is the sight of this Muslim terrorist held in the brig of a naval vessel, shackled, naked, possibly cowering, possibly in a stress position, being bombarded with loud music. Agent Gibbs of NCIS arrives and is able to extract the necessary information by more amiable methods. But the audience has been familiarised with, or should that be anaesthetised to, the alternatives. And on television the prisoner is always guilty, a real culprit responsible for actual evil. A similar scenario turns up in the series *Criminal Minds* (2005–) about the work of the FBI's Behavioral Analysis Unit. The show's regular cast members, who normally specialise in profiling the worst kind of murderers and serial killers, set off for Guantánamo Bay to help with the interrogation of a terrorist, part of a sleeper cell in possession of a chemical dispersal device. The team's superior psychological training, plus the fortuitous fact that one of their number is fluent in Arabic, enables them to elicit the vital information that the blunt instrument of the usual treatment – dehumanising torture – had failed to achieve. Here television offers a double desensitisation: the harsh regime becomes familiar, an accessible aspect of normality; and where it fails, other tactics and expertise are readily available to ensure public safety. So, by whichever means, all is for the best; the outcome, as it always is on television, is satisfactory.

When it comes to implementing the 'by any means necessary' rule, no one is more prepared to do whatever it takes than Jack Bauer. No series more completely encapsulates the new rules of engagement with terrorism than *24*, of which Jack, the most complete reconfiguration of the television action hero, is the star. To date, Jack Bauer has had six 'worst days' of his television life as he encounters relentless terrorist threats which turn into actual attacks on America. In the world of *24*, terrorists have access to the most sophisticated technology; they exclusively launch attacks with nuclear, chemical and biological weapons. They succeed in building a nuclear bomb in Los Angeles, which Jack ensures is 'safely' exploded in the desert. They gain the technology to compromise all the nuclear power plants in America, and succeed in making one plant go critical, with the resulting release of lethal radiation into the atmosphere. They release a toxic nerve gas into a shopping mall, as well as decimating the staff of the Counter Terrorist Unit (CTU) by planting a canister in its Los Angeles office. They acquire and release a genetically engineered virus with no known antidote into a Los Angeles hotel. Ultimately they succeed in exploding a suitcase nuclear bomb in a suburb of Los Angeles – the programme can hardly be said to be doing much for the City of Angels tourist industry! Standing between the terrorists and full realisation of their plans is the Los Angeles office of the CTU, equipped with an array of computers from which it can interface with satellites, seemingly all computers everywhere, and all intelligence agencies in the US and around the world. Through the power of technology, the analysts at CTU can know what needs to be known and can do most of what needs to be done. But actually catching the terrorists still needs field agents, and CTU appears to have teams of them deployed around the city and ready to be despatched from headquarters at a moment's notice, equipped with a small arsenal of weapons. When apprehended, terrorists are brought back to CTU for interrogation by a battery of techniques – everything from being blindfolded and subjected to white noise, to chemical agents which inflict 'an inhuman amount of pain'. In the CTU office or in the field, the agent par excellence is Jack Bauer. Jack has spent his whole life defending his country from terrorists. In this cause he has sacrificed his family, his relationships and his friendships, and ultimately is ready to sacrifice his own life, demanded by a terrorist in exchange for information that the government considers vital, because Jack knows the distinction between dying for something and dying for nothing.

But it is not Jack Bauer's willingness to suffer or inflict pain and sacrifice on himself which made 24 leap in the ratings, or which made him a hero with American troops serving in Iraq and the quintessential model for the new rules of engagement. It came about because Jack Bauer will do whatever it takes – Jack Bauer will kill and use the entire repertoire of torture techniques to elicit the urgently needed information to foil the ticking time-bomb threats that are the premise of the non-stop pulsating action of each series of 24.

The show's popularity took off in season two (first screened October 2002 to May 2003) when a dishevelled Jack Bauer, still grieving over the loss of his wife and estrangement of his daughter, is brought back to CTU because only he has the contacts to infiltrate a gang of criminals who may be aiding terrorists. Jack marks his return by bursting into an interrogation room, shooting a shackled prisoner, and announcing 'I'm going to need a hacksaw' as he checks that the man is dead. He then takes the severed head of his victim as a peace offering to establish his bona fides with the criminals. Now that's whatever it takes! The complicated interweaving plotlines of this second series also boosted the ratings by focusing on the hot-button, old familiar zeitgeist issue: Muslim terrorists constructing and seeking to explode a nuclear bomb on American soil. And worst of all, in the lexicon of popular paranoia, a mainstay of this plot is a modish, blonde California girl who has been brainwashed into believing that America is the root of all evil around the world and must be taught an atomic lesson to make it change its ways.

Torture is the signature theme of 24. It is ordered by President Palmer, supposedly the model of an honest and honourable leader and incidentally the first black president. It is institutionalised in the practice of the CTU where, when all else fails, the enigmatic Blake is summoned with his suitcase full of extremely large hypodermic syringes containing truth serum or concoctions which simply inflict pain to make people talk. The greatest conceit of 24 is not that its action takes place in real time over the course of one 24-hour period, each episode of the season being one hour of one day, timed by a running clock which even accounts for the gaps taken up by commercial breaks. The greater conceit on which all its storylines rely is that torture works. And that is what caused such concern that in November 2006 a delegation headed by the dean of the US Military Academy at West Point flew to California to express their fears to the creative team responsible for the programme, as reported in *The New Yorker*.[20]

Brigadier General Patrick Finnegan, dean of West Point, has taught a course on the law of war to senior students. He told

The New Yorker that it had become increasingly difficult to convince some cadets that America had to respect the rule of law and human rights, even if terrorists did not, and identified one of the reasons as the misconceptions spread by *24*, which was exceptionally popular among his students. The most significant misconception that the delegation, consisting of three highly experienced military and FBI interrogators, sought to tackle was that torture works, when the overwhelming evidence is that it does not. Tony Lagouranis, a former army interrogator in Iraq who accompanied Finnegan, is quoted as saying:

'In Iraq, I never saw pain produce intelligence. I worked with someone who used waterboarding. I used severe hyperthermia, dogs and sleep deprivation. I saw suspects after soldiers had gone into their homes and broken their bones, or made them sit on a Humvee's hot exhaust pipes until they got third-degree burns. Nothing happened.'

The article also quotes a report of December 2007 by the Intelligence Science Board, an advisory panel to the US intelligence community, which declared: 'most observers, even those within professional circles, have unfortunately been influenced by the media's colourful (and artificial) view of interrogation as almost always involving hostility.' It is this aspect of the Jack Bauer effect which has been explored by Philippe Sands QC, a lawyer and professor of international law at University College London. Sands highlights the fact that far from being the isolated activity of a few bad apples, such as those prosecuted for events at Abu Ghraib, the problem of torture is systemic, comes from the top and has been influenced by *24*.

In his books and articles Sands has followed the documents, such as the declassified memo written in March 2003 by John Yoo, a deputy in the department of justice's office of legal counsel, in which the justice department told the Pentagon that presidential authority overrode numerous laws banning torture or cruel treatment of prisoners in US custody. The memo endorsed assault, maiming and even administering mind-altering drugs to prisoners. In an interview with *Democracy Now!*, Sands explains how he discovered the influence of *24*.[21] When interviewing Diane Beaver, a lawyer at Guantánamo Bay, the academic lawyer scribbled a note '24 Becker' which did not ring any bells. When he Googled the phrase, 'it came up with "*24* – do you mean *24* Bauer"? So I typed yes.' Having learnt of the existence of Jack Bauer, Sands then spoke with Beaver and her boss Mike Dunlavey in greater detail:

> ... as she described it to me, the TV program *24* had many friends down at Guantánamo. And the timing is fascinating. The abusive interrogations started in November 2002, just three weeks after the start of the second season of *24*. And it seems that there is a direct connection between that program and the creating of an environment in which individuals felt it was permissible to push the envelope, as it was put to me.[22]

If professional lawyers and those being trained for military command in the field are influenced by the worldview of Jack Bauer, why quibble about its influence on the general public? What works the Bauer effect is patriotism, as Brigadier General Finnegan noted: 'The disturbing thing is that although torture may cause Jack Bauer some angst, it is always the patriotic thing to do.'

Patriotism is central to Jack Bauer's character, the motive force which drives him to do whatever it takes. He is the one exception to *24*'s rule that everyone breaks. Jack returns in season six after nearly two years of being tortured in a Chinese prison, during which time not only did he not break, he spoke not a word. And on his return he is ready to do whatever his commander-in-chief, the president, asks, which in this instance is that he hand himself over to a terrorist to be killed. This is the unquestioning patriotism that infused the action movie genre.

And in *24* and the character of Jack Bauer it is mixed with a streak of insubordination, a defiance of any rule or authority that interferes with what must be done, just as in the action heroes of the 70s and 80s. But again there is the implicit question: if this kind of patriotism is the ideal, what is actually left of the idea of America as the rule of law or respect for human rights and enduring values? The scenarios that *24* deals with surmount this disturbing thought by invoking the justification of a higher good, served by choosing between bad options: torture works to defuse or circumvent the ticking time-bomb when there is no time for other means, therefore it saves lives. However beloved it is as a classroom conundrum, the ticking time-bomb scenario – you have in custody the one person who knows for certain the location of a bomb primed and ready to explode and cause the death and suffering of innocents: what would you do? – never occurs in reality. The use of torture has become familiar to American audiences. Human Rights First estimates that in the year 2000, 42 scenes of torture were shown on prime-time US television, while in 2003 there were 228.[23] The Parents' Television Council has counted 67 torture scenes in the first five seasons of *24*.[24] And whereas torture was once the cinema's signifier of villainy and barbarism, the practice of the enemy, in the cause of national security it has been appropriated by the hero, another of the parallels with the action movie genre. On *24* it is simply 'a dramatic device to show you how desperate a situation is', in the words of Joel Surnow, the show's creator. Who adds: 'America wants the war on terror fought by Jack Bauer. He's a patriot.'[25] In which case, what other freedoms and liberties can also be overturned in the cause of vanquishing terror?

A noticeable feature of the first five seasons of *24*, during which lethal nuclear radiation, nerve gas and a genetically modified virus have been unleashed on the American public, is the lack of interest taken in the effects of these incidents. The government is always counting on CTU, or more often Jack Bauer alone, saving the day rather than causing panic by an evacuation and thus taking citizens out of harm's way. The body counts caused by the show's scenarios are script points. The fear of terrorism is pervasive, but how society responds to it is not a democratic debate, it's taken care of by Jack Bauer. In season six, responding to complaints not just about torture but also regarding its portrayal of Muslim terrorism, the show decided to debate the wider issues.

The season opens by setting the scene: there have been ten terrorist attacks in eleven days across America. The public are urged to be vigilant and report anything suspicious. A discernibly Arab man carrying a rucksack is walking to a bus stop on a crowded street; all eyes turn suspiciously to him. When the bus arrives, the driver refuses to open the door and let him board. The Arab man protests that he has rights too. But this precautionary fear by the bus driver is in vain – the suicide bomber is already aboard. The bus explodes. In Washington the show's second African-American president, and second President Palmer, younger brother of the assassinated David Palmer, wrestles with conflicting advice on how to respond. Everyone agrees that Jack Bauer must be sacrificed, but the chief of staff and national security advisor have radically different views on what else should be done. The national security advisor insists that once Jack's blood sacrifice is delivered to the terrorist Abu Fayed, along with $25 million, he will provide the location of the terrorist responsible for the attacks, Hamri al Assad. Once Assad is killed, she argues, lopping off the head of the terrorist network will mean that the attacks stop. The chief of staff disagrees and proposes a slew of measures targeting the Muslim population among whom and from whom the terrorists gain support. There is plenty of precedent: Lincoln suspended habeas corpus and Franklin Roosevelt interned Japanese Americans during World War II. President Palmer observes that everyone considered the internment of 200,000 Japanese Americans to be a grave mistake: 'But they don't say how many Japanese this prevented from carrying out acts of sabotage on this country', the chief of staff ripostes.

When Jack is delivered to Fayed, he discovers that Assad, far from ordering the terrorist attacks, arrived in America to stop them. He wants to negotiate a ceasefire and bring his and other terrorist organisations into the mainstream of the political process. The real culprit is actually Fayed, the unrepentant terrorist, who has five suitcase nuclear devices as well as a horde of potential suicide bombers at his disposal. Learning this truth re-energises Jack, whose task becomes stopping Fayed and tracking the source of his nuclear weapons. This becomes the main storyline. But two subsidiary threads are interwoven. On a suburban street in Los Angeles, neighbours watch as the FBI arrest an Arab American on suspicion of involvement with terrorism. His son loudly protests his innocence. When two neighbours begin menacing the young man, another intervenes to protect him, insisting he take refuge in his house. But the young man, Ahmed, and not his father, actually is a terrorist charged with the mission of collecting the vital piece of equipment that will permit Fayed to arm his nuclear weapons. The idea of a terrorist living quietly on a suburban street is not new to 24. In season four an entire family of terrorists – father, mother and son – have been living quietly for five years in suburbia preparing for the day when they will strike at the heart of America by assisting in the plot to attack its nuclear power plants. The threat within the Muslim American population, the 'potential enemy within' scenario, is familiar. The other sub-plot concerns the head of the Islamic American Alliance (IAA). The FBI arrives at the organisation's headquarters and demands its personnel records to add to the database it is compiling to check against its watchlist. The lawyer for the organisation happens to be none other than the sister of President Palmer, who vigorously argues the civil liberties case not only with the FBI but directly on the phone to her brother. When the head of IAA suggests that they should just comply since they have nothing to hide, Sandra Palmer replies:

'We may have nothing to hide but we do have something to protect.' For the sake of the right of privacy she deletes the records from the organisation's computers and is arrested along with her boss, and both are taken to a detention centre. The Constitution is indeed being treated as a list of suggestions and Muslim Americans are being rounded up. Ethnic profiling means that all Muslim Americans, including Nadia who works for CTU, are to have restricted access to security-sensitive information. We also learn that there is a Guantánamo-like prison which is operated on American soil. Eventually, the head of IAA becomes suspicious of some of his fellow inmates – who speak Arabic, which he cannot understand – and passes a vital message to CTU, which informs them that Fayed has not one but five nuclear devices. He becomes a mole for the FBI, trying to gather more information on his fellow detainees. They turn out to have read the vital information from the internet and are merely disaffected citizens with latent support and sympathy for the terrorists.

Back in Washington, the argument over whether and how to tear up the provisions of the Constitution continues. Another sub-plot concerns those within the administration who plan to kill the president and blame it on Assad, so that the hawkish vice president can take over and bring detention centres for Muslim Americans and all the other proposals into effect. When this bomb injures but does not kill President Palmer, we are back in a 25th Amendment scenario, which also bedevilled the first President Palmer in season two. To be ousted by one cabinet might be thought unfortunate, but two President Palmers ousted by two cabinets looks less like carelessness than the obsessions of tired scriptwriters. The point of sidelining presidents who trust and rely on the powers of Jack Bauer is to advance the case for military retaliation against Muslim countries that sponsor terrorists. So however it unwinds its sub-plots, 24 makes it clear that Muslim terrorism is a clear and present danger that has somehow to be tackled at home and abroad. And if the major thesis is that safety comes from doing whatever is necessary to stop terrorists, the audience is invited to become familiar with and accustomed to the full repertoire of measures that might be needed.

24 is not breaking new ground in considering the domestic consequences of responding to terrorism. It was the subject of the movie *The Siege* (1998). It is worth examining the differences in the way 24 and *The Siege* handle the question, separated as they are by the watershed of 9-11. Both are considering the appropriate treatment for people who exist in popular memory as the 'ideal candidates for the metaphysical enemy'. Academic orthodoxy, the Lewis Doctrine, as the *Wall Street Journal* has called it, rests on the proposition that the West is now in the last stages of a centuries-old struggle for dominance and prestige with Islamic civilisation. But Islam, once Europe's enemy without, now resides within Western nations, as evidenced by the growing Muslim population of America. So how would or should America regard Muslim Americans if Muslim terrorists began sustained attacks on the homeland?

Like 24, *The Siege*'s opening scenes set up the arrival of Muslim suicide bombers in the United States. At first, lead FBI agent Anthony Hubbard (Denzel Washington) thinks he is dealing with conventional hostage situations. A first incident is defused. Agent Hubbard is confident: 'We can take it', he says, comparing New York's capacity to maintain its balance in face of the threat of terrorism with that of other major cities such as London, Paris, Athens, Rome, Belfast and Beirut. A second incident occurs, terrorists hijack a New York bus and again Hubbard tries to negotiate the release of the passengers. But national security agent Elsie Kraft (Annette Bening) arrives convinced that this is no conventional incident. She warns that the terrorists are waiting for the TV cameras aboard the media helicopters that service 24-hour news channels to arrive, because they want everyone watching. They need to be taken down by sniper fire immediately, she urges. The bus explodes, killing all its passengers, hijackers included. Suicide attacks have arrived in America.

The tension and cross purposes between the covert world of secret intelligence and the overt common sense of ordinary law enforcement is played out in the relationship between Hubbard and Kraft. As the scale of the attacks increases, remorselessly and graphically, we learn that the government is well aware of the existence of terrorist cells in the United States. Kraft not only runs a supposed agent within this nexus but also explains its origin. The terrorist threat to America is 'blowback', the term coined by the CIA for unintended consequences of American foreign policy engagements and action. Indeed, the terrorists in *The Siege* are a group previously recruited, trained and financed by the US to help in the overthrow of Saddam Hussein. When that plot was foiled, Kraft helped to get the members of the group student visas to come to America. The script point is underlined by the sequence in which Kraft is shown to be having an affair, literally sleeping with the enemy who is her principal informant. The lover/enemy eventually turns out to be the last and most dangerous member of the terrorist cell.

But irrespective of how the terrorist threat originates, how is it to be countered? In Washington there are frantic discussions about the possible need for martial law. Enter General Devereux (Bruce Willis), the military man ready to tackle the problem by any means necessary. The casting of Willis is a subtle link between *The Siege* and the conventions of the action movie genre in which Muslim terrorism has played such a prominent part. Incidentally, *24* used the martial law scenario in season five. In *The Siege*, Devereux warns that the last thing America needs is to militarise the problem: it is not an option to be taken lightly. But the general has his own agenda. The objective of the terrorists' campaign is not just to attack America but also to secure the release of their sheikh, their spiritual leader, who they believe is being held by the US. Their claim is indeed true. The sheikh was kidnapped in a covert military operation planned and supervised by Devereux, who is holding him incommunicado.

The Siege is notable for some remarkable visual imagery. The terrorists succeed in blowing up the New York headquarters of the FBI, in a sequence that visually references the attack on the Federal Building in Oklahoma City, America's worst incident of home-grown domestic terrorism. With the infrastructure of crime prevention and detection disabled, panicked politicians invoke the War Powers Act and call in the military. Tanks rumble over the Brooklyn Bridge to occupy the borough that is home to the majority of New York's Muslim citizens, another potent image. House-to-house searches are accompanied by the rounding up of all Muslims profiled as being of likely age and character to be either terrorists or terrorist sympathisers, including the son of one of the FBI agents working with Hubbard. These civilians are confined in a mass detention centre hurriedly constructed in a football stadium. Again, there are amazing visual references which recall that other 9-11, the coup on 11 September 1973 in Chile when America connived in the military junta's overthrow of Salvador Allende's elected government. As the Chilean coup progressed, dissidents were held at a football stadium where thousands were tortured and disappeared. With stunning prescience, the visual imagery in these scenes also prefigures the cages of Guantánamo Bay! As the search for the remaining terrorists and their nuclear device gathers pace, in the bowels of the football stadium General Devereux gets set to torture a captive to discover where the weapon is hidden. In scenes that foreshadow Abu Ghraib, we see this naked man humiliated, and then physically abused to death.

The denouement of the film begins when Hubbard discovers the general's intention to torture his captive. He rounds on Devereux:

What if what they really want is for us to herd our children into stadiums like we're doing? And put soldiers on the street and have Americans looking over their shoulders? Bend the law, shred the Constitution just a little bit? Because if we torture him, General, we do that and everything we have fought, and bled, and died for is over. And they've won. They've already won!

The doctrine of necessity, of doing whatever it takes, however, prevails. When the general emerges, literally with blood on his hands, Hubbard arrests him. Denzel Washington, Hollywood's decent man, gets to deliver a ringing peroration on respect for law and the American way that would not come amiss from James Stewart in his role in the classic 1940s movie *Mr Smith Goes to Washington*:

You have the right to remain silent. You have the right to a fair trial. You have the right not to be tortured, not to be murdered, rights that you took away from Tariq Husseini. You have those rights because of the men who came before you who wore that uniform. Because of the men and women who are standing here right now waiting for you to give them the order to fire. Give them the order, General.

Dared to make murderers of his ordinary soldiers, after a tense moment the general tells them to stand down and submits to arrest. All that remains is for the FBI to save the day by conventional law enforcement. The conclusion includes a last-ditch piece of heroism by Kraft, which results in the death of her all-too-equivocal and complicit character. And thus, in its traditional manner, Hollywood secures a happy ending and vindicates traditional American values.

But that is not what has happened in America post 9-11, with the rush to grant the president war powers, to pass into law the Patriot Act, and the arrest and detention in America of some 1,100 Muslims, both citizens and residents, and the launching of the war in Afghanistan. What distinguishes *24* and *The Siege* in dealing with the same issues is that *The Siege* attempts to place events in a political and historical context, and to suggest how they relate to the genesis of Muslim terrorism. In doing so, *The Siege* became a much more important film after 9-11 than it was on its first release. At that time, its potent imagery of Muslim Americans being ethnically profiled and herded into detention camps both frightened and angered the Muslim community, who complained that the film was racist, despite having been consulted during its making. It set out an argument of complicity which in response to 9-11 many Americans were unwilling to concede, and still earnestly reject. After 9-11 it holds potent questions about how the domain of the popular has been influenced by the writing of cultural history, the conventions of the movies we have seen.

The top box office hit at cinemas across America for two weeks in April 2000 was *Rules of Engagement*. It is not a terrorist genre movie. It uses the format of a courtroom drama to tell a story about radicalisation by fundamentalist Islam as a total phenomenon that spares no member of Muslim society. The opening scenes of the film show an elite Marine unit despatched to extract a US ambassador and his family from the US embassy in Yemen, which is threatened by hostile demonstrators. While a large angry crowd protests outside, Marines guarding the evacuation from the embassy's rooftop come under sniper fire and get pinned down. Marine Colonel Childers (Samuel L. Jackson) orders his men to open fire. 'Are you ordering me to fire into the crowd?' asks one of his men. 'Yes. Waste the motherfuckers!' he replies. After the burst of automatic gunfire, the scene falls silent. The camera pans to reveal the entire square littered with dead and dying civilians; no one has escaped.

Once back in the US, Colonel Childers faces a court martial. In the kind of revisionist aside that action movies made commonplace, he will be defended by a military lawyer who is an old army buddy from their service in Vietnam. The court proceedings revisit the shooting incident three times, each time revealing more of the context and content of the event. In the second reprise we learn that snipers with high-powered rifles are hiding behind black-robed, chador-wearing women on the rooftops surrounding the embassy. The ultimate reprise reveals the entire crowd in the square to be armed; women whisk automatic weapons from beneath their chadors and even the doe-eyed, one-legged little girl, an enigmatic presence throughout the film, wields a weapon to fire at the Marines. The court martial is played an audio tape found in the wreckage of the embassy, another copy of which was found at the nearby children's hospital: 'This is a declaration of Islamic jihad against the United States ... We call on every Muslim who believes in God to kill Americans and their allies, both civilian and military. It is the duty of every Muslim everywhere. To kill Americans is a duty.' Colonel Childers is exonerated, his actions legitimated. The metaphysical enemy is returned to prime position in the public consciousness with a vengeance. As Peter Brunette noted in his review for film.com, 'the audience I saw the film with cheered when the Marines slaughtered the civilians'. The audience response was ready and waiting for its appointment with real events. Indeed, so realistic and convincing was this film in placing its action in America's recent past that, according to the Yemeni ambassador to the US, many people were asking when exactly the event happened.[26]

As Hollywood understood so well in the 1930s, the media, the movies and television are an important influence on the life of the nation. Reading the cultural and strategic histories written since 9-11 and following the trail of the impact and influence they have made on popular memory, they present little evidence that America will change. 24 ended its sixth season less interested in resolving the questions it raised about how Muslim terrorism and the war on terror impact on domestic community relations than in prefiguring its connection to coming threats to American dominance. The Russians are back in vogue, renegade Soviet loyalists relishing the prospect of supplying Muslim terrorists with WMD to target America. And the Chinese are now firmly on the radar of the culture of fear, eager to appropriate the technology which will make them not merely an economic but a genuine strategic threat. If America is to change, then how it thinks and informs its popular memory about the rest of the world has to change. And so too does its view of dominance, its willingness to entertain an imperial mindset. Cultural and strategic histories are but two sides of the same coin. How they have marched together over the years are the footsteps we need to trace to determine if America can or will change.

CHAPTER FOUR

American Myths and Myth-Making in America

In America the footprints of history have been overlaid by the creation of mythic narratives that convey the idea of America. How America thinks about its place in the world is a direct expression of its idea of national mission, a story explained by its mythic tradition which has determined how its cultural and strategic history has advanced since 9-11. As Robert Kagan, foreign policy analyst and *Washington Post* columnist, has argued: 'America did not change on September 11. It only became more itself.'[1] There was not just an outpouring of national solidarity in the face of tragedy; there was conscious and conspicuous resort to the icons and imagery that symbolise the story of the nation, from the unfurling of flags to law-makers gathering on the steps of Congress to sing 'God Bless America', to President Bush reprising the language of America's western frontier. It was the idea of America which was mobilised for war in response to 9-11. Three wars on – Afghanistan, Iraq and the global war on terror – if America has not changed, then understanding the making of America, how its idea of itself and its view of the rest of the world came into being, is essential to determining not only if America will or can change but what constitutes a real agenda for change.

For Kagan, America's response to 9-11 is the persistence of

a project that it has been engaged in not just 'over the past decades but for the better part of the past six decades and one might even say the better part of the past four centuries. It is an objective fact that Americans have been expanding their power and influence in ever-widening arcs since even before they founded their own independent nation.'[2] According to Richard Haass, a state department director of policy and planning, the projection of this power and influence seeks to integrate 'other countries and organisations into arrangements that will sustain a world consistent with US interests and values and thereby promote peace, prosperity and justice'.[3] Pre-emptive war, retaliation, regime change and democracy-building are all expressions of this unifying project. If this project is foundational to the very idea of America, the essence of its mission statement, it is hardly surprising that Americans are blind to the imperialist nature of their national undertaking. Indeed, Clyde Prestowitz argues that this arises from the 'implicit belief that every human being is a potential American, and that his or her present national or cultural affiliations are an unfortunate but reversible accident'.[4] Enveloping the whole world in its self-interested and self-serving embrace is the very meaning of America. And it is the precise cause of the rest of the world's difficulties with America, the content of the substantive change they hope America can make. If all other identities are mere 'reversible accidents', what place does the idea of America allow for plurality, difference and autonomy – indeed, self-determination for anyone else?

America assumed the status of leader of the free world not by the happy accident of emerging from World War II as the richest nation, unscathed by the ravages of war on its own soil and with its productive capacity enhanced, its military might unquestioned and deployed around the globe, and its political and diplomatic position decisive in establishing the new order of the post-war world. America acquired this dominance by virtue of its accumulation of political, military, economic and cultural power and influence, as the realisation and full meaning of its history, the manifest destiny inherent in the idea of America. As Kagan suggests, this vision preceded the foundation of the nation. To trace the origins of the idea of America and its relationship to the rest of the world we have to look beyond America to the worldview that defined the expansion of Europe, the process which brought the United States of America into being. In the cultural and strategic history of Europe's expansionist worldview is to be found the bedrock of America's mythic narrative.

American belief in its own national myth as a model for all nations is something other than simple altruism. This was the substance of what is known as the Wolfowitz Indiscretion. In 1992, following the success of Operation Desert Storm, the annual review of the Defense Planning Guidance prepared by Paul Wolfowitz, then under-secretary of defence for policy, openly argued that calculations of power and self-interest rather than altruism and high ideals provided the proper basis for framing American strategy for the operation and maintenance of its unquestioned pre-eminence. When this leaked to the press there was fulmination from affronted and aghast critics. Senator Alan Cranston saw it as a proposal to make America 'the one, the only main honcho on the world block, the global big Enchilada', and that was most of all un-American.[5] When the document was published, all traces of such candour had disappeared. As Andrew Bacevich notes, no other responsible official of that Bush administration or any subsequent one repeated the mistake: 'The calculus of power that is inherent in the very nature of politics did not disappear, but it remained hidden from public view.'[6] Mythic narrative shrouds harsh realities, overlaying them with benign goodness, but the essence of the story of America is the construction of a new imperialism, different but not distinct from all other varieties that have gone before. The pursuit of the American dream on a global basis subsumes the rest of the world as its own backyard, to be known and engaged with in purely American terms. This is an expression of patriotism which sees all other nations as either failed examples of what a nation should be, or inferior and incapable examples desperately in need of remedial education. The more uncritical this patriotism is in shaping popular imagination and public discourse, the more insulated, special and different Americans become. The more it holds a distorting mirror to itself and the rest of the world, the more incomprehensible the rest of the world becomes, full of inarticulate, hostile elements, true barbarians. The term 'barbarian' originated among the Ancient Greeks. To Greek ears, foreign languages sounded like 'ba-ba'. The word came to refer to anyone incapable of speaking Greek, and carried the implication that barbarism was a defect of reason. Not a bad analogy for how the rest of the world conceives – with justification – that America thinks of itself: as the type-site of all that is reasonable and good, while all others are incomprehensible barbarians who just will not see what's best for them. You might say this is the Joe Bing view of the world that we encountered in the pages of *The Ugly American*.

The origins of America are not at all mythic; they begin with the ideology that bred imperialism as a deliberate, conscious undertaking shaped by the history, ideas and identity of Western Christendom. America begins with a pragmatic response to an old problem, the strategic geo-political problem that for centuries posed an economic dilemma for Europe. When Columbus presented his novel plan to find the East, the land of Cathay, by sailing westward, he was, in his own mind, hoping to open a new front in an old war, a seventh Crusade. In his journals Columbus explicitly linked the success of his own endeavour with the hope that it might make possible the recapture of Jerusalem. The so-called 'Age of Discovery', in particular the single generation from 1492, when Columbus made landfall on Hispaniola, to 1526, when Ferdinand Magellan completed the first circumnavigation of the earth, was momentous for Europe. Not only were all the old textbooks rendered incomplete by the new discoveries, but the way in which Europeans thought about this information, what it meant in terms of the origins and purpose of the world, was reformulated. In one generation, two quantum leaps occurred. As knowledge of the terrestrial world was expanding, so the spiritual world was undergoing a Reformation. But behind this burst of exploratory activity was a strategic manoeuvre in the continuing power rivalry between Christendom and Islam, and its legacy is the legitimation of persistent imperialism. It forged the ideas and attitudes that became fundamental to the making of America.

Like the Cold War, the power struggle between Christendom and Islam was ideological. It was not inevitable, not based on something inherent in religion, either Christianity or Islam, per se. It was a product of Christian ideas and outlook based on a particular understanding of religion at a particular time in history. For Europe, it shaped an understanding of the world rooted in enduring enmity and pervasive fear. All ideological systems produce a distinction between 'Them' and 'Us'. The ideological underpinnings of the Cold War of the 20th century were a definition of differences in ways of life, principles and values, organisation of economy, society and politics. Things were no different in the earlier era when all of these differences were seen as natural outcomes of difference in religion.

The Crusades began on 27 November 1095, when Pope Urban II preached at Clermont in France. In both surviving accounts of this sermon, by Robert the Monk and Fulcher of Chartres, the Pope describes the enemy in familiar ideological terms: 'a despised and base race, which worship demons'; 'an accursed race'; 'unclean nations'. The enemy was, supposedly, attacking Christians in the Middle East, throwing them off their lands, despoiling and destroying Christian altars, appropriating churches for the rites of their own religion. In Robert the Monk's version, the Pope presents the Crusade as the special mission of the Franks, the French people, and also an opportunity for this special people to escape the confines of lands 'too narrow for your large population'. Europe, Urban argued, was riven by conflict within. It was right that Europeans should turn from this sinful rivalry to their proper mission by attacking the pagans and infidels. The Crusade would be a Holy War in two senses: it would be for the advance of Christian society; and it would be an armed undertaking that would earn the expiation of sins for all who took part. Those who took the Cross, becoming Crusaders, would be set on the road to paradise. This conflict was steeped in history, 'a war that should have been begun long ago'.

Through planting a settler society in the Middle East, the life of the Muslim world became known to Europe as opulent, provided with technological sophistication, scientific learning, literary and philosophic achievement and a cornucopia of resources far beyond anything available in the West. To acquire these goods and techniques, Europe was dependent on trade with its adversary. The terms of medieval trade were hugely weighted in favour of the Muslim world. Acquiring the gold to pay for these goods only added to the problem. The gold came from West Africa along the Muslim trans-Saharan trade routes to the Maghrib, the region of present-day Morocco, Algeria and Tunisia, from where it was traded to Europe. It then circulated around Europe before flowing out again in trade with the Muslim ports of the Levant, the eastern Mediterranean terminals of the Muslim-dominated trade routes which stretched to the Spice Islands of the Indies and China in the Far East.

The Crusades are not five or six separate events – they are the context and set of ideas that shaped five centuries of European history. The experience of this first expansion beyond Europe was gradually shaped into a coherent worldview that not only defined the identity of Europe but also produced a clear definition of who and what was the Other – the unbaptised, non-Christians – and how relations with such peoples should be organised. The footprints of these old ideas not only determined the creation of America, they find their echoes in the role and power accumulated by America's imperial presidency as well as the justifications and agenda offered for the war on terror. The implicit assumptions of today's arguments are lineal descendants of the way of thinking established by Sinibaldo Fieschi (died 1254), who in 1243 became Pope Innocent IV. Already a noted canon lawyer, Innocent IV turned his attention to the question of the rights of other peoples, or more correctly the right of the peoples of Christendom to intervene in the affairs of other peoples for anything from a little regime change to creative nation-building of an imperialist kind. He was not concerned with justifying the Crusades but rather with establishing whether Christians could legitimately seize lands other than the Holy Land occupied by Muslims.

It is in the development of medieval canon law that we see how Europe thought about its relations with the rest of the world. Explicitly, Innocent IV conceived the papacy to have a responsibility for all people, a duty of care. Within the bounds of Christendom the secular power had autonomy but, at the same time, the Pope had an overriding right in Europe and especially beyond its bounds to intervene in secular affairs under certain conditions. The conditions depended on whether or not the natural law known to all men was being upheld and properly observed. Now exactly what this natural law consisted of was often vague; but always a useful construct, it could be invoked as self-evidently obvious without necessity for strict definition because it comprised the essential values and cultural norms of Christendom – how else should good people everywhere want and aspire to live? It is not unlike the familiar rhetoric invoking the natural yearning of all people everywhere for liberty, freedom and democracy articulated by George W. Bush.

For Innocent, pastoral responsibility for all mankind meant the right to judge infidels in cases where they violated natural law if their own rulers failed to punish them. Infidel rulers who neglected to do so failed in the very purpose for which rulers existed – to make justice. Further, the sins of infidels could call forth Christian armies blessed by the Pope, who might then adopt the law of conquest as developed by the Crusaders in the Holy Land: the right to appropriate whatever they laid claim to, while undertaking the business of forcing infidels to adhere to natural law. The Pope also maintained the additional right to send representatives, missionaries, to instruct non-believers in the proper ways of worship. Any infidel ruler who blocked such efforts could face invasion. Any infidel ruler persecuting, or presiding over those who persecuted, Christians was again fit for military invasion. It was, of course, ultimately only the leader of Christendom who could authorise attacks and interventions to enforce adherence to natural law. Deciding what violated natural law proved to be both a subjective judgement and endlessly open to manipulative re-interpretation according to circumstances and strategic interests.

Not all other people were the same. This was made clear in the works of a contemporary of Innocent IV, St Thomas Aquinas (c. 1225–74). It was Innocent who intervened to ensure that Thomas should join the Dominican order against the wishes of his family. Aquinas became the leading theologian and philosopher of his day. He was much influenced by the works of Muslim philosophers, for which enormity he was excommunicated after his death. But within 50 years his reputation was restored and he was pronounced a saint of the Church. In his work on ethics, Aquinas distinguished four kinds of law: eternal, natural, human and divine. His definition of natural law was based on first principles: that 'good is to be done and promoted and evil is to be avoided'. It reads exactly as the formula is understood by all Muslims of his or any day, for it is the constant theme stated in exactly these terms in the Qur'an. But in the contradictory convolutions typical of the European worldview, Aquinas also developed a definition of two categories of non-Christian peoples: the vincibly and invincibly ignorant. The vincibly ignorant were those Others who had knowledge of Christianity but had consciously rejected inclusion. As clearly set out in canon law, this group comprised Jews and Muslims.

Jews were the Other who existed within the boundaries of Christian society, discriminated against and persecuted for their otherness. Muslims were the Other without, those not expected to exist within European society whose lands and territories bounded and constrained Europe. The invincibly ignorant were those Others who had never encountered the message of Christianity. These were the distant peoples who lived beyond the encircling Muslim lands, only vaguely known from the writings of classical antiquity, but who might be converted and made subject to the polity of Western Christendom. The invincibly ignorant were barbarians, and included savages – people who could legitimately be enslaved. The institution of slavery was a survival from Roman times that never fully disappeared from medieval Europe. The word 'slave' derives from 'Slav', referring to the Slavic peoples of eastern Europe. Among this second category of the invincibly ignorant, Europe hoped to find allies in its battle against Islam. If only it could find a way to circumvent the Muslim lands.

Following from the basic framework established by Innocent IV, ideas justifying intervention and the use of coercive power became even more forthright. Another contemporary, Henry of Segusio, known as Hostiensis (c. 1200–71), based his arguments on Ecclesiastes 10:8: 'lordship passes from one people to another because of injustices and wickedness and outrages and other kinds of evil.' Not surprisingly, it was taken to mean that infidels could be dispossessed of their lordship and property, and was the most complete justification for imperialism. This worldview depended on the conviction that Europe was innately and inherently superior, founded as it was on the unshakeable assurance that it possessed the only proper meaning of natural law and the values and practices founded on this basis. The propositions of canon law were interwoven with a whole set of conventional ideas, stereotypes and representations of Other peoples formed from an amalgam of classical sources and biblical references, as well as biblical anthropology and archaeology. For example,

Muslims were considered the descendants of Ishmael, a wild ass of a man (Genesis 16:12), a term that conjured images of the lack of and opposition to civilisation as Christendom knew and interpreted the concept. For Oldratus de Ponte (died 1335), these nomads, the descendants of Ishmael, were always at war with settled peoples inhabiting agricultural land, so 'against them the hands of all people were turned since they deserved to be subjected to the bridle of civilisation'. Disposed to natural violence, they had to be pacified so that they might be led to the natural law, otherwise known as the way of life of Christendom.

Finding a way around the lands of Islam would provide Europe with open, direct access to the source of all those goods from the 'Indies' that were becoming staples of European life. It would undercut the economic stranglehold that Muslim civilisation had over Europe. When the Crusades faltered in their objective of securing a European presence in the Middle East and Europe felt threatened by a new wave of expansion by the emerging Ottoman empire, the venture of exploration began in earnest. In 1492, a few days after the completion of the Reconquista – the reconquest of all Spain, achieved by the fall of the last Muslim sultanate, Granada – Their Most Catholic Majesties, Ferdinand and Isabella, summoned Christopher Columbus and finally gave their approval for his novel proposal to continue the Crusade against the infidel, seeking the East by sailing westward across the Atlantic.

Like the explorative ventures of the Portuguese, Columbus' voyages were ultimately under the auspices of the leader of Christendom, the Pope. They were conducted under terms of reference set out in a series of Papal Bulls which became the substance of the charters issued by individual monarchs to those they licensed to make so-called 'voyages of discovery'. The Papal Bulls encapsulate the propositions of canon law developed in the context of the Crusades. Their terminology and content show that the basic premise of Western expansionism was an oppositional ideology informed by its sense of superiority, and superior right, and the enduring otherness, difference and inferiority of the Rest. These documents justified Europe's right to attack, appropriate and possess lands and peoples who, from their own perspective, had every right to believe they were the owners of their own land, property, persons and destiny. This process, once begun, leads inevitably to imperialism in all its guises, and continues to operate in the hyper-imperialism of America today.

Dum Diversas is the earliest in the series of Papal Bulls, granted to the Portuguese monarch in 1453. It authorised the king of Portugal to attack, conquer and subdue 'Saracens', pagans and other unbelievers who were inimical to Christ; to capture their goods and their territories; to reduce their persons to perpetual slavery; and to transfer their lands and properties to the king of Portugal and his successors. Similar Bulls were granted to the Spanish monarchs Ferdinand and Isabella before Columbus set sail. Columbus' discovery of what he claimed were the islands of the East created friction by seemingly infringing the rights already granted to Portugal. In 1493, Pope Alexander VI mediated between the Iberian rivals and issued the Treaty of Tordesillas. In light of his prerogatives under canon law, the Pope neatly divided rights to discovery and conquest of the entire world between Spain and Portugal, all that was found westward of a line a few hundred leagues from the Azores being granted to Spain, and all to the east of that line going to Portugal. The familiar terms of the Papal Bulls appear in the charter granted by Henry VII of England to John Cabot in 1482 before his voyages exploring North America, the basis for all subsequent English claims to what became the United States. The Cabots were licensed to occupy and set up the king's banners and ensigns 'in any town, city, castle, island or mainland whatsoever, newly found by them', anywhere in the 'eastern, western or northern sea', belonging to 'heathens and infidels, in whatsoever part of the world placed, which before this time were unknown to all Christians'. The Charter empowered them 'to conquer, occupy and possess' all such places, on condition of paying the king 'the fifth part of the whole capital gained' in every voyage.

Columbus set sail armed with conventional European learning and ideas. He sailed west inspired by a newly reprinted error, the under-calculation of the circumference of the earth by the ancient Greek scholar Ptolemy. Columbus annotated profusely his copy of *The Travels of Sir John Mandeville* and the works of Pierre d'Ailly, books containing the repository of contemporary European ideas about the world and its peoples. Full of marvels, wonders and perversions of natural law, they contain the familiar stereotypes which inscribed Other peoples as different and inferior when not wholly demonic. And lo, these images came alive before his eyes in the poor Indians he encountered. The real peoples beyond Europe became configured, defined and described according to the expectations and ideas Europeans brought with them, and were treated according to the character notes assigned to them. This was a terrorism of culture whose consequence was imperialism, colonisation, despoliation and dispossession. The representational language of Europe was overwritten on the lands and peoples beyond Europe to make sense of their newness. The Europeans who settled the newly found continent of America brought with them the motifs, ways of thinking and self-perceptions of Western Christendom. In this new location, old ideas and reflexes began a new career of colonial domination.

The torch of civilisation, of reason and scientific understanding, the mantle of innovation, the mission of Christianity, moved west. It was taken up by new hands, those of the European nations who were pushing the boundaries of Europe ever outward. The new reformed religion provided new authority for individuals to search and inquire in the books of God, the Bible and Nature, armed with human reason. The Protestant Reformation broke down old structures of authority and created new ones. Individual conscience became the basis of a new kind of civil compact, and the idea from which centuries of endeavour to establish individual civil liberty took its inspiration. The Reformation began as a movement to overcome the corruption, abuses and inaccuracies of the received religion of the Universal Roman Catholic Church. A new world, a promised land of faithful observance of a proper relationship to God, opened before those who made the spiritual and intellectual journey into reformed theology. Armed with their new approach to the Bible, within the fold of a reformed Body of Christ, adherents of the new denominations would build a New Jerusalem in their civic society on earth. The pilgrims who ventured to the New World truly saw themselves as New Israelites seeking the land of Canaan. But the project they engaged in appropriated the worldview and prerogatives so familiar from medieval canon law, Papal Bulls and charters. It was the authority that devised and issued these instruments, the Pope, not their content, meaning and application, that reformed religion rejected.

With high purpose, the pilgrims set out to establish a new society. 'What need we fear', wrote John Rolfe in 1617, of the 'zealous work' of establishing the Virginia colony, 'but to go up at once as a peculiar people, marked and chosen by the finger of God to possess it'.[7] As he sailed for America in 1630, John Winthrop wrote: 'We must consider that we shall be a City upon a Hill, the eyes of all people shall be upon us.'[8] Rolfe, a founder of the tobacco industry in the Virginia colony, and Winthrop, who became governor of the Massachusetts colony, define the perceived purity, manifest destiny, righteousness and innocence of America. And their careers contained the contradiction that so troubles observers of America. As the Native American writer Jimmie Durham says:

Even now one may read editorials almost daily about America's 'loss of innocence' at some point or other, and about some time in the past when America was truly good. That self-righteousness and insistence upon innocence began as the US began with invasion and murder.[9]

For Durham, America has from the beginning had nostalgia for itself because of actual guilt. The United States, he argues, was the first settler colony to establish itself against, and through the denial of, its original inhabitants. 'It developed thereby a narrative that was more complete, more satisfying ... That narrative has generated new cultural and political behaviour which has been a main influence in the modern world.'[10]

'The great myth', as Peter Mathiesson calls it, used to justify and sustain the seizure of America, is that what was 'discovered' was a vast wilderness. 'The New World: fresh, virginal, unaltered by human hands. And in consequence of believing in the unspoiled nature of the land found here, all culture on this continent was considered then, and is considered now by many, to have been transplanted from the "advanced" civilizations of Europe, the "Old World".'[11] The earliest settlers wrote that they had found a new Eden, the land of Canaan, an earthly paradise. Here they could begin a new experiment in society, superseding and resolving the problems, corruption, imperfections and failings of the 'Old World'. The freedom that the settlers appropriated for themselves is directly related to the freedom they denied to the original inhabitants of an already peopled, settled, cultivated land, a landscape that was the product of the interaction of man and nature. Once established, the new society advanced in an ever-widening arc across the continent by the practice of imperialism within. What for other European nations was the exercise of colonial policy in foreign lands was for America the internal activity of nation-building: appropriating ever more land, overspreading the continent, state funding of the infrastructure of building roads, bridges and railways and so forth. America was not different from the imperial powers of Europe, except in the location where these ideas were practised: at home, not abroad.

The denial that Durham refers to begins with the question of whether the native inhabitants of the New World were human beings possessed of souls at all. What is clear is that old and familiar reflexes of thought shaped in the medieval power rivalry between Christendom and Islam were extended to manufacture the ideas, attitudes and means of dealing with Native Americans.

Spain, the first imperial power in the New World, earnestly debated the status of the native inhabitants. The debates were not a disinterested search for understanding of a new people. They were directly related to justification of the right to appropriate and possess their territory, to create and possess an empire in the more complex political realities of a post-Reformation world. The arguments were deeply indebted to the framework and ideas established by Innocent IV and, in particular, Hostiensis.

The first debate produced the Requimiento, the requirement to read out, in a language they could not understand, a formal declaration offering the Indians a choice. They could submit to Spanish rule and allow the preaching of the Christian faith. If they refused, the Spaniards were empowered to undertake punitive measures and enter their land with fire and sword. 'We shall take you and your wives and your children, and shall make slaves of them, and as such shall sell and dispose of them as His Highness may command; and we shall take away your goods, and shall do all the harm and damage that we can, as to vassals that do not obey.'[12]

In the 1550s, great debates took place at Valladolid in Spain between the philosopher-theologian Juan Gines de Sepulveda (1490–1573) and the Dominican friar Bartolomé de Las Casas (1474–1566, known as 'the Apostle' to the Indians). At issue was whether the Indians were natural slaves, as defined by the Ancient Greek philosopher Aristotle – one part of mankind set aside by nature to serve those born for a life of virtue free of manual labour – and given biblical warrant by the sons of Ham, destined to be 'hewers of wood and drawers of water'. On the other hand, 'All mankind is one', Las Casas insisted, and went on to argue: 'And the savage peoples of the earth may be compared to uncultivated soil that readily brings forth weeds and useless thorns, but has within itself such natural virtue that by labour and cultivation it may be made to yield sound and beneficial fruits.'[13] This is the case for Indians as 'natural children' to be taught, converted and brought to civilisation. The trouble with this all-embracing colonial framework proved to be the lack of any passing-out exam. And it is rather difficult to accept the tutelage and pedagogy of one's murderers, oppressors and despoilers. The idea of the natural child was a polite fiction founded on deep racial arrogance, even when it came from a good and saintly man such as Las Casas, who wished only to expose the genocidal brutalities of his contemporaries.

In the 16th century, the idea of the 'natural child' was embraced by colonial rulers, not from altruism but self-interest. As persons with souls, capable of being instructed, the native inhabitants of America legally possessed sufficient competence to assign their lands, property and persons to the authority and administration of a colonial power. Slaves who were themselves property could have no property or rights to agree to cede.

The debates in Spain were avidly followed by English enthusiasts for empire. Terms and ideas mined from disavowed Catholic canon law were appropriated, suitably modified, in the early English colonial literature. The familiar negative description of the native peoples, 'They have no ...', became the argument of *'Meum'* and *'Teum'*. The Indians, having no true concept of possession, no 'Mine' and 'Thine', were users of their land rather than owners. Therefore, by law, they could be dispossessed of the land they occupied. There were also Puritan clergy who asserted that the Indians were children of the devil who might profitably be wiped out and their lands appropriated. The approach with fire and sword was legitimated by the instructions to early colonists, in for example the guidelines laid down for the establishment of the Virginia colony, and honoured in their practice. Resistance was not only not tolerated, it was futile. And when no actual hostility was offered – as was the case in King Philip's War, the campaign in the Massachusetts colony (1675–6) that marked the major turning point in relations between the colonists and Indians, as Francis Jennings argues in his book, *The Invasion of America* – a little 'black ops' on the part of the settlers could manufacture an offence to justify overwhelming military response. Or the exercise of democracy could simply vote the problem of appropriating rights of ownership out of existence. In 1640, one New England assembly passed an eminently straightforward series of resolutions:

1. The earth is the Lord's and the fullness thereof. *Voted*
2. The Lord may give the earth or any part of it to his chosen people. *Voted*
3. We are his chosen people. *Voted*.[14]

The debate is epitomised by John Rolfe's 'mighty war with his meditations'. Rolfe was enamoured of Pocahontas, not the Disney animated reformulation, but the actual woman. In a letter written in 1614, he presents his detailed justification for marrying Pocahontas. It reads as a forensic dissection of the justification for empire. Rolfe depicts himself and his fellow settlers as charged with the duty to make a new society, separate from the errors and corruption of Europe. To come out and be separate was a New Testament text (1 Corinthians 6:17) with a significant dual meaning in America. Pilgrims separated themselves from Europe to develop a pure and more perfect society. But this and other biblical texts (Ezra 10:10 and Genesis 9:25) had direct import concerning marriage across ethnic and religious lines, marriage with unclean, accursed races, and therefore should have been a complete bar to the marriage that he intended. Rolfe needed another line of argument to overcome what seemed an insurmountable obstacle. He found his alternative argument in the idea that Pocahontas, while clearly the daughter of an unclean, barbarous people, was nevertheless willing and able to be instructed and thus brought within the fold of Christianity, and therefore his marriage would precisely fulfil the missionary purpose of settling this New World. Pocahontas was the first and most notable convert to Christianity in what became the United States of America. It is the baptism of Pocahontas that is depicted in the Rotunda of the Capitol building in Washington DC. The baptismal image is more important, conceptually and legally, than Captain John Smith's self-serving tall tales.

A soldier of fortune, Smith was among the leaders of the first successful English colony, Jamestown, in what became the US. He wrote a number of popular books about his experiences as advertisements to attract new settlers to the colonies. The sensational story, the mythic encounter, relates events when Smith, captured by Powhatan Indians and about to be executed, was saved when the chief's daughter, Pocahontas, laid her head on his and demanded that his life be spared. Indeed, this may be the only legend of Pocahontas that most people know. It formed the centrepiece of Disney's 1995 animated film. But Pocahontas married John Rolfe, and it is Rolfe's thinking, which is an individualised mirror of the arguments central to the great Spanish debates, and not the popular myth, which tells the story of the project of imperialism in which America was born.

Old ideas brought the New World within European conventions. Native peoples and their possessions could then be appropriated, subsumed and removed to create the actual, philosophic, legal and cultural space for the idea of America and its birth in innocence. It was an innocence that permitted the most repugnant triumphalism of all. The pilgrim settlers soon found that native populations were dying at an alarming rate. The great pathogen invasion of new diseases – introduced by European settlers, and to which the natives had no natural resistance – devastated whole communities and peoples. Disease and death seemed to be opening up the country, making the land available. It was understood in the writing of the pilgrims as the Hand of Providence operating to advance the 'zealous work' of the 'chosen people'. It has been estimated that at the time of first contact there were between 20 and perhaps 50 million native inhabitants of the land that became the United States. By the 1890s, at the end of the Indian Wars and after the cataclysm of disease and the depredations of taming and settling the wilderness, the Native American population numbered 250,000.

The 'Hand of Providence' argument gave way in the 19th century to the nostalgic romance of the 'vanishing Indian'. The vanishing Indian was a lamentable figure, another myth overlaid on the real people of the 'New World'. The 'Noble Savage' was another invented abstraction, one of the ways in which those who had appropriated Native Americans' land and possessions could more completely appropriate their existence and being to justify dominance by drawing new contrasts between that state of nature in which native peoples had lived and the civilisation which was to be brought to the lands they once owned. Whether the concept of the savage was used to denigrate the natural law of their existence or the idea of the Noble Savage was used to romanticise their existence and criticise the shortcomings of industrialising civilisation made little difference. The objective of the exercise was always to vindicate the superiority of the Western perspective. In the process of intellectualising real people as abstractions, increasing distance was being created between the West and the rest of the world, the remnants of those earlier stages of social life that the West had transcended in its rise to dominance. The passing of the Noble Savage could be regretted while real people were hounded to the verge of extinction by design, by law and by political will. Both of these abstractions prefigured 'the survival of the fittest', the social-Darwinian idea of civilisations, peoples and races as being destined by nature to adapt or perish. It is not just in human law but in the framing of laws of nature – in biologising social philosophy and breeding the disciplines of modern knowledge – that Western civilisation has generated what the Native American scholar and academic, the late Vince Deloria Jr, called 'abstractions that idealise human rationality in order to give to events and incidents a sense of meaning which they would not otherwise enjoy'.[15] Native Americans are one example, internal and instrumental to the idea of America, of a general condition that has afflicted the Third World. In fact, their adaptation (conversion, civilising missions, development) was enforced by denial of general freedom and individual liberty, while they were pushed to extinction by acts of commission (warfare, starvation and malign neglect) and acts of omission (strategies of benign neglect, exclusion from full participation in the economy, politics and society) whose effects were as pernicious as war. And as can be seen, the process worked in fidelity to the original conceptions developed in medieval canon law.

Jimmie Durham explains the process and its consequences in terms that are familiar, that echo in the experience of the peoples of the developing countries and that are reflected in the war on terror:

> The Master Narrative of the US has not (cannot be) changed. It has been broadened. It has been broadcast. This narrative is only superficially concerned with 'taming the wilderness' and 'crossing new frontiers'. The US has developed a concept and reality of the state, I might say 'statism', because US culture is so completely ideological ... The Master Narrative of the US proclaims that there were no 'Indians' in the country, simply wilderness. Then, that the 'Indians' were savages in need of the US. Then, that the 'Indians' all died, unfortunately. Then, that the Indians today are a) basically happy with the situation and b) not the real 'Indians'. Then, most importantly, that that is the complete story.[16]

What Durham says of Native Americans could be said of Muslims, Indians of the Subcontinent or innumerable other peoples: 'The world knows very well who we are, how we look, what we do and what we say – from the narrative of the oppressor. The knowledge is false, but it is known.'[17] For anyone who wants to understand other people, within or beyond the West, this is the most essential and awkward question to confront. 'Knowledgeable ignorance' is the education handed out with authority by the West to itself and to the Rest. Education, the bedrock of development programmes designed to modernise developing nations, consists of learning their history through the prism of 'knowledgeable ignorance', and thus learning why they are inferior. It is the essential premise of the strategic decisions in the war on terror: that tutelage in democracy is necessary and can be imposed, at the point of a gun, upon people incapable of achieving this stage of development on their own recognisance and in their own terms, whose leaders have failed in their essential duty and can thus be overthrown with justification and impunity. The missionary duty of today's leader of the free world thus parallels the ideas of an earlier leader of the West, the Pope, who framed the earliest conception of the relationship between Europe and the rest of the world.

The ideas that made the American myth came out of Europe. They had been fashioned by European experience of its 'Hot War' with Islam and the war psychosis it produced. European identity was shaped and defined in opposition to other people, particularly Muslims, the vilified and demonised enemy. Attitudes forged over centuries on the frontier of European civilisation's fault-line with Islam were transferred to America, where they provided the motifs which made the new society possible. These old and familiar assumptions are not just history. They operate today in the unthinking reflexes, ideas and attitudes of hyper-imperialism. They are embodied in American rhetoric and policy. They are recycled in every intervention America has made in the affairs of other countries.

The truly awkward issue is not simply the recognition that invasion, murder and oppression have been done, but that institutions, values and ideas that are taken for the 'exercise of virtue' were, have been, and are responsible for the continuation of exclusion and marginalisation; and that they provide us with examples of the way in which 'sin grows by doing good'. America is a nation of immigrants, of diverse people – but everything that makes the idea of America is exclusively European, descended from a Western civilisation which is seen as superior to all the rest of the world. The point is epitomised by the neo-conservatism of the liberal historian Arthur Schlesinger Jr:

> Whatever the particular crimes of Europe, that continent is also the source – the unique source – of those liberating ideas of individual liberty, political democracy, equality before the law, freedom of worship, human rights, and cultural freedom that constitute our most precious legacy and to which most of the world today aspires. These are European ideas, not Asian, nor African, nor Middle Eastern ideas, except by adoption.[18]

The only option this offers the rest of the world is to submit, as natural children should or must be made to do, and keep on taking the lessons. This is ignorance on a grand scale masquerading as knowledge. The outright denial that any ideas about freedom, justice and other virtues could come from non-Western people makes dialogue with other cultures irrelevant. Such ignorant arrogance is pernicious and dangerous. It presents a two-tier world, and fuels global hatred of America. Out there, in the rest of the world, being cast into the enduring darkness of barbarism creates popular support for extreme groups whose only programme is to aggressively oppose the dominant hyper-power. The challenge for the USA, the essence of substantive change, is to accept that all civilisations have the same right to exist, the same freedom to express themselves, and the same liberty to order their society guided by their own moral vision. Moreover, all other people of the world have the right and the freedom to peacefully disagree with America.

But there is a problem. The mythic narrative, the story of America that Americans tell themselves, may hide the realities of calculations of power and self-interest, the logic of dominance and hence the right of imperial oversight that the US appropriates for its exclusive use. Yet the mythic story has no compunction in insisting that the ever-widening arc of the project of America was achieved by righteous violence. At the heart of these narratives is the power of the gun, itself mythologised into a redemptive force on which the peace, prosperity and security of the nation depends. To be coy about the uses of power and dominance while eulogising the coercive use of force does not make for clear-sighted debate and consideration of any agenda for change. The mythic tradition serves to assure Americans that violence is instrumental in realising the nation's manifest destiny because in the hands of a hero it is always wielded to secure high ideals, for good ends. It is a dangerous presumption, but one that is central to the writing of America's cultural history. A nation blind to its own imperialist attitudes that is simultaneously indoctrinated with the logic and high purpose of redemptive violence is ill prepared to contemplate the perils and pitfalls of its strategic behaviour. In the making of the nation, popular memory knows that all difficulties were removed, all good things made possible by resort to violence. It is the story of the taming of the wilderness, the establishment of settler society and the defence and remaking of the constitutional perfection of an ever-closer union: the beatitude of America expressed in 'America the Beautiful'.

The opening scene of the classic western *Shane* (1953) visualises the patriotic song. A sweeping landscape of 'spacious skies' and 'purple mountain majesties' is revealed, encircling a fertile, fruited plain, threaded with streams where antelope roam and drink deep. In this vast expanse a tiny figure on horseback is at first barely visible. Director George Stevens pays homage to the conventions of 19th-century American art, where enormous canvases depict the virgin wilderness, dwarfing whatever microscopic images of human activity are included. In this imposing natural setting the film will play out one particular phase of the ever-widening arc of the idea of America: the creation of security for the 'pilgrim feet' to beat 'a thoroughfare of freedom' across the wilderness and bring forth the bounty of the 'amber waves of grain'. But the transition will only be achieved courtesy of the violence dispensed by the equivocal figure of the hero, that tiny figure on horseback, who enters this idyllic but troubled scene.

What to Americans reads as an iconic vision of simple virtues made safe by a knight-errant of the wilderness is for the rest of the world full of the ambiguity at the heart of America. American political rhetoric may circle its wagons around old familiar ideas of national self-identity, with clear and certain recognition of the need for self-preservation and security. But beyond the comforting woodsmoke and firelight, outside that circle, the meaning is plain: other people will have to die. When Shane rides into the homestead of the terrorised settlers, he brings the reflexes of violence with him. Eventually he will provide the proper response to danger, lead the defence against the onslaught of evil, and at the barrel of a gun bring the security that makes the land safe for the virtues of social progress and the fulfilment of national mission. He will do this with ruthless brutality, dealing death to those who oppose the future course of America.

Shane is often cited as a 'coming-of-age' myth. This has less to do with the character of little Joe, the young boy who watches the approach of Shane and quickly becomes his devotee, than with the idea of America itself. The film deals with the transition from the era of cattlemen, who replaced the trappers and woodsmen and are now to be displaced by the civilising virtues of homesteading. *Shane*, then, is a myth about that old familiar issue: the legitimation of the right of possession, the appropriation of just claims to righteous ownership of the land. Its themes are summed up in the arguments of the cattleman, Ryker: that blood is the bond with the land. He means the spilling of blood through violence. What *Shane* establishes is that violence is a redemptive act of justice by which civilisation is secured and advanced.

Shane is a nostalgic elegy on how the 'manifest destiny' of the mission of America came to be. The western, the definitive American genre, is not merely a hymn to violence – it is a view of the essential, inescapable and enduring necessity of violence to preserve civilisation. The western advances the myth that evil is intractable and can only be eradicated, that justice eventually comes down to the willingness to spill blood, that liberty resides in the right to make armed response, that the use of violence is the legitimate and only secure way to resolve a conflict. The whole world has experienced the western, and underlying its popularity elsewhere is a different reaction: fear.

It is the fear that America's political outlook continues to be too readily and uncritically shaped by the myth of the redemptive, regenerative powers of violence. At the heart of this mythic vision stands the question: does America cherish a double standard concerning the victor and victim? In the western it is the hero – what he defends, vindicates and saves – who alone evokes poignant reflection, while the vanquished are unmourned; they do not require a moment's regret, for as agents of evil they are by definition of less human worth. As American popular culture increasingly enfolds all stories, all histories, within its own authority and authorial power, it re-inscribes its mythic passion and moral coding onto more complex and morally challenged situations around the world. The subtext of American storytelling in relation to these other settings is abundantly clear: the gooks, the towel-heads and camel jockeys are of a piece with the Red Indians, the cattle barons and comancheros.

The western is a mythic space in which the history, idea and themes of America are explored. Richard Slotkin, professor of English at Wesleyan University, has examined the way in which the western genre has been manipulated in succeeding phases of American history as a powerful metaphor for the nation's political communication and policy.[19] Slotkin argues that one source of the worldview of the western is to be found in a subtle re-ordering of the traditions of Puritan literature. This literature was concerned with the interior struggles of the Puritan conscience and brought forward themes of insecurity, weakness and a sense of isolation as motive forces inspiring dependence on God, the search for the surety of divine warrant for human action, and certainty of doing God's work in building the civilised life of community. Western narratives externalised these themes and found their resolution in the project of appropriating the land and taming the wilderness. The western hero embodies all of the virtues and certainties of this project, along with all of the ambiguities and the sublimated guilt that it implies. He also resolves the ambiguities of violence, an essential part of heroic response to the challenge of the wilderness.

Shane embodies these themes. When he rides into the valley, Shane is dressed in buckskins and wearing a gun, symbols of appropriation of the land. He tries to adapt to the settled life of subduing the wilderness with hard work, until the climactic moment when he must again put on his buckskins and gun to resolve the conflict between civilisation and its adversaries by shooting the bad guys. Then, Shane rides off, leaving behind a community legitimated, regenerated, preserved and secured by violence. The quest of the homesteaders is purified by the hero's violence, the insecurities and weakness inherent in their struggle to tame the land have been resolved by it, and the dead cannot be mourned since they embodied all that was antithetical to the good and pure that was destined to triumph by its inherent worth. In short, we have all the essential elements of America's manifest destiny.

The western genre has been central to the growth of American popular culture, a mainstay of its forms of popular entertainment. There was no getting away from the western, therefore there was no way of evading the ethic on which the western was built – and its effect on the key battleground, the domain of the popular and the consciousness of American popular memory. As John Wayne so famously said, in his role as the Ringo Kid in the film *Stagecoach* (1939): 'There are some things a man just can't walk away from.' What he meant was the violent showdown, the gun battle in which the hero legitimised the mission of America by killing whomsoever stood in his, or its, way. The heyday of the cinematic epic and television western was the era when America founded its national security state on the principle of opposition to the evil of communism (the 'evil empire', as one-time 'B' western star, then President Ronald Reagan, insisted it should be called), and began its career as chief marshal in the global gun battle that this rivalry inspired. The writing of cultural and strategic histories coalesced in the era when America globalised the worldview of the western as its political outlook on international affairs; when America kept finding threats it could not walk away from in all the local bush wars and frontier conflicts across the Third World; and when it practised the doctrine that, in foreign policy, violent response was the first and only means of reliable conflict resolution.

The western as myth and epic drama expresses America's manifest destiny. The idea was first enunciated by the polemicist John L. O'Sullivan in his political magazine *Democratic Review*. O'Sullivan stated, in his frequently quoted formulation of 1845, that Americans had

> the right of our manifest destiny to overspread and to possess the whole of the continent which Providence has given us for the development of the great experiment of liberty and federaltive [sic] development of self government entrusted to us. It is the right such as that of the tree to the space of air and the earth suitable for the full expansion of its principle and destiny of growth.[20]

This continental expansion of America was merely a precursor to the fuller meaning O'Sullivan had given to 'manifest destiny' in 1839. The process of internal colonisation and the imperialist mindset it developed had a universal sense: it foretold the coming dominance of America as sole possessor of the truth and of universal human values:

> [O]ur national birth was the beginning of a new history, the formation and progress of an untried political system, which separates us from the past and connects us with the future only, and so far as regards the entire development of the natural rights of man, in moral, political and national life, we may confidently assume that our country is destined to be the great nation of futurity. ... We are the nation of human progress, and who will, what can, set limits to our onward march? Providence is with us, and no earthly power can. ... For this blessed mission to the nations of the world, which are shut out from the life-giving light of truth, has America been chosen; and her high example shall smite unto death the tyranny of kings, hierarchs, and oligarchs, and carry the glad tidings of peace and goodwill where myriads now endure an existence scarcely more enviable than that of beasts of the field. Who then can doubt that our country is destined to be the great nation of futurity?[21]

O'Sullivan might as well have stated that America is formed as the full and proper meaning of natural law and thereby, as of right, assumes a duty of care for all humanity. Both elements of O'Sullivan's populist ideas are comfortably accommodated in the mythic space of the western. Myth draws on the historical experience of a culture and its sources of feeling, fear and aspiration; and, as Richard Slotkin argues, it 'can be shown to function in that culture as a prescription for historical action and value judgement'.[22] The western genre is infused with the greatest confidence in the future that is being made on the frontier, the classic locale of value judgement. Yet the future is presented as being made by isolated, vulnerable and insecure outposts, constantly under threat, harassed and terrorised by agents of evil who appear in many guises but are all discernible as enemies of true civilisation. The ambiguous relationship between insecurity, the need for self-preservation, and the moral imperative of future greatness resolves itself in the same prescription for historic action in all westerns: the hero with the gun, the man who by moral necessity is quicker on the draw and who eradicates the problem.

So we arrive back in the valley with the simple, vulnerable homesteaders in *Shane*, anxious to secure their future through individualism and hard work. The coming-of-age experience for young Americans in the early 1950s, when *Shane* was released, included regular drills hiding under their school desks to save themselves from nuclear fallout deposited by Russian warheads: paranoia and insecurity as the basis of normal life, just like the homesteaders who expected daily terrorism from the cattlemen. In *Shane*, the other coming-of-age story is that of little Joe, the proto-America. The deeply troubling fact is that this youngster is presented as eager for violence, constantly impressed by violence, fascinated by weaponry, anxious to learn how to use the gun. It is little Joe who runs after Shane to witness gleefully the brutality of his fight with the evil-doers and the final shootout, and who provides the most poignant and memorable of film endings, plaintively calling to Shane to come back as he rides off into the great beyond. What does he say as his voice resounds to the echo? 'Pa's got things for you to do, and Mother wants you. I know she does. Shane. Shane! Come back! Bye, Shane.' The lost hero has provided redemption, security and the preservation of the fledgling community through violence. He is longed for and desired. This is not a final goodbye: such heroes and such tactics will be needed again. The reconfiguration of the hero in the films of the 1970s and 80s and of the television hero of the noughties draws upon the familiar character notes and themes to be found in the western heroes of old movies. The western heroes were always loners, men apart because they knew and were prepared to provide what settled society requires for its safety and security: violence, the law of the gun, victory by whatever means are necessary.

The story that the western mythologises is the story of America. It began by internalising the imperial project of colonisation, of European expansion, while externalising the angst and guilt associated with its motives and necessary actions. But while it worked to complete this internal project, the very idea of America contemplated and contained a wider global and universal mission. How that mission and its inseparable methodology, the use of coercive force and military means, has shaped America's relations with other people around the world is a story that can no longer be subject to the obscuring mantle of myth. It needs to become the substance of scrutiny and debate. It is the agenda that urgently calls not for the restoration of America's global leadership but for fundamental change.

CHAPTER FIVE

The Endless Expansion of the American Frontier

For the last six decades America has known that it is the 'indispensable nation', the hyperpower with the duty of care for how the world order operates. In consequence, as then secretary of state Madeleine Albright explained: 'If we have to use force it is because we are America. We are the indispensable nation. We stand tall, we see further into the future.'[1] Whatever polite fictions are used to hide the use of its power and influence from the American public, that public has been comfortable with their country's role as leader of the free world because, as we have seen, it is and always has been inherent in the idea of America. If America is the Great Nation of Futurity, the role model of the human future, then it is destined to lead the way. In a sense, dominance is what America is for.

The idea of America, in all the familiar rhetorical formats invoked by its politicians of all persuasions, provides the underlying consistency of its policy towards the rest of the world. 'The consensus is so deep seated that its terms have become all but self-evident, its premises asserted rather than demonstrated.'[2] The question of whether America will change is not about the electorate turning against the policies of the Bush years. George W. Bush will leave office, as he must, the most unpopular president ever. However, as Bacevich argues:

Charging George Bush with responsibility for the militaristic tendencies of present day US foreign policy makes as much sense as holding Herbert Hoover culpable for the Great Depression: whatever its psychic satisfaction, it is an exercise in scapegoating that lets too many others off the hook and allows society at large to abdicate responsibility for what has come to pass.[3]

If America became more itself on 9-11, then it is the terms and premises, not the immediate expression, of its foreign policy that is at issue. Change depends not on the unpopularity of how the Iraq war was conducted but on whether there is electoral mileage in debating how and why the Dubya years were a continuation of the foreign policies that went before.

Whether America can change depends on the willingness of politicians and public to examine the origins and consequences of the two props which have sustained US policy towards the rest of the world over the course of more than a century, and possibly even since before it became a nation. Is America ready to reconsider the open doors it demands from the rest of the world?; is America ready to rethink its addiction to militarism as the necessary means of its engagement with the rest of the world? Change in either of these premises would require Americans to recognise and reconsider the sense of entitlement that underwrites the lifestyle known as the American Dream which the US seeks to secure through the working of its foreign policy. Substantive change requires Americans to become aware of the consequences of the category mistake they have been encouraged to accept: that America is the world; and the world is America. The greatest impediment to real change is that most characteristic attitude endlessly repackaged by politicians, be they Republican or Democrat: that what is good for America is good for the world.

America began with the project of establishing a 'British empire'. The term was first coined by Dr John Dee, the exotic scholar, alchemist and advisor to Queen Elizabeth I. He was also a friend and correspondent of the leading cosmologists and map-makers studying the information made available by Europe's new encounters with the wider world. Elizabeth, the Virgin Queen, began the process of empire by unleashing her seadogs, the likes of John Hawkins and his cousin Francis Drake, to harry, plunder and trade with the Spanish empire. Thus, in 1562, did Hawkins found the Atlantic slave trade, authorised to kidnap West Africans to be sold in the Caribbean islands. In 1585 Elizabeth authorised her favourite Walter Raleigh to establish a colony in North America, the failed Roanoake experiment. In 1600 she issued the charter for the East India Company, the merchant venture enterprise which became the basis of Britain's eastward expansion. In 1606, her successor James I issued the charter for the Virginia Company, named, as was its colony, in homage to Elizabeth. Plunder and trade gave way to organised projects of settlement. These endeavours gave a Protestant reformulation to what was essentially a worldview and practice derived from medieval canon law. The objective was a British empire to rival those of Portugal and Spain, the country whose leadership of Catholic Europe posed a direct national security threat to the existence of Protestant Britain. In whatever denominational form, the purpose of empire was territorial possession, trade and enrichment.

In the Americas, settling European people was the means to dominance over the native inhabitants, to securing territory, managing the extraction of wealth and the development of new industry. The empires established were, however, strictly tied to the oversight and management of the European metropolis, their trade constrained by the restrictions of the mercantilist theory of empire. The rebellion for 'no taxation without representation' which led to the birth in war of the United States was the transfer of the mission of empire from the metropolis to the independent colony. The founding fathers of the US were insistent on their own rights to self-government but had no difficulty in envisaging their new republic as an imperialist project. An ever-widening arc of territorial possession under their power and influence was the idea of America they repatriated from Britain. George Washington, the first president, saw the new nation as 'a rising empire'. In 1786 Thomas Jefferson envisaged 'our confederacy' as the nest from which all America, north and south, should be peopled; the waning Spanish empire holding on until, piece by piece, 'our population shall be sufficiently advanced to gain it from them'. The terminology was widespread. In the year that the Constitution came into force, 1789, Jedidiah Morse wrote in his book *American Geography*: 'we cannot but anticipate the period, as not far distant, when the AMERICAN EMPIRE will comprehend millions of souls, west of the Mississippi.'[4] The *Boston Herald* in that year described the new Constitution as 'nothing less than a hasty stride to Universal Empire in this Western World'. In 1803, the now President Thomas Jefferson made large strides to realise Morse's prediction, establishing an 'empire of liberty' as far as the lands around the Mississippi by negotiating the Louisiana Purchase.

But the revolutionary war of independence did not merely release the energy of the new nation to found its own polity and overspread its own continent. It also released Americans to pursue their trading activities on a global scale unencumbered by the restraints of British regulation. America was open for business. All that remained was to ensure that the world was opened to American enterprise. Even before securing the Louisiana Purchase, in 1801 the US became embroiled in a war with Tripoli, in North Africa, to secure its shipping from the depredations of the corsairs, the local naval privateers usually known as Barbary pirates. William Eaton approached the US government with the proposal to achieve this by means of a little regime change. President Thomas Jefferson had misgivings about interfering in the internal affairs of another state. But his secretary of state James Madison argued that the principle of non-intervention should be countermanded by that of 'just war'; what was 'just' being the self-evident proposition that all the world should be open to American activity, free from the bribes (tribute or tax) that were the customary cost of doing business in the region. Eaton's covert operation to overthrow Yusuf Karamanli, Pasha of Tripoli, in favour of his brother Hamet would be financed by tribute that Hamet would elicit from Swedish, Danish and Dutch shipping – the flags of convenience used by Europeans in North African waters – once installed on the throne courtesy of American military backing. The entire project was an utter disaster, and anyway was made redundant by the American consul in Algiers who negotiated a settlement allowing Yusuf to keep his throne in exchange for a pledge not to molest American shipping. But the easy conjunction between opening the world to American power and influence and the use of military means was established. It was evidence of the seamless appropriation of the ethos of the British empire by what had been its American colonies.

By the 1820s America had naval squadrons in Mediterranean, Pacific, African and South Atlantic waters. Their function was to exert power and influence to keep the world open to US national interests by protecting Americans and their commerce. This could mean anything from ensuring the rights of American seal-hunters in the Falkland Islands to punishing Sumatrans for stealing opium from American traders; and it was hardly distinct from the gunboat diplomacy that the British empire was earnestly engaged in practising. In 1823, President James Monroe issued what became known as the Monroe Doctrine – henceforth, the American hemisphere was off-limits to European adventurism, any example of which America would view as 'dangerous to our peace and safety'. What happened in the Americas was defined as of direct concern to the United States, and on this premise there is hardly a Latin American country that has not experienced the exertion of US power and influence on behalf of its commerce and national security, much to the detriment of the independence, self-determination and economic well-being of the people of those countries.

The 1840s saw the beginning of a century of American patrols in the Yangtze River to enforce the trade concessions and access for missionaries it had wrung from China. In this, America was acting no differently from the British empire, which at the same time was extracting trade concessions from China by means of the opium wars and securing possession of its safe harbour base in Hong Kong. In 1846, the US went to war with Mexico after annexing Texas in support of American citizens who had moved into the territory and then objected to becoming Mexicans, much as happened previously when Americans moved into Spain's Florida territory. As a result of the Mexican war, the US acquired not just Texas but the whole of the southwest – New Mexico, Arizona and California. It was the war in which so many of America's military personnel acquired the experience they would so fatefully bring to bear on opposing sides in the Civil War.

If China could be intimidated into opening its doors, why not Japan? In 1853, America's Commodore Matthew Perry sailed into Tokyo Bay with his fleet of 'Black Ships' and their promise of coercive force, bombardment or possible invasion, if Japan would not open its markets to American trade. In 1871, the same stratagem was used, but with less success, against Korea by Admiral John Rodgers. American missionaries first arrived in Hawaii in 1821. They were fruitful, multiplied and pursued the Protestant ethic in a variety of business ventures by which they came to dominate the economic life of the island group. The eventual prognosis for the islands was long self-evident: that Hawaii was intimately connected to America's commercial and naval supremacy in the Pacific was acknowledged by one of its admirals in 1851. Various treaties and failed attempts to negotiate acquisition followed, including that of 1884 which gave the US exclusive control of the harbour on the Pearl River in Oahu. Technically Hawaii was an independent nation ruled by a Hawaiian monarchy. But Jingo Jim, the Maine Republican James G. Blaine, a notoriously corrupt congressman and then senator for the railroad interest and advocate for imperialism, pointed to that old familiar: 'the gradual and seemingly inevitable decadence and extinction of the native race.'[5] This might leave the islands, long declared an American preserve, open to colonisation by other powers. In 1891 Queen Liliuokalani ascended the throne and attempted to introduce a new constitution which would undercut the political dominance of the sugar-planters. A cabal of leading American Hawaiian business interests planned a coup, with the assurance of 'the protection and assistance of the United States forces there', who came ashore to patrol the streets in support of the plot. One month after the coerced abdication of Queen Liliuokalani, annexation papers were signed, though the changed administration in Washington was not yet convinced of the argument for empire. Actual annexation did not come until 1898, by which time imperialist fever was in the ascendancy. The following year another Polynesian island group, Samoa, subject of American attention since whaling interests had ventured there in the 1830s, suffered a similar fate. It was partitioned between Germany and the US. American Samoa included Pago Pago, 'the most perfectly landlocked harbour that exists in the Pacific Ocean',[6] and conveniently placed on a number of major trade routes across the Pacific.

The Adams family – Samuel, his cousin John (second president, 1797–1801) and John's son, John Quincy Adams (sixth president, 1825–9) – all shared the view that putting the US on a sound footing necessitated territorial expansion on its own continent – by which they meant, at various times, Canada, Quebec, Florida and Cuba. By the 1890s the American frontier, excluding Canada and Cuba, was famously declared closed. The process of internal colonisation achieved by war, territorial possession and the practices of imperialism was complete. But a world open to the rising power of American commerce and industry suggested that the internal process should shift its horizons outward and unashamedly embrace imperialist aspirations.

And at last the Spanish empire was in terminal decline, just as Jefferson had predicted. One piece, Cuba, looked especially ripe for falling into American hands. On 11 April 1898, President McKinley sent a message to Congress proposing 'the forcible intervention of the United States' to end 'the barbarities, bloodshed, starvation, and horrible miseries' in Cuba, where an insurrection was under way against Spanish rule and especially the brutality of Spain's General Valeriano (Butcher) Weyler. Intervention was also necessary for the 'protection and indemnity' of American 'life and property' and to prevent 'very serious injury to the commerce, trade, and business of our people'. War fever had been rising since January of that year when the American vessel *Maine* had exploded in Havana harbour. Events in Cuba – such as the taking of San Juan Hill by Theodore Roosevelt's Rough Riders – were restaged at the Orange, New Jersey studios of Thomas Alva Edison. The raising of Old Glory in Havana was the subject of one of the newfangled motion pictures, the craze that was captivating urban American audiences.

The Spanish-American war of 1898 is the point from which the modern terms and premises of American foreign policy are usually traced, the essence of the policy being contained in the 'Open Door Notes' issued in 1899 and 1900 by secretary of state John Hay. The Notes declared a commitment to the territorial integrity of China, and America's determination to claim the same concessions from China as those enjoyed by the European powers and Japan. The principle enunciated could be used elsewhere, indeed everywhere, and sold to the American public as the pursuit of fairness, a level playing field. However, it was well understood that in reality the playing field would tilt in America's favour. As Woodrow Wilson admitted, it was 'not an open door to the rights of China, but the open door to the goods of America'.[7] And it should not be forgotten that the policy was immediately followed by American military participation in an international coalition, the other major participant being Britain, to protect foreign nationals and property threatened by the Boxer Rebellion, a popular movement to defend China from the concessions being forced upon it by foreign powers.

The twin props of openness and force in American foreign policy have always had a single object: 'at no time has the United States refused to defend American commercial enterprise in any part of the globe.'[8] As fundamental to the story of the US as territorial expansion is the global expansion of American commerce, providing the outlet for the goods, services and finance generated by and necessary to sustain the expansion of its economy and underwrite the rising living standards of its people.

The Spanish-American war was prosecuted not only in Cuba but also, as we have seen, in the Philippines. Despite the assurances given to the Filipinos, it resulted in the US acquiring a colony in the traditional sense. The taking up of 'the white man's burden', as was poetically urged by Rudyard Kipling, colonialism in the conventional European sense could be explained to Americans in the familiar terms of their own western frontier experience. This is exactly the analogy employed by Theodore Roosevelt:

> Every argument that can be made for the Filipinos could be made for the Apaches. And every word that can be said for Aguinaldo could be said for Sitting Bull. As peace, order and prosperity followed our expansion over the land of the Indians, so they'll follow us in the Philippines.[9]

However, the open door policy offered an alternative approach to empire, that of non-colonial imperial expansion. In whatever guise, the future trajectory and implications of US foreign policy were made clear by Senator Albert Beveridge of Indiana, in his famous 'March of the Flag' speech to the Republican convention of 1898: 'The conflicts of the future are to be conflicts of trade – struggles for markets – commercial wars for existence. And the golden rule of peace is impregnability of position and invincibility of preparedness.'[10]

Roosevelt's successor as president, William Taft, showed the presentational flexibility of the principles of foreign policy with his handy soundbite – 'dollar diplomacy': 'The diplomacy of the present administration has sought to respond to modern ideas of commercial intercourse. This policy has been characterised as substituting dollars for bullets. It is one that appeals alike to idealistic humanitarian sentiments, to the dictates of sound policy and strategy, and to legitimate commercial aims', he declared in December 1912. The first recipient of dollar diplomacy was Nicaragua. Ruled by the dictator José Santos Zelaya, the country had a habit of refusing American requests for a naval base, a concession for a second canal route, and proposals for new business opportunities for American firms. Antagonism to openness had its consequences. In his state of the union address of 1909, Taft held Zelaya responsible for keeping 'Central America in constant tension and turmoil'. America would act on behalf of those beset by the troubles Zelaya created. Covertly, American businesses in Nicaragua began financing and supporting a revolution – with the total agreement of the state department. Washington broke relations with Zelaya, refused to recognise his properly elected successor, and paid its custom duties to the rebel regime. When the rebels were defeated by forces loyal to the Nicaraguan government, the US landed Marines to protect the rebel force while it reorganised. In August 1910 the rebels triumphed and entered the capital, Managua. The realities of dollar diplomacy then got under way in earnest. A state department representative arrived to negotiate a pact with the new regime. A constituent assembly would be selected; America's favoured candidates would be elected president and vice president. A commission satisfactory to the state department would settle outstanding financial claims. Nicaragua would accept a loan from American bankers secured in part against customs receipts which would be collected by a US agent. Control of customs receipts, as the US had learned from experience in Santo Domingo, meant effective control over the entire economic life of a country.

Within months, the American minister in Managua noted that 'the natural sentiments of an overwhelming majority of Nicaraguans is antagonistic to the United States, and even with some members of [President] Estrada's cabinet I find a decided suspicion, if not distrust, of our motives'.[11] The National Assembly sought to amend the constitution to preclude foreign bank loans. President Estrada was forced to resign. The American minister wired the state department that if it wished the vice president to succeed him, 'a war vessel is necessary for moral effect' – it was duly dispatched. In June 1911, a $15 million loan from American financiers and operation of the customs houses under American supervision was agreed. Most of the loan would go to settle Nicaragua's external debts to Europeans and Americans, while US banking firms would oversee improvement of the national railways and build a new one which they would control. Not even the US Senate was prepared to acquiesce to these terms, refusing to ratify the agreement on three occasions. A new and more modest agreement was then worked out by which two American banking houses would acquire a 51 per cent stake in a reorganised Nicaraguan National Bank. A slimmed-down loan was to be secured by a lien on customs and a liquor tax. This time the arrangement was effected by executive order. The mechanisms of dollar diplomacy were adopted, adapted and implemented throughout Latin America. As President Taft commented in 1912, the year US Marines were sent to Cuba: 'While our foreign policy should not be turned a hair's breadth from the straight path of justice, it may well be made to include active intervention to secure for our merchandise and our capitalists opportunity for profitable investment.'[12]

But far more importantly, such a policy could be sold to the American people as an exercise of virtue in and of itself because it could be bundled comfortably with values inherent in the idea of America: 'Expanding the marketplace enlarged the area of freedom. Expanding the area of freedom enlarged the marketplace.'[13] The project of ensuring an open world was not only benign, it was a precondition of freedom and democracy and the stability, peace and security this would bring. Such thoughts could be, and variants indeed were, uttered by American presidents from William McKinley to George W. Bush. The open door policy legitimated a familiar idea: 'the endless expansion of the American frontier in the name of self-determination, progress and peace.'[14] It produced a consensus across the entire spectrum of opinion because, as William Appleman Williams has argued, imperialists believed that such an American empire would be humanitarian, while most humanitarians believed that doing good would be good for business. Of course, implicit in this worldview is the corollary that resistance to openness is evidence of untrustworthiness if not outright antagonism that distinguishes friend from foe.

With this guiding light to its foreign policy, America could present itself as a reluctant superpower, intervening militarily only in self-defence or in defence of those too weak to defend themselves. The myth of the reluctant superpower operated much as the fiction that sustained the idea of the British empire: that it was acquired in a fit of absence of mind, the result of circumstance not intention, and certainly not deliberate policy – but events nevertheless imposed responsibilities which then could not be shirked. By whatever presentational terms, myth or polite fiction, what is clear is that in essence the premises of US foreign policy have long served to foster the worldview that America is the world and the world is America.

Immediately after 9-11, Zoltan Grossman, an American peace activist and regular contributor to the radical magazine *Counterpunch*, published a list of 'A Century of US Military Interventions from Wounded Knee to Afghanistan', based on congressional records and the Library of Congress research service. Grossman lists 134 interventions, small and big, global and domestic, covering the 111 years between 1890 and 2001. Clyde Prestowitz makes the point that Americans 'don't like to think of ourselves as a warlike people, but can we expect others to accept us as "peace loving" when it is really only in arms we trust?'[15] By his tally, since the signing of the US Constitution in 1789 there has scarcely been a year when the US was not engaged in some overseas military operation: some 235 separately named events, of which 25 or 30 could be characterised as full-scale wars, the Iraq war not included. But the most telling statistic comes from the US Commission on National Security: 'Since the end of the Cold War the US has embarked upon nearly four dozen military interventions … as opposed to only 16 during the entire period of the Cold War.'[16]

With the demise of communism the basic premises of US foreign policy have reasserted themselves with a vengeance. Indeed, the terms and premises of the policy reached their apotheosis in the new buzzword: globalisation – an open world by another label, calling for continuity and not change in America's stance. 'It is important to reach out to the rest of the world,' wrote George Herbert Walker Bush, first president of the new era, in *A World Transformed*, the book co-authored with his national security advisor Brent Scowcroft, 'even more important to keep the strings of control tightly in our hands.'[17] In an open and interdependent world where peace, prosperity and security were all intertwined, 'the scope of US interests was limitless. There was nothing that did not matter.'[18] But Americans could be confident of the outcome: 'You know we're going to do very, very well as the world becomes more interdependent', Bill Clinton assured a student audience in December 2000 when he delivered a speech on foreign policy in the global age.

Throughout the Cold War, the containment of communism was the self-evident justification for American pursuit of openness and consequent presence around the globe, as well as the legitimation for intervention, whether overt or covert. As Andrew

Bacevich notes, 'The Big Idea guiding US strategy is openness, the removal of barriers to the movement of goods, capital, people and ideas thereby fostering an integrated international order conducive to American interests, governed by American norms, regulated by American power and above all satisfying the expectations of the American people for ever greater abundance'.[19] It was not merely containment of communism but the climate of fear and imminent existential threat posed by an alternative to the American dispensation that so seamlessly interwove a policy of openness with the building and maintenance of the greatest military power the world has ever seen. But the mighty arsenal that America amassed to face down the global communist conspiracy did not make the nation more secure once the communist bloc evaporated.

Globalisation in the post-Cold War era, American politicians quickly assured the American public, brought with it a whole new set of menaces to fear. 'The very openness of our borders and technology also makes us vulnerable in new ways', President Bill Clinton explained in May 2000. The theme was taken up by Madeleine Albright, who explained what this would mean: 'we must plot our defence not against a single powerful threat, as during the Cold War, but against a viper's nest of perils.'[20] As the definition of peril exploded, what constituted national security and its defence had to expand:

> Trade became a full fledged national security issue. So too did offshore money laundering and the price of oil, along with refugees, environmental degradation, large scale violations of human rights, drug cartels and computer hackers. By the close of Bill Clinton's second term, with his administration classifying climate change and the spread of AIDS as imminent threats to American well being, the range of security concerns to which the US must attend in a global era was virtually without limit.[21]

And there was one other item the Clinton administration worked tirelessly to emphasise: terrorism, but especially terrorists using weapons of mass destruction. It would be, said Bill Clinton in January 1999, 'the enemy of our generation'. This fear preceded rather than followed events. Clinton's warning was issued despite the state department's annual report on terrorism showing that international terrorist activity had declined substantially with the end of the Cold War. From a peak of 665 incidents worldwide in 1987 the number of attacks fell by 29 per cent in the 1990s. In 2000, 423 incidents occurred, fewer than half directed at Americans or US facilities, and the majority targeted property and caused no casualties. America acquired full spectrum fear as a continuation of its way of viewing the world. It was the consistent build-up of this fear and accompanying sense of vulnerability that prepared the way for America to become more itself after 9-11.

The only salve for full spectrum fear is the US military. As analyst Joshua Muravchik notes: 'The bedrock of America's global leadership is military might.'[22] Or as secretary of defence William Cohen explained: 'when people see us, they see our power, they see our professionalism, they see our patriotism, and they say that's a country that we want to be with.'[23] That people might conclude that America was a power they had no option to oppose was the alternative interpretation, the 'what if' question not asked, its potential meaning not given reasoned consideration. In the global age now declared, American forces needed to be capable of much more than ever before: 'our soldiers, sailors, airmen and Marines, all our services must be trained to do everything', Cohen argued. The Pentagon responded with 'Joint Vision 2010', which appeared in 1996 and was subsequently revised as 'Joint Vision 2020', committing the US to establishing 'a level of military mastery without historical precedent'. It was summed up in the phrase 'Full Spectrum Dominance'.[24]

Militarily, by design, the US is the most powerful country in history. Even if all the other states in the world put all their military resources together, they would not be able to mount a credible threat to the US. The colossal US military is more than two-and-a-half times larger than the militaries of the next nine largest potential adversaries combined: Russia, China, Iran, North Korea, Iraq, Libya, Syria, Sudan, Cuba. US defence spending, before the Iraq war, accounted for 40 per cent of the global total, a percentage that is set to rise. There is no equivalent in the world in sheer concentration of power to a US carrier task force: the nuclear-powered carrier group that forms around the USS *Enterprise*, for example, has a combined flight deck almost a mile in length and a superstructure twenty storeys high; it concentrates more military power in one naval group than most developed states can manage with all their armed forces. The US possesses twelve such carriers – with another, the USS *Ronald Reagan*, under development. 'Nothing', writes Paul Kennedy, professor of history at Yale University, 'has ever existed like this disparity of power; nothing.' The US has accumulated more power than Charlemagne, the Roman empire, and Britain at its imperial height. Not surprisingly, the US spends more on defence than any other country in history. While the European powers cut their defence spending after the fall of the Berlin Wall, China held its spending in check, and the Russian military budget simply collapsed, the US budget continued to increase from $260 billion in the middle of the 1990s to a staggering $329 billion in 2002. And this in a democratic country that claims to despise large government! 'I have returned to all of the comparative defence spending and military personnel statistics over the past 500 years that I compiled in *The Rise and Fall of the Great Powers* [1989], and no other nation comes close', says Kennedy.[25] The satirists at *Bremner, Bird and Fortune* have offered on British television, just as Jon Stewart has in America, more telling and insightful analysis than mainstream news and political coverage. They prove that if news and entertainment merge, there is no reason why entertainment should not become the purveyor of the real news that journalists and pundits neglect to bring the public. Bremner et al. calculated, by careful addition from public sources:

> Since the end of the Second World War, the Americans have spent US$19 trillion on what they call 'defense', which they spell differently. And define very differently. That means that if you were to spend US$26 million every day since the birth of Christ, you'd still have spent less than the Americans have spent on defence since the end of the Second World War. Put another way, if you had funded a small military invasion (helicopters, small arms, infantry support) each and every day for the last two thousand years – that's nearly 750,000 wars – you still would not have matched what the USA has spent on defence in the last fifty.[26]

Despite its unmatched military might and the astronomical figures of its defence budget, money buys insecurity. The US still feels threatened – so much so that it insists on militarising outer space. The US Star Wars programme, aimed at the 'control of outer space', 'domination of outer space' and 'superiority in outer space', envisages deploying space-, land- and sea-based antiballistic missile systems, and a variety of orbiting systems that could strike terrestrial targets. Even US arms manufacturers, such as aviation giant Lockheed Martin, are having problems in finding appropriate enemies at which to aim American military might. However, this has done little to constrain their commercial activity. Since the end of the Cold War the US share of the global arms trade has roughly doubled. America now sells half of all weapons sold around the world. In 1999 this amounted to $26.2 billion, a 49.1 per cent share of the market (the UK accounted for 18.7 per cent, France 12.4 per cent and Russia 6.6 per cent). The French describe US military evolution as *'gigantisme militaire'*, a phrase that incorporates the scale of US military ambition as well as the idea that it is a pathological condition: an organism that has grown so large it is sick. Yet in the election of 2000, both Republican and Democratic candidates promised to increase military spending. They were responding not just to the anxiety of the military, which concluded that it had been subsisting on half rations and demanded more money; it was also the plaint of academics and pundits publishing books lamenting America's 'military weakness' and the drift of public opinion. Gallup found that the number of Americans thinking the US was spending too little on defence had grown from 9 per cent in 1990 to 40 per cent in August 2000.

Apart from the hardware, with an increasing emphasis on information technology and its ability to deliver mastery by 'seeing through the fog of war', as William Cohen termed it, America's defence budget buys it a global footprint, a presence everywhere. There are more than 700 US military installations around the globe, located in some 73 countries. The bases established at the end of World War II to administer the transformation of the vanquished enemies, Germany and Japan, are still there. The end of the Cold War and the declaration of a global war on terror has increased the opportunities for new countries to play host to the American military. Wherever American forces are stationed, they live cocooned in enclaves provided with the abundance of the norms of an American lifestyle, which tend to be surrounded by the sleazy detritus of bars, clubs and strip joints that cater to overly healthy young men far from home with money to spend. But wherever they are, American military personnel are covered by SOFA, status of forces agreements, which ensure that they are subject only to American jurisdiction for whatever excesses of behaviour they commit. As Chalmers Johnson documented in *Blowback*, the military bases cause friction with the local population, whether it be in disputes over land or the apparent exemption from justice enjoyed by US service personnel charged with anything from vehicular manslaughter to rape and murder. Suspects in crimes against the indigenous population are likely to be shipped back home, where their fate remains a mystery to the victims of crime, their family and community.

American overseas military bases are about the projection of American power and influence. For the American public they are testimony to America's global leadership and a necessary part of 'the endless expansion of the American frontier in the name of self-determination, progress and peace'. But they also have another implication, diagnosed by Michael Sherry in his interpretative history of the US since the Great Depression, *In the Shadow of War*: that America harbours a pervasive sense of anxiety and vulnerability. War itself has become a metaphorical constant, national security the axis around which the American enterprise has turned. Therefore, militarism 'reshaped every realm of American life – politics and foreign policy, economics and technology, culture and social relations – making America a profoundly different nation'.[27] If this was indeed change, it was not accomplished in a fit of absence of mind while the American public was distracted. It did not come about because of 9-11. It was not the work of a small group of fanatics. It developed as conscious policy with considerable support from a public easily roused to even greater fiscal exertion and paroxysms of fear by goading politicians, or placated and massaged for electoral advantage by those same politicians. The terms and premises of American foreign policy are a reflection of America and how America views the world.

As long ago as the 1930s, the American historian Charles A. Beard foresaw a number of problems with this way of thinking. He argued that the more America sought to open the world, the more opposition it would encounter. It relied on an over-simplified view of other people, 'the exclusion of their national cultures – ideas, loyalties, passions, political traditions, the development and clash of races and nations'. The world was not that malleable, and would not obligingly conform to American preferences. To insist otherwise was to court perpetual conflict.[28] Resistance to America's opening of doors to its trade and investment would lead to the US increasingly having to resort to force, and to the growth of militarism at home and a nation 'compelled to devote immense energies and a large part of its annual wealth production to wars, to preparation for wars, and to paying for past wars'.[29] Beard's views did not find favour and his reputation went into decline when he was perceived to oppose America's participation in its 'good war', World War II, being branded an apologist for fascism. Yet the consistent objective of an open world by whatever means necessary is the lodestone of American foreign policy. The development of the military-industrial complex that President Eisenhower warned of in his farewell address in 1960, and the growing antipathy to the overt and covert exertion of American power and influence by those on the receiving end, are matters that cannot be wished away. They comprise the debate that America consistently balks at having with itself. The consequences of US foreign policy, of the full spectrum dominance it has pursued, the outcomes that this has had on the lives of ordinary people around the globe, remain obscured, unknown, under-reported, doubted and denied, and highlighting them is seen as evidence of pure envy when not an open declaration of outright anti-Americanism. It is to the consequences and effects of this policy for the people of the world that we need to turn our attention.

CHAPTER SIX

Full Spectrum Dominance

Full spectrum dominance is more than a military strategy – it is the effect that America has around the globe. As a military strategy it is just one manifestation of what we call the hamburger syndrome. There is hardly a place in the world where one cannot get a hamburger. Even in the remote jungles of Sarawak, the rainforests of Brazil, the deserts of North Africa, one cannot escape the 'golden arches' of McDonald's, the 'flaming grills' of Burger King, the cute little girl of Wendy's and other signs and symbols of American food chains. But hamburgers are more than ubiquitous. While the mass-produced hamburger is promoted as food, it is essentially junk, food confected with a whole series of additives that diminish the nutritive value of the whole. Moreover, while a hamburger is certainly fast food, it is not, as is commonly claimed, the only or indeed the first fast food the world has ever seen. Every culture has its own fast food. The shawarma (a form of rolled-up sandwich) in the Middle East, aloo-puri chaat in India and nasi lamak (rice with dry fish) in South-East Asia, good old British fish and chips, and the French baguette with cheese and ham are good examples. So, both as food and as a cultural product, the hamburger pretends to be something it is clearly not.

The hamburger is the single most concentrated, or should that be congealed, symbol of the entire complex that is America. Like the hamburger, the idea of America has a number of separate ingredients: there is the government, the most powerful government on earth, or the sole hyperpower as we have termed it; there are the consistent terms and premises of foreign policy operated by successive American administrations and their consequences for countries and people beyond America; there is the enormous power of US corporations in whose commercial interest and by whose influence the policy of American government is shaped, while the corporations remain beyond the reach of or accountability to any government; there is the power and wealth of American academic institutions which, along with health services, industry and business, purchase the brightest and best from wherever they can be found, draining away the talents and expertise nurtured at great cost by other countries; then there are the concepts, philosophy and ethos characteristic of the American worldview – such things as individualism and belief in personal freedom – that are like the relishes that flavour the hamburger; and there are Americans themselves, with their particular blend of self-belief, seeming lack of interest in the rest of the world, and certainty that their way of life is the biggest, boldest and best for everyone. Like the hamburger, this multidimensional America is experienced as a standardised, massproduced, packaged brand. Each aspect of America may have its own distinctive character, and many, taken in isolation, have more good attributes than questionable or negative connotations. But, like the burger, the essence of America is that the individual aspects of its influence seldom occur in isolation. A true hamburger is a superabundant, multi-layered compound entity. It comes with the lettuce, ketchup, pickle and tomato included, whether you like them or not, whether you want them or not. It is sold as a compound feast. If you don't want the lettuce or the pickle you get them anyway and then have to dispose of them on your own recognisance. It is the degree to which America proclaims and glories in itself as a compound whole that makes the hamburger such a powerful metaphor for the nation, and such a potent symbol and focus for criticism of

America in the rest of the world. The hamburger is more than its ingredients – it is, indeed, a way of life.

As a way of life, the hamburger is a seductive novelty with discernible, and deleterious, consequences. Not just because it is an omnipresent con-trick, but also because the consumerism it embodies is seen as a clear cultural threat. It personifies the way in which America is taking over the lives of ordinary people in the rest of the world and shrinking their cultural space – their space to be themselves, to be different, to be other than America. And America projects itself on the rest of the world as though it were a hamburger: a commodity, a brand, out to capture all cultural space for itself. It sees any negative aspects of its international image not as something rooted in its foreign policy or cultural hegemony, but simply as a communication problem. After 9-11, the Bush administration appointed Charlotte Beers as under-secretary for public diplomacy. Beers, whose career included heading two of the world's advertising behemoths, Ogilvy & Mather and J. Walter Thompson, became famous for 'branding' products like American Express. 'Well, guess what?', secretary of state Colin Powell told senators on the Foreign Relations Committee. 'She got me to buy Uncle Ben's rice and so there is nothing wrong with getting somebody who knows how to sell something.' The 'something' Beers was to sell was 'an elegant brand' called 'the US', and the president and secretary of state are the 'symbols of the brand'.[1] Beers told *Business Week*: '[T]he whole idea of building a brand is to create a relationship between the product and its user. ... We're going to have to communicate the intangible assets of the United States – things like our belief system and our values.'[2]

But a well-established 'relationship' between 'the product and its user' already existed: a relationship based on more than half a century of experience of how corporate America has sold itself to the rest of the world. One outcome of the spread of American hamburgers, and the philosophy associated with them, is that it has spread standardisation throughout the world. A Big Mac is made by the same process, packaged in exactly the same containers, weighs the same, and is sold in the same way in similar restaurants throughout the world. There may be regional variations to capture the local palate and cultural imagination – Curry Burgers in India, Samurai Burgers in Japan, Rendang Burgers in Malaysia and Indonesia – but the product is the same, despite its McDonaldised 'diversity'. This is exactly what the rest of the world has experienced from American foreign policy: with the US you get a standardised theory and practice in its dealings with the world. The theory is always about 'our values', which are placed on a global pedestal: justice, democracy, human rights, freedom, civic concerns, compassion, resolve, responsibility – all the great virtues of Western civilisation. But the practice consistently contradicts these values. In other words, politically, America relates to the rest of the world in terms of double standards.

The world's perception of America is based on experience – for example, how the US behaves at international forums such as the United Nations. As the former UN secretary-general Boutros Boutros-Ghali writes in his book *Unvanquished: a US–UN Saga*, the UN is now the sole property of a single power – the US – which, through intimidation, threats and the use of its veto, manipulates the world body for the benefit of its own interest.[3] When it suits the US, it uses the UN to seek legitimacy for its actions, to build coalitions and impose sanctions on 'rogue states'. When world opinion goes against the US, it treats the UN with utter contempt. In the aftermath of World War II, the US was the prime mover in establishing the UN – and such UN initiatives as the Universal Declaration of Human Rights – to further 'democracy' and 'freedom' on the Western model as a global norm. Throughout the history of the UN, America has consistently vetoed any resolution or declaration that did not reflect US priorities or business interests. 'With noteworthy regularity', writes William Blum in *Rogue State* (2001), 'Washington has found itself – often alone, sometimes joined by one or two other countries – standing in opposition to the General Assembly resolutions aimed at furthering human rights, peace, nuclear disarmament, economic justice, the struggle against South African apartheid and Israeli lawlessness and other progressive causes'. Blum lists some 150 incidences between 1984 and 1987 when the US cast a solitary 'no' vote against General Assembly resolutions.[4]

American cynicism towards and criticism of the organisation exists despite the fact that the US did not pay its UN dues for decades. When it finally agreed to pay past dues in return for a reduction in its assessments, it refused to fulfil the promise. The resentment against the US at typical UN meetings is so intense that it can be felt in the air. It was this resentment that led the UN's Economic and Social Council (ECOSOC) to oust the US from the 53-member Human Rights Commission (HRC) in May 2001. It was the first time this had happened since the Commission was created in 1946. The ECOSOC voted in a secret ballot, and one would expect such a move to be led by Third World nations with long lists of grievances. In fact, it was the vote of a number of European 'friendly nations' that eventually ousted America. The US suffered a similar defeat in 1998 when it was ejected from, but later reinstated to, the UN Advisory Committee on Administrative and Budgetary Questions (ACABQ), a key committee that deals with funding the whole body. The relationship reached its nadir, or perhaps revealed its essential character, with George W. Bush's temporary recess appointment of John Bolton as US ambassador to the UN, a man whose open contempt for the organisation is summed up in his aphorisms: 'If you lost ten storeys [from the UN building in New York] today it wouldn't make a bit of difference'; 'There is no United Nations. There is an international community that occasionally can be led by the only real power left in the world, and that's the United States';[5] 'The United Nations is an instrument to be used to advance America's foreign policy interests, not to engage in international social work.'

The US has consistently opposed important human rights initiatives of the United Nations. It is one of only two countries – the other being pre-invasion Iraq – that has still not ratified the 1989 landmark UN Convention on the Rights of the Child. It also held back ratifications on the treaty to ban landmines and the treaty to establish an International Criminal Court. According to the UN Committee against Torture, which oversees and monitors the actions of parties to the convention, the US has consistently violated the World Convention against Torture: the Green Berets routinely tortured their prisoners in Vietnam during interrogation, the CIA frequently tortured suspected infiltrators of Soviet émigré organisations in Western Europe, the US trained and maintained SAVAK, the notorious secret service of the Shah of Iran, and trained and equipped the intelligence services of Bolivia, Uruguay, Brazil and Israel with techniques and technologies of torture – to give just a few examples that precede the current unilateral redefinition of torture by the Bush administration. As Blum notes, in 1982 and 1983 the US was alone in voting against a declaration that education, work, healthcare, proper nourishment and national development are human rights. It would appear that even thirteen years later, official American attitudes had not 'softened'. In 1996, at a UN-sponsored World Food Summit, the US took issue with an affirmation of the 'right of everyone to have access to safe and nutritious food'. The United States insisted that it does not recognise a 'right to food'. For the people of developing nations, these rights – set out and championed by the world community as global norms – are part of their defence against tyranny, corruption and injustice practised within their nations and by agencies and corporations of foreign nations. Within the context and history of Third World nations, establishing these principles as rights opens debates about the legacy of injustices that still create inherent inequalities, poverty and lack of equal opportunity; and it opens the prospect of change. Washington, instead, has championed just one cause: free trade – the eternally open door.[6]

In general, the US takes little interest in bodies such as the United Nations Development Programme (UNDP), the United Nations Educational, Scientific and Cultural Organisation (UNESCO) and the United Nations High Commission for Refugees (UNHCR). One institution in which America maintains total control is the World Trade Organisation (WTO). Indeed, it has been suggested that the WTO is a major instrument of American 'neo-imperialism'. Today, technology is the glue that binds production, distribution and marketing systems, connects producers, designers and consumers, and enables capital and cultural commodities to whiz around the globe without any regard for borders. It is the all-embracing reach and omnipotence of its technology that enables America to function as a hyperpower. In a hyperlinked world, in which $1.5 trillion change hands in a single day, all the aces are held by those who generate both the technology and the information – all of which leads to a new, heightened hyper-imperialism.

The forums of choice for maintaining US hyperpower, and technological hyper-imperialism, include not just the WTO but also the International Monetary Fund (IMF) and the World Bank. There are two main reasons. First, the WTO, IMF and World Bank are the most untransparent and undemocratic of global institutions. The secrecy surrounding their decision-making processes makes them ideal bodies for keeping the rest of the troublesome world firmly at arm's length. Second, both the WTO and IMF have effective mechanisms for the enforcement of obligations, particularly those of the developing countries: the WTO through the threat of retaliation against their export of goods, and the IMF through loan conditions, which are imposed ruthlessly. The US uses these mechanisms to keep developing countries in line, and to smooth the progress of its own multinational companies by removing obstacles and giving positive encouragement. By American-imposed convention, the top jobs at the WTO, IMF and World Bank are shared by the US and Europe. When the first person from a developing country,

Supachai Panitchpakdi of Thailand, emerged as a viable candidate to head the WTO, all hell broke loose. The then US president, Bill Clinton, threatened permanent gridlock at the WTO unless America's chosen candidate was accepted. 'In evaluating the candidates', he explained, he had 'focussed on their positions on issues of importance to us'; this consideration, according to Clinton, was synonymous with 'what we believe would best serve the needs of the WTO'.[7] This is the operational end of the theory that what's good for America is good for the world, and is presumably what Clinton meant when he assured students that America would do very, very well from globalisation. Not surprisingly, 'a United Nations-appointed study team has labelled the World Trade Organisation a "nightmare" for developing countries', said the *Financial Times*. Its activities 'reflect an agenda that serves only to promote dominant corporatist interests that already monopolise the area of international trade'.[8] And according to the *Economist*, the business bible of the establishment, 'the Fund and Bank ... have become a more explicit tool of western, and particularly American, foreign policy'.[9]

What all this means is that the world's economy functions largely for the benefit of the US and the US-led Group of Seven (G7), which with the addition of Russia became G8. What the functioning of this global economy means for developing nations is the continuation of structural arrangements that operate to keep them disadvantaged. While such structures continue to operate, development, as known and understood, is the problem and not the cure. The demands of conventional development create the vicious spiral of conditions that work against the interests of the poorest. 'Development' seldom amounts to anything more than developing countries importing expensive – and frequently out-of-date – technologies from the US and other industrialised countries; technologies they can seldom manage or maintain. Often these technologies undermine local techniques and age-old manufacturing capabilities and end up further marginalising the poor. This is a paradox that has been known, argued, advanced in pleading terms, but still has not had any effect on the policy stance of the US. If the whole world is read according to one single vision and one set of simplistic 'values', then the complicating conditions of each particular country – its history and how its economic fortunes have been shaped into misfortunes – disappear. The misfortunes of the poorest, however, are a direct by-product of the self-interest of the richest. As the proper prelude and context for the Iraq war-induced predicament of the US and the global economy, we need to examine the underlying continuities of the last six decades, during which eight types of manipulations have ensured that the US accumulates the wealth of the world.

1. The US has been financing domestic growth through the savings of the rest of the world. 'Ever since the abandonment of the gold standard,' says Ed Mayo, the director of the London-based think tank, New Economic Foundation (NEF), 'the US has benefited from being the currency leader. This means that it benefits from the seignorage, i.e. free money, of issuing dollars for use as cash around the world. It benefits from the right to set interest rates in its domestic interests rather than global interests. One catastrophic effect was when, at the start of the monetarist years of Reagan and Thatcher, the US raised interest rates sky high, precipitating the collapse of Mexico financially and the start of the debt crisis, which has hit poorer countries hard. Since then, many countries have been caught in a debt trap. Many states are trapped in a vicious spiral of either allowing their currency to float, a tough proposition in the face of the power of the dollar, yen and euro, or tie it to the dollar, so-called dollarisation that came horribly unstuck in Argentina. When countries like Argentina end up in debt, they suffer from capital flight ($130 billion, almost equal to her total public debt), as their US-educated elites transfer money out of the country

and into US banks', says Mayo.[10] The debt trap is the simple economic equation that devastated small farmers in the US. They were encouraged to borrow cheap money to invest in 'development', new equipment, seeds and so on, but however much they borrow or improve, they cannot compete with large-scale operators whose size and resources allow them to control production and the market. So the debt burden grows, and countries – like American small farmers – end up paying, or owing, more in interest than they can possibly earn, however hard they work.

2. The US denies democratic control over their own economic destinies to over two-thirds of the world's population. Most of the world has no say at the IMF and little power to initi-ate positive change at the WTO. In particular, policies tied to IMF loans lead the way to foreign ownership and domina-tion of the economy, especially in the manufacturing and financial sectors. For example, after the South-East Asian economic crisis, the IMF imposed on Thailand and South Korea the condition that they must allow higher foreign ownership of their economies – at the insistence of the US. This was strategically the most crucial of the IMF's condi-tions, an 'extra bonus' outside of its normal macro-economic conditions (such as raising interest rates and reducing govern-ment expenditure and current account deficit). As part of the deal with the IMF, Thailand was asked to allow foreign banks to own more equity in the local banking sector. Through such 'loan conditions', American businesses and technology corporations ended up wholly or partly owning banks, financial institutions and key technology sectors in the developing world.

3. The US interprets 'trade liberalisation' to mean one-way, open access for American multinationals and businesses. Trade lib-eralisation – that is, removal or reduction of barriers to

international trade in goods and services – has been going on since the 1980s. Under the WTO's Agreement on Agriculture (AoA) and the World Bank/IMF-imposed structural adjustment programmes (SAPs), developing countries have to make significant changes in their food and agriculture policies, and open their economies to cheap food imports, while reducing and limiting support for their farmers. While the AoA itself requires WTO members to reduce tariffs on food imports by 24 per cent over a ten-year period, most SAPs require more sweeping liberalisation measures as well as demand-related measures such as privatisation of state-run enterprises, elimination of subsidies and price controls, and abolition of marketing boards. Ostensibly, the WTO and its Agreement were arrived at by consensus and with the participation of developing countries. In fact, the whole agreement was stitched up between the US and the European Union. AoA has been described as 'an act of fraud' (by Oxfam, among others) which intensifies rural poverty and destroys smallholder livelihoods. It enables the US and the EU to export their goods cheaply to developing countries in which farmers, unable to compete, are put out of business. The cheap imports come from commercial channels and dumping of food sold below the cost of production to dispose of surpluses. In Ghana, for example, local farmers are unable to get an economic price for their produce such as corn, rice, soybeans, rabbit, sheep and goats, even in village markets. The farmers are forced to pay heavily for inputs – expensive imported fertilisers and pesticides and sometimes even seeds – and usually receive less for their produce. But food prices for the consumers do not fall. Rural people suffer, despite increases in production, and there is significant deterioration in living standards, primarily among the rural poor. As a result, countless farmers are forced to move to already overburdened cities to eke out some sort of living. Thus, local agriculture is destroyed, domestic food production shattered, and the food security of the country is seriously compromised. The story repeats itself from one country to another.

4. The US promotes a type of 'economic freedom' that actually destroys the economic freedom of poor people. It has caught the developing countries in a classic pincer movement: on the one hand, it has opened the terrain for American technology-driven businesses to enter freely and capture the markets of the world; and on the other, it has inhibited the efforts of developing countries to boost their own products and exports, and bars them from US markets. This is what is known as the free market economy. It also goes under the guise of neo-liberalism, which implies a return to 19th-century liberal or 'laissez faire' economics in which the state took a firmly hands-off stance to economic regulation. In fact, the state plays a decisive role in promoting its corporations and businesses. Thus, so-called 'free trade', so aggressively promoted by the WTO and IMF, 'amounts to little more than highway robbery, benefiting only the rich, while making the poor more vulnerable to food insecurity', says Andrew Simms, head of the global economy programme at NEF. 'As a consequence of American policies, in a single day under globalisation, poor countries lose nearly $2 billion due to rigged international trade, 30,000 children die from preventable diseases, and $60 million drains from poor to rich countries in debt.'[11]

5. The US systematically undermines the efforts of the least-developed countries to combat poverty and feed their populations. It has imposed massive tariffs on key agricultural items such as rice, sugar and coffee; on groundnuts, for example, it has imposed tariffs of over 100 per cent. These trade restrictions cost the poorer countries of the world a staggering $2.5 billion a year in lost foreign exchange earnings. The overall effects are nothing short of disastrous. In Haiti, for example,

the liberalisation of the rice market and subsequent surge in subsidised US imports has not only destroyed local rice production and the livelihoods of countless farmers, but also undermined national food security. In country after country, in such labour-intensive and job-creating areas as textiles, footwear and agriculture, the dumping of American products, often at below the cost of production, has shattered the livelihood of vulnerable populations and reduced them to abject poverty.

6. The US defrauds the least developed countries, thus increasing their poverty. Consider, for example, how the Africa Growth and Opportunity Act (AGOA), signed into law by President George W. Bush in October 2001, defrauds the countries of Africa. AGOA is supposed to provide African economies with duty- and quota-free access for their products to the American market in exchange for certain concessions to the US and its firms. So what do the African countries actually get? The American government grants access only to those goods that it decides may not negatively affect US producers. Hence, coffee, sugar and other products of economic benefit to African countries are not covered. In particular, AGOA offers duty- and quota-free access for African textiles and clothing to the American market – but, in fact, only products using fabric and yarns produced in America have easy access to the US market. Textile products made from materials produced in African countries and other areas are subject to severe constraints. Access in these cases is granted only on a yearly basis, and cannot exceed a total of 3.5 per cent of all apparel imported into the US in eight years. Moreover, the US government can withdraw even this benefit at any time, if it determines that there is a sudden surge in imports of textile products into the US which threatens its own domestic industries. The requirement for US raw material to be used in their products not only undermines the

African countries' own domestic raw materials industries, but importing US raw materials for textile production in Africa is expensive, given the transport and other costs involved, which means that African textile products exported to the US end up being uncompetitive. It is not that they cannot compete, but the rules ensure that they will always be unable to compete fairly on a level playing field. And what does the US get in return? The AGOA demands that African countries must, among other things: (1) eliminate barriers to all US trade and investment in Africa, treat American firms as equal to African firms, and protect US intellectual property to international standards; (2) pursue further privatisation and remove government subsidies and price controls; (3) guarantee international labour standards and set a minimum age for child labour; and (4) not engage in any act that undermines US national security and foreign policy interests. Thus, while America gains real, concrete benefits from AGOA, the benefits for Africa are illusory. Such 'agreements' are largely responsible for the increase in absolute poverty in Africa over the last two decades.

7. The US has consistently worked to bring down commodity prices in the developing world. 'Anti-inflation is supposed to be one of the key successes of the US economy over the past decade', says Mayo. 'But the major contributor to low inflation has been the consistent decline in prices for commodities, exported by indebted countries, encouraged to get into exports as a way out of debt by WTO and IMF. For many products such as tea, coffee and groundnuts, the aid- and debt-fuelled oversupply is such that increasing exports from Africa lead to lower overall returns. While the WTO- and IMF-backed push for exports has led to structural oversupply, no cartel of export producers exists, except in oil, to balance power between supply and demand. When cartels have emerged, they have been taken out by US interests, as in the aborted

banana cartel in the 1970s, when following the model of OPEC, banana-producing countries in Central and Latin America thought they could do the same. Unfortunately bananas are not like oil, you can't leave them in the ground to restrict supply – they go bad – but even so, the prime reason for the break-up was the activities of US banana companies like Chiquita that sought to undermine the deal any way they could. It is a buyer's market, in which the principal buyer is the US consumer. It is a recipe for deflation, by which US citizens benefit from price stability and the shock waves are felt in the producer countries – that is, the US has structured a global political economy that, come heads or tails, feeds the US economy.'[12] The lifestyle of the richest nation in the history of the world, based as it is on cheap food, is effectively subsidised by the hard work and continuous effort of the poorest.

8. If all this wasn't enough, the US imposes unilateral coercive economic measures, otherwise known as 'sanctions', with regularity. During the past 80 years, such sanctions have been imposed on various countries on 120 occasions, 104 of them since World War II. In 1998 alone, the US had sanctions against 75 countries, accounting for 52 per cent of the world's population.

The beneficiaries of these manipulations of the global economy are American consumers. When Americans survey the world, they see poverty and under-development that refuses to change. They believe, as they are regularly told by politicians and the media, that America is the world's most generous nation. This is one of the most conventional pieces of 'knowledgeable ignorance'. According to OECD, the Organisation for Economic Co-operation and Development, the US gave between $6 and $9 billion in foreign aid in the period between 1995 and 1999. In absolute terms, Japan gave more than the US, between $9 and

$15 billion in the same period, though Japan's totals have since declined. In 2007 the US remains the largest donor with some $21.9 billion. While this dwarfs all other countries (the next highest official development assistance (ODA) comes from Germany with $12.3bn), it should be noted that America's total includes war-related reparations to Iraq and Afghanistan and increased aid to 'war on terror' allies such as Pakistan. But the absolute figures are less significant than the proportion of gross national income (GNI) that a country devotes to foreign aid. On that league table, and despite recent war-related increases, the US continually ranks 22nd of the 22 most developed nations. As former president Jimmy Carter commented: 'We are the stingiest nation of all.'[13] In 1970 the United Nations passed a resolution recommending that wealthy nations annually provide 0.7 per cent of GNI in official development assistance to fight poverty. In 1980 this target was reaffirmed by the Brandt Commission Report which produced the North-South Dialogue on Development, held at Cancun. The pressure to increase official assistance was maintained by the Live Aid initiative, and it was again part of the UN Millennium Challenge and the Gleneagles Agreement of 2005. However, as the OECD report for 2007 comments: 'Overall most donors are not on track to meet their stated commitments to scale up aid and will need to make unprecedented increases to meet the targets they have set for 2010.'[14] And bringing up the rear on the league table, with the furthest to go, is the US. Its massive-seeming 2007 contribution represents just 0.16 per cent of its GNI, equal with Greece. Only five nations actually exceed the UN target of 0.7 per cent. In 2007 the table was headed by Norway (0.95), followed by Sweden (0.93), Luxembourg (0.90), Denmark (0.81) and the Netherlands (0.81). Apart from being the least generous nation, the US is highly selective in who receives its aid. Over a period of decades, more than 50 per cent of its aid budget went to middle-income countries in the Middle East, with Israel being the recipient of the largest single share. And America routinely included military assistance in its 'development' aid totals. More importantly, as the official website of the US Agency for International Development (USAID) used to proclaim: 'The principal beneficiary of America's foreign assistance program has always been the United States.' In 2000, the website explained that nearly 80 per cent of USAID contracts and grants go 'directly to American firms', and that USAID programmes have helped to create new markets for American goods and 'hundreds of thousands of jobs'. That proportion is now calculated to be 70 per cent and is mandated by legislation passed by the US Congress. Far from being a burden on American citizens, aid is that arm of US foreign policy which ensures that the poor are paying a 'tax', effectively subsidising the jobs and companies of the wealthiest nation on earth.

America's earnings from the eradication of poverty are matched by its rejection of any international agreements which might hinder its own industrial and commercial interests. As President Bush Snr told the Earth Summit held at Rio de Janeiro in 1992: 'the American way of life is not up for negotiation.' Hence the subject of limiting carbon emissions was off the international agenda. And that is where it has remained from the perspective of the United States, despite the controversy over the Kyoto protocol. The protocol, adopted at the third session of the conference of the parties to the United Nations Framework Convention on Climate Change (UNFCCC) in Kyoto, Japan, on 11 December 1997, sets specific targets for the reduction of carbon dioxide emissions to combat global warming. The agreement requires industrialised countries to reduce emissions, by 2012, to an average 5.2 per cent of 1990 levels. But targets vary from country to country; the nations of the European Union, for example, have to reduce emissions to 8 per cent over the period 2008 to 2012, compared to 1990 levels. In March 2001, to the dismay of the international community, the US administration announced that it would not implement the Kyoto protocol on the grounds that it is not the right tool to deal with the challenge of climate change at a global level – thus putting the whole process of the protocol in jeopardy. In its place, the Bush Jr administration proposed a 'cap and trade' system that would set limits for emissions of three major air pollutants – but not carbon dioxide. Whereas the Kyoto protocol sets out mandatory reductions, under the Bush plan, permits would be assigned for each ton of pollution. By cutting emissions, firms would save up these permits for use at a later date, or to trade with other businesses. The European Union estimated that the Bush plan would allow the US to actually increase emissions by up to 33 per cent!

World reaction to the US proposal was unanimous. President Bush's statement was 'the announcement of the death of the Kyoto protocol', said Mohammed Al-Sabban, energy advisor to the Kingdom of Saudi Arabia. 'No one has the right to declare Kyoto dead', declared Sweden's environment minister, Kjell Larsson. EU Commission president Romano Prodi announced that 'tearing up the agreement and starting again would be a tragic mistake'. 'I appreciate your point of view,' President Bush replied, 'but this is the American position because it's right for America.' And, just to make the point clear, he added: 'We will not do anything that harms our economy, because first things first are the people who live in America.'[15] In a letter to Republican senators who had urged him to abandon the Kyoto pledge, George W. Bush explained the reasons for his decision. A new energy department review had concluded that carbon dioxide regulation would lead to significantly higher electricity prices; and he did not want to take action that would harm American consumers during a period of electricity shortages. So the price of electricity in California is far more important than the depletion of the ozone layer, the disappearance of the polar ice caps, the rise in global temperature and the havoc caused throughout the world by climate change. Not only are the needs of Americans greater than those of the rest of the world, but even the dangers to the planet as a whole must be subordinated to the sensitivities of American consumers.

American consumers are not to be scorned. The shopping habits of ordinary Americans account for two-thirds of the US economy and are the engine of the global economy. However, living the American Dream has direct consequences for the resources of the world. UNDP's Human Development Reports note that Americans consume over half of all the goods and services of the world; that its people spend over $10 billion annually on pet food alone – $4 billion more than the estimated total needed to provide basic health and nutrition for everyone in the world; that their expenditure on cosmetics – $8 billion – is $2 billion more than the annual total needed to provide basic education worldwide; or that the three richest Americans have assets that exceed the combined gross domestic product of the 48 least developed countries. Having cornered most of the world's resources, America now has its eyes firmly set on the last remaining resource of developing countries: the flora, fauna, biodiversity and the very DNA of the indigenous people of the world.

American biotechnology corporations, researchers and speculators are engaged in a quest to appropriate the ancient knowledge and wisdom of indigenous people. These technologies, processes and knowledge have developed over thousands of years. Indigenous peoples have been domesticating and cross-pollinating plants, taming wild animals, developing plant and herbal medicines, and using techniques we nowadays associate with biotechnology – employing living organisms, or parts of organisms, to make or modify products, and improve breeds of plant and animal. For example, the Igorot people in the Cordillera region of the Philippines have been fermenting their own tapey (rice wine), which is made with a native yeast called bubod, and basi (sugar cane wine), prepared with forest seeds called gamu, for millennia. They have been cultivating and breeding a wide variety of camote (sweet potatoes), a staple crop before rice was introduced. Then they developed numerous varieties of rice for different environmental conditions and terrains – a single village may have up to ten varieties of rice seeds planted for different weather and soil conditions. They have similarly developed other varieties of crops such as cassava and taro. While knowledge produced in the US and Europe is aggressively protected, this traditional knowledge has no protection. The WTO's Agreement on Trade-Related Intellectual Property (TRIPs) does not include specific provisions related to the protection of systems, practices, naturally occurring plants or products that are the basis of traditional and indigenous knowledge. So, American multinational companies, agribusiness and biotechnology firms can appropriate this knowledge and learning with impunity.

Plants that have traditionally been used by indigenous peoples are now the subject of predatory intellectual property claims. It began with the neem plant, which is used in India for making a wide range of medicines for diseases such as ulcers, diabetes, skin disorders and constipation, as well as a potent insecticide effective against locusts, brown plant-hoppers, nematodes, mosquito larvae and beetles. In 1985, a pesticidal neem extract called Margosan-O was patented by a US timber merchant and then sold to W.R. Grace and Co., the multinational chemical corporation. The floodgates were open. Between 1985 and 1995, over 37 patents were granted in Europe and the US to use and develop neem products, including a neem-based toothpaste! So, something that was free and widely available (there are an estimated 14 million neem trees in India alone), something that had been developed and used for centuries by South Asians, became the property of an American multinational corporation. Neem was quickly followed by ayahuasca and quinoa from Latin America, kava from the Pacific, and the bitter gourd from the Philippines and Thailand – all widely used by indigenous peoples, but now their ownership is claimed by American business.

This predatory behaviour not only deprives people of what is rightly theirs, but could also have devastating consequences for their future. Consider, for example, what could happen with quinoa (*Chenopodium quinoa*), a high-protein cereal which has long been a staple in the diet of millions of people in the Andean countries of Latin America. It has been cultivated and developed since pre-Incan times. Two researchers from the University of Colorado received US patent number 5,304,718 in 1994 which gives them exclusive monopoly control over the male sterile plants of the traditional Bolivian Apelawa quinoa variety. So, suddenly, Andean people cannot use a plant that is a part of their natural ecosystem. Bolivia currently exports this variety to the US and Europe, a market worth US$1 million per year. But if this hybrid variety is used for large-scale commercial production in the US, the Bolivian exports will be prevented from entering US and European markets. This will lead to the displacement of thousands of small farmers, most of whom are indigenous Indians. The other possibility is that their land will fall into the monopoly control of corporations who own the patents (or their subsidiaries in Bolivia), who will produce quinoa using the hybrid commercial varieties. Genetic erosion of the diverse quinoa varieties developed by local farmers over centuries will take place, diminishing forever genetic diversity. Many farming communities are facing a similar plight throughout the world.[16] Mexico is the original home of maize. Despite a national ban on the cultivation of genetically modified crops, in April 2002 a Mexican government-commissioned study reported to the biodiversity convention at the Hague that as many as 95 per cent of maize fields in the states of Oaxaca and Pueblo contain evidence of GM contamination. The report confirmed that genetic contamination of wild Mexican varieties is taking place.[17] Mexico faces a double threat from GM maize. Since the signing of the NAFTA free trade agreement, Mexico is open to imports of heavily subsidised US maize, about 30 per cent of which is produced from transgenic seeds. This undercuts the livelihood of indigenous Mexican farmers, though it is good for urban-dwelling Mexicans, the country being a net importer of corn. On the other hand, its long-term implications could be devastating for Mexico and the world as a whole. It is estimated that up 20 million Mexican campesinos farming traditional varieties of maize by traditional techniques could be forced to abandon the land. This has implications for global crop improvement, which relies on the range of corn varieties that exist in Mexico. Dr Exequiel Ezcurra of the Mexican National Ecology Institute says: 'Basically, crop improvement is based on traditional varieties. Losing those traditional varieties [through GM contamination] could be an issue of great concern.'[18] To campesino farmer Aldo Gonzales the compound effect has a clear meaning: 'We believe the free market is a lie, because the US is subsidising farmers ... That's not a free market, that's not free competition, that's not fair competition.' But his concern is more than economics: 'The indigenous people of Mexico have farmed corn for 10,000 years. The security of the world's food should not be in the hands of corporations. It should be in the hands of farmers.'[19]

US bio-piracy is not limited to medicinal plants and crop varieties – it also extends to the DNA of indigenous people. The patent application of the US Department of Commerce for the T-cell line infected with human T-cell lymphotrophic viruses (HTLV) type 1 – which might help in the development of a cure for cancer – of a 26-year-old Guaymi woman from Panama was the first attempt to patent genetic materials from indigenous peoples. The application, submitted as early as 1993, was eventually withdrawn after an international outcry and campaigns led by various non-governmental organisations. This, however, did not stop the US National Institute of Health from patenting the DNA of a man from the Hagahai people of the highlands of Papua New Guinea. The patent covered a cell line containing unmodified Hagahai DNA – and it too had to be withdrawn after international pressure. Since then, attempts to patent the DNA of indigenous people have multiplied – and one can now openly buy Amazonian Indian blood cells on the internet from US companies.

Indigenous knowledge is, of course, not new knowledge. Genetic engineering is a new science that generates new technology. But the US denies that genetic technology is a new departure from conventional biotechnology, or that it brings with it new environmental and health problems. While it is happy to appropriate ancient knowledge, the US does not want the new technology to be regulated in any way. It has consistently opposed the Convention on Biological Diversity, the first international effort to set legal standards and norms for genetically modified organisms (GMOs) and products derived from or containing GMOs. First, at US insistence, the term 'GMOs' was changed to 'living modified organisms' in the draft protocol. Second, as scientific evidence mounted on the environmental and health hazards of GMOs and GMO-related products, the US opposed the rest of the world on the question of making the 'precautionary principle' the basis for the protocol. Underlying this principle, first formulated at the 1992 Climate Change Convention, is the assumption that biotechnology can generate potentially dangerous outcomes, and that we should proceed with caution. The principle, now enshrined in many international regulatory statutes, has become the guiding spirit of the European Union's science policy, and is increasingly used in policy-making where there is a perceived risk to the environment or to the health of humans, animals or plants. The US – the biggest developer and exporter of GMOs – is the sole country that rejects the precautionary principle. Those developing countries working for a strong bio-safety agreement and promoting the Convention on Biological Diversity are routinely accused by the US of blocking international trade, and are threatened regularly with being referred to the WTO.

Almost every concern of the world, from the risks and safety of GMOs to climate change and biodiversity, from the protection of indigenous knowledge and resources to the reform of undemocratic and authoritarian global institutions like the WTO and IMF, to global justice and fair trade, is reduced by the

US to a question of 'free trade' – meaning America should be free to do as it desires. Over the last few decades, so-called 'free trade' has increased exponentially. Today, one day's trade equals a whole year's commerce in 1949. But while international trade is growing, the regulations designed to manage trade and promote equity are being progressively removed at US behest. In its treatment of the rest of the world, the US acts like an overgrown teenage bully, constantly expressing indignation at having to accept limits on its behaviour while refusing to understand why this behaviour might have real consequences in the lives of others. If it doesn't like a country's economic policies, it crushes them using the WTO and IMF. And if that doesn't work, it imposes sanctions or simply arranges to overthrow its leaders in a coup (Iran, Chile, Guatemala). Authoritarian countries whose leaders are tyrants and brutes who trample on human rights are called friends and allies if they have the right economic policies (Saudi Arabia, the Philippines, El Salvador). The problem is that America's behaviour, its insistence on being free to do as it chooses, not only places serious constraints on the freedom of others to choose their own way of life – it is actually placing their very survival in jeopardy. It should not surprise anyone that America is perceived as having declared a war on the non-European world, including the poorest, the weakest, and most disadvantaged.

But this is a perception of America that Americans seldom have come to terms with. As Jim Dator, professor of political science at the University of Hawaii and well-known futurist, notes: 'The exclusion of the rest of the world from American sight is one of the most disturbing facts about American society. Even with its gigantic media system operating with state-of-the-art technologies, the US functions as a society closed to information, facts and the opinions of the rest of the world.'[20]

The American media is notoriously parochial. With the exception of a couple of national newspapers, foreign news is, by and large, conspicuous by its absence. Television, the medium that US citizens use more than any other, ventures outside its national boundaries only to report disasters and American-led wars. As the American media has acquired a global reach, it has simultaneously, and paradoxically, become even more parochial and banal. Diverse and dissenting voices have been filtered out to create a bland media monoculture dedicated to promoting consumerism, business and the interests of the government and the power elite, and to keeping the masses entertained and docile. This is not the outcome of a 'free market' operating as a natural law – it is the product of conscious state policy.

Since the days of the Reagan administration, the United States has been deregulating its own media industry, and leading an onslaught on international regulation, with the natural consequence that global media power is aggregating into fewer and fewer hands. In 1983, when Ben Bagdikian published *The Media Monopoly*, media ownership was concentrated in the hands of 50 trans-national conglomerates.[21] By 2002, only nine trans-national firms dominated US and global media: AOL Time Warner, Disney, Bertelsmann, Viacom, News Corporation, TCI, General Electric (owner of NBC), Sony (owner of Columbia and TriStar Pictures and major recording interests), and Seagram (owner of Universal film and music interests). So one global super-industry now provides virtually everything that Americans see and hear on the screen, over the airwaves, in print and on the web.

These media giants function as a powerful political lobby at national, regional and global levels. In Washington DC alone, they spend hundreds of millions each year lobbying against owner-ship restrictions. They not only have a hand in drafting national laws and regulations, but also play an important part in shaping and directing international rules and regulations. In 2000, for example, the corporate media giants led the lobbying effort to open up trade with China, and fought against those who raised concerns about free speech and a free press. Earlier, they used US levers to open up Indian markets to satellite television.

Much of what this media cartel purveys to America, Mark Crispin Miller notes in *The Nation*, 'is propaganda, commercial or political'. Under AOL Time Warner, General Electric, Viacom and others, the 'news is, with a few exceptions, yet another version of the entertainment that the cartel also vends nonstop'. These entities, writes Miller,

> are ultimately hostile to the welfare of the people. Whereas we need to know the truth about such corporations, they often have an interest in suppressing it (as do their advertisers). And while it takes much time and money to find out the truth, the parent companies prefer to cut the necessary costs of journalism, much preferring the sort of lurid fare that can drive endless hours of agitated jabbering ... The cartel's favored audience, moreover, is that stratum of the population most desirable to advertisers – which has meant the media's complete abandonment of working people and the poor. And while the press must help protect us against those who would abuse the powers of government, the oligopoly is far too cozy with the White House and the Pentagon, whose faults, and crimes, it is unwilling to expose. The media's big bosses want big favours from the state, while the reporters are afraid to risk annoying their best sources. Because of such politeness (and, of course, the current panic in the air), the US coverage of this government is just a bit more edifying than the local newscasts in Riyadh ...
>
> In short, the news divisions of the media cartel appear to work against the public interest – and for their parent companies, their advertisers and the Bush administration. The situation is completely un-American. It is the purpose of the press to help us run the state, and not the other way around. As citizens of a democracy, we have the right and obligation to be well aware of what is happening, both in 'the homeland' and the wider world. Without such knowledge we cannot be both secure and free.[22]

Such a highly concentrated and controlled media system can hardly be described as a 'free press'. The American media functions primarily to keep its American audience ignorant of the rest of the world; it is interested in producing happy consumers, not informed, free-thinking citizens who question the foreign policy of their government. It performs this function largely through self-censorship and subtle bias. The point was made, before his fall from grace, by then leading American newscaster, Dan Rather – but only when talking outside the US to the BBC's *Newsnight* programme, in a burst of introspection which got only limited coverage in America. 'It starts with a feeling of patriotism within one's self. It carries through with the knowledge that the country as a whole, and for all the right reasons, felt and continues to feel this surge of patriotism within themselves. And one finds one's self saying, "I know the right question but you know what, this is not exactly the right time to ask it."'[23] Rather went on to argue that apart from giving the administration an easy time, the media had become a willing adjunct to politicians and the military leadership that had woken up to the Hollywoodisation of the news and almost everything else in society and were now offering the Hollywoodisation of war, with reality-style programming about the troops overseas but scant journalistic scrutiny of policy.

Hyper-commercialism has implicit bias against political action, civic values and anti-market activities, and tends to regard consumerism, class inequality and so-called 'individualism' as natural and benevolent. The genius of the American media, as Robert McChesney notes, is its 'general lack of overt censorship. As George Orwell noted in his unpublished introduction to *Animal Farm*, censorship in free societies is infinitely more sophisticated and thorough than in dictatorships, because "unpopular ideas can be silenced, and inconvenient facts kept dark, without any need for an official ban".'[24]

Most Americans take it as a self-evident truth that America has a 'free press', that the US is promoting freedom and human rights across the globe, that the rest of the world is jealous of America's freedom and democracy, that American wealth is a consequence of 'free trade', that the American way of life is the best ever devised in the history of humanity and so America should be loved and admired by everyone; that America, in Lincoln's famous phrase, is 'the last best hope for mankind'.

The anger directed at the US and voiced from Argentina to Zambia is based on the belief that while its foreign policy demands 'consistency and discipline' from everyone else, America is far from consistent and disciplined itself; while it sells democracy and diversity to the rest of the world, it is in fact deeply undemocratic in its behaviour and deeply intolerant of any state that disagrees with its actions or offers an alternative to Washington's chosen path. The anger and resentment of the rest of the world comes, as Naomi Klein notes in the *Guardian*, 'from a clear perception of false advertising. In other words, America's problem is not with its brand – which could scarcely be stronger – but with its product.' But once a 'brand identity' is established by a corporation,

> it is enforced with military precision throughout a company's operations. The brand identity may be tailored to accommodate local language and cultural preferences (like McDonald's serving pasta in Italy), but its core features – aesthetic, message, logo – remain unchanged. This consistency is what brand managers call 'the promise' of a brand: it's a pledge that wherever you go in the world, your experience at Wal-Mart, Holiday Inn or a Disney theme park will be comfortable and familiar. At its core, branding is about rigorously controlled one-way messages, sent out in their glossiest form, then sealed off from those who would turn corporate monologue into social dialogue.[25]

The 'one-way message' that the US sends out to the rest of the world is that its own cultural and social reality is the only reality that really matters. Just because Americans eat on average three burgers a week (according to *The Dictionary of American Slang*, the suffix 'burger' means 'any hot sandwich served on a bun, often toasted, with many condiments'), some 38 billion annually, accounting for nearly 60 per cent of all sandwiches eaten in the US, then the rest of the world's people should also eat burgers. Of course, no one forces the rest of the world to eat them – they are undeniably popular – but the desire for American burgers is created through massive advertising, tie-ins with other American cultural products such as Disney films, and their association with the glamour and power of American civilisation. And burgers are not just fast food; they are also a fast culture economy. One in ten Americans works for a fast food outlet; and nearly 7 per cent of the US workforce had their first job at McDonald's. If all space is American space, then the cultural space of the globe belongs to the American burger. McDonald's alone has sold twelve hamburgers for every person in the world.

But hamburger chains do not just purvey hamburgers to the world. They carry with them the principles and processes that make fast-food restaurants possible: clinical efficiency, total predictability, callous calculability and complete control through the replacement of human with non-human technology. How could local cultures compete with such an onslaught? To survive, local cultural products have to emulate the imposed American cultural commodities. Local restaurants, for example, end up looking like McDonald's:

Examples abound including Juicy Burger in Beirut with J.B. the clown standing in for Ronald McDonald and the chain Russkoye Bistro in Russia which is consciously modelled after McDonald's and regards it like a big brother. The most famous restaurant in Beijing – Quanjude Roast Duck Restaurant – sent its management staff to McDonald's in 1993 and then introduced its own 'roast duck fast food' in early 1994. In a sense, it is the largely invisible incursion of the principles of McDonaldisation into local institutions that is a far greater threat to indigenous cultures than the spread of McDonald's itself (and other American fast food restaurants) to other nations.[26]

In Europe, this 'invisible incursion' has made McDonald's a metaphor for the corrosive influence of American consumer culture, and the target of local anger and anti-American campaigns. For example, a postal worker and a gardener from London, Helen Steel and Dave Morris, were taken to court by McDonald's for alleging that the corporation 'exploits children' with its advertising, is 'culpably responsible' for cruelty to animals, pays its workers exceptionally low wages, and is 'antipathetic' to unionisation. The court case, which came to be known as the 'McLibel' trial, ran for two-and-a-half years, one of the longest trials in English history. Giving his verdict on 19 June 1997, the judge, Mr Justice Bell, ruled that Steel and Morris, who had defended themselves, had indeed libelled McDonald's but had also proved many of their allegations. The defendants had shown that McDonald's exploited children, falsely advertised its food as nutritious, and risked the health of its long-term customers, and that the corporation was indeed anti-union and cruel to the animals reared for its products.

Two years later, on 12 August 1999, José Bové, a French farmer and former union activist, trashed a McDonald's building site in Millau, south-west France. Bové's trial turned into an anti-McDonald's festival: supporters (some on tractors), demonstrators and members of the public turned up to a family day out for all variety of McDonald's-haters. In court, Bové objected to the way the food sold by McDonald's is farmed, sourced and processed; he was concerned about the bland homogenisation of culinary culture as represented by the hamburger; and there were community concerns about litter, and the impact of a multinational on local businesses. But more than anything else, he was opposed to the practice of feeding hormones to cattle to artificially speed up their growth. Like the McLibel trial in Britain, Bové's trial gave birth to a major anti-McDonald's campaign in France. Bové himself went on to co-author a best-selling book, *The World is Not for Sale* (2001), which outlines an alternative vision of sustainable and humane farming. He is now regarded as one of the leaders of the international anti-globalisation movement.

George Ritzer, professor of sociology at Maryland University and author of *The McDonaldization of Society*, argues that American culture has acquired 'obscene power' in the process of replicating itself around the world. Australian cultural critic and science writer Margaret Wertheim, who lives in Los Angeles, suggests that to much of the rest of the world, 'American culture seems like a virus, a particularly pathological one at that. We might, not without some justification, compare American culture to the AIDS virus, HIV. Like that brilliantly adapted organism, US culture is endlessly self-replicating and alarmingly adept at co-opting the production machinery of its hosts. The reason HIV is so hard to stop is precisely because it harnesses its host's cellular functions, turning the body's power against itself to produce ever more copies of the viral invader. So too, American fast food culture, pop music, films and television infect the cultural body of other nations, co-opting local production machinery to focus their efforts on mimicry. This pattern of viral replication repeats itself the world over, with American pop cultural norms choking out and stifling native flora and fauna.'[27]

The 'virus' of American culture and lifestyle replicates so readily because it is founded on a promise of abundance, the lure of affluence. Material well-being is universally appealing, irresistible to those who have, or are close to having, sufficient means to buy into the dream. It is the upwardly mobile, those busily working to distance themselves from poverty, who find the prospect of ever-expanding material horizons truly intoxicating. There is no mystery, nothing in the least difficult to understand, in this most human of motivations. There is no known human constituency that wishes to vote for poverty. And given the fact that so many people aspire to their lifestyle, it is no surprise that Americans feel that their way is the best and the only way.

The global projection of American affluence, the coded texts of all its popular cultural products, is a permanent advertisement for the goods, services and material endowments that are potentially available, how they can be possessed and how they will make us better, happier, more attractive and more modern. What it costs to acquire this cornucopia is less apparent. The costs will be intangible – alterations to cherished traditional values and lifeways, undermining of the unquantifiable worth of long-established identities with their sensibilities and refinements – a pitfall that is never mentioned. What is sold is the prospect of choosing to have whatever one's heart can desire. Everyone believes that sensible choices can and will be made. But that all choices carry unintended, and often undesired, consequences is a realisation that comes after the event. It is a predicament that only gradually became apparent to America and other developed nations. To replicate American abundance – the choice of goods, the service and lifestyle that it permits – does not involve a free choice of means, but adaptation to the constraints of the 'virus': a particular kind of economic organisation, particular political and social forms, that inevitably compromise the 'immune system' of the host. This has been the story of all developed nations, and it did not stop them from seeking more and more abundance. It is the same story for all of the less- and least-developed, and would-be-developing, nations.

'When I was growing up in suburban Australia,' says Wertheim, 'America strobed like a lighthouse on our horizon.' She loved the 'flash and trash' of American culture, epitomised by such sizzling 1960s television shows as the dada spy-spoof *Get Smart* and the subversively feminist *Bewitched*. 'I was entranced; and yet at the same time I felt suspicious of America. Culturally speaking, it was the sixty-pound gorilla in the room; we were bombarded with their films, their television, their music, their celebrities, and their fashions, but ours were utterly invisible to them. A quarter century later, that largely remains the state of affairs', she says. To survive, the Australian film industry started to ape Hollywood. 'This almost proved fatal. In the late 1980s, the Australian film industry almost died after a spate of botched attempts at producing American-style dramas. No one wanted this cynical fare, least of all the Americans at whom these mish-mashes were largely aimed.'[28] If the Australian government had not stepped in with state funding, the result could have been devastating. It is not that Australians and New Zealanders in the film industry do not thrive. The current contingent, led by Mel Gibson, Nicole Kidman, Russell Crowe, Cate Blanchett, Baz Luhrmann, Peter Jackson, Sam Neill, Peter Weir, Jane Campion and others, all have sparkling careers and notable successes to their names. But their success is found in Hollywood. It comes about by working in the product that Hollywood determines is fit for the global audience. In order to work they acquire semi-American, vaguely trans-Pacific accents, homogenising out their distinctiveness or subduing it to the imperative for standardisation.

As Wertheim asks, 'if rich, white Anglo and European nations feel threatened, how much damage has the onslaught of American cultural hyper-imperialism already done to cultures and peoples of developing countries?'[29] The simple, and truly frightening, answer is that the ascendancy of 'hamburger culture' has meant the eradication of indigenous Third World cultures everywhere. Sylvester Stallone, Bruce Willis, Britney Spears, Madonna, Brangelina and Homer Simpson dominate the airwaves and screens the world over. Local products have to compete not only against vast US production budgets but also equally lavish promotion budgets. The home-grown culture industries just don't stand a chance. Of course, there are always exceptions to general rules. The Iranian film industry has thrived largely because Hollywood products are not allowed into the country. Bollywood, as the Indian film industry is known, has succeeded by imitating the style and content, and sometimes even the production values, of Hollywood. But these are exceptions, and in any case we are talking about much more than simply film and television, pop music and videos, fast foods and electronic gadgets. In traditional societies of developing countries, identity is shaped by history, tradition, community, ancestors and extended families. American-led globalisation seeks to replace all this with American cultural products. The tsunami of American consumerist culture assimilates everything, exerting immense, unstoppable pressure on the people of much of the world to change their lifestyles, to abandon all that gives meaning to their lives, to throw away not just their values but also their identity, stable relationships, attachment to history, buildings, places, families and received ways of doing and being.

The 'obscene power' of hamburger culture places local cultures in a vice-like grip. American multinationals promote their products through a multiple strategy using pop music, local television channels and specially produced style products, thus occupying all available cultural space. Cigarette companies, for example, don't just sell cigarettes: they sell cigarettes as a total style and identity package. The cigarette-hawking cowboy, 'The Marlboro Man', has disappeared back home in the United States, but in Asia it is almost impossible to escape his craggy all-American mug: it is slapped up on billboards, peering through magazines and newspapers, flickering across television screens. He is 'sponsoring' American movies and television series, gazing at everybody in crowded shopping malls, selling 'Marlboro Classic' clothes in shops done up in the style of Wild West saloons, and enticing the young to smoke in malls and bars where young women dressed as cowgirls offer free cigarettes to passing youngsters. Desire is incubated among the young not only to smoke a particular brand of cigarette but also to buy designer clothes stamped with the brand logo ('Salem Attitudes', or 'Pall Mall Action Gear'), shop at the brand's record shops, grace pop concerts sponsored by the brand ('Salem Power' or 'Salem Cool Planet'), and even take high-concept vacations designed to solve all their identity problems ('Salem Cool Holidays', or 'Mild Seven', or 'Peter Stuyvesant'). Even those companies that sell nothing but cigarettes promote a packaged identity: in Malaysia, for example, 'Kent Vacations' won't take you anywhere, for despite its heavy advertising presence on the television it doesn't actually exist; and since no one in Kuala Lumpur could work out what 'Benson and Hedges Golden Gallery' actually sold, it has been replaced by a high-concept bistro hosting regular jazz sessions at which local and American musicians play together. The multitude of style products are used for the construction of images and signs that portray American culture as a bastion of 'freedom' and 'individualism', the only way to be 'cool' or 'hot'. The added seductive pull is the concept that 'the consumer is god', crystallised in the American Dream – sold without irony or doubt. And if there is any doubt, the latest teenage flick from Hollywood playing at the local multiplex will confirm that the American way is the only way to be.

In many developing countries, local television programming has almost been eradicated. This is not because these countries cannot make their own programmes, or that they do not wish to do so; it is largely a function of the economics of programme-making, combined with the agenda of American multinational advertisers, which tilts the playing field against local programmes. Just as America dumps cheap commodities on developing countries, thus forcing locally produced commodities and goods to the wall, so television programmes are dumped on the Third World. The system works like this. A single episode of a hit television show such as *Alias* or *Dark Angel* might cost, by way of example, $5 million to make. This money is recouped by selling the show to a single network in the United States and Canada. The European sales are pure profit. Once the American and European markets are sewn up, the programmes are dumped on Third World television stations according to a long-established formula for payment. The higher a country's per capita income, the higher it is on the ladder of 'development', the more it pays. Thus, while a British channel might pay £200–250,000 for an episode of a high-rating show like *The Simpsons*, Malaysia would acquire the same show for less than US$70,000 and Bangladesh for only US$25,000. Thus a programme with exceptionally high production values is sold for peanuts, while local programming, working on modest to miniscule budgets, will always look inferior to imported shows. Everything that reflects the culture and reality of the locale appears unsophisticated, old-fashioned, somehow tawdry, even backward. Modernity, sophistication, true professionalism and expertise – these are images, lifeways and ideas that have to be acquired; they do not come with a familiar face, but must be copied or parodied as showcased in the imported wares. And programmes are not bought individually; they are bought in package deals. So a major proportion of the prime-time seasonal output of a local channel in a developing country may consist primarily of imported shows.

Moreover, each programme of the package will be subsidised or 'sponsored' by a multinational company: the programme will be associated with its name or with one of its brand products. As a general rule, American multinationals do not sponsor local programmes, even if they attract high ratings. They sponsor only those programmes – *Models Inc.*, *Melrose Place*, *Baywatch* – which promote images of American culture: images of high consumption, of unrestrained freedom, of the young individual as the consumer. Thus, television channels in countries with 'open economies', such as South Korea, Taiwan, Malaysia, Singapore, Thailand, Indonesia, Hong Kong, are dominated by American companies. When what is being shown on terrestrial television is combined with what is beaming down from satellites – 24-hour MTV, QVC (the 'Quality, Value, Convenience' shopping channel), old American movies on TCM, endless repeats of situation comedies on the Paramount Comedy Channel, and American reality and quiz shows – we get a more accurate picture of the displacement of indigenous culture.

Much the same can be said for the internet, which was hailed as a great boon for democracy, including cultural democracy (all new technology is initially sold with this false promise). Yet, much of the content is largely controlled by two American giants – AOL Time Warner and Microsoft. Both AOL and Microsoft force their subscribers to remain in their high-pressure bazaars, where their own and their partners' cultural products are hawked night and day. In most Asian middle-class homes, the internet is accessed through the set-top box and the television screen – all three media are dominated by American multinationals. For example, Rupert Murdoch's Star TV, which has almost total control over coaxial cable and satellite, transmits content to around 40 cable channels across Asia. Much of this is American cultural output; and even the Asian material such as pop songs and quiz shows are tawdry imitations of American originals.

The impact of hyper-imperial American culture is not limited to laying waste to indigenous cultures. It also represents an onslaught on indigenous identities. Among Asian youth, for example, the imitation of American culture is more than style. They want to look and sound like disaffected black urban youth in the States – but they imbibe the representation of the psychological profile as well. So crime, truancy, drug addiction and promiscuity, along with breakdown of parental authority, are all on the rise in societies in which 'youth' was never a separate concept and the extended family and disciplined personal behaviour were the norm. The most notable feature of this culture of disaffection in Asia is that it is confined to those with the most prolific purchasing power – the children of the privileged, affluent elite. Western pop music, MTV and television programmes, notes *Asiaweek*, 'have created a money minded youth culture that demands instant gratification and thrives on audio-visual bombardment ... [A]s pre-schoolers they start out with Christian Dior sneakers. Then they want *Beverly Hills 90210* spectacles. They even use designer pencil boxes.'[30] But these goods only generate disaffection, for the accent in imported culture is on constant and continuous disaffection. Disaffection is the youth culture of the haves who would like to find meaning in the outrage of the have-nots. Thus the interests of affluent youth everywhere in Asia seem to mirror that of the *lepak*, as Malaysia has dubbed its most recently identified social problem – loitering around malls and having all the goods that go with the lifestyle, but a lifestyle in which style signifies meaninglessness, in which a designer fashion-plate is the essence of disaffection. And beyond that lies the flirtation with self-destructive addictive behaviour.

Thus, American-led globalisation uses pop music, television and style products to transform the identity of young people in the developing world into a commodity. The package is sold with the allure of 'freedom'. But this notion of 'freedom' – or more appropriately, libertarian individualism which promotes every individual's potential for fulfilment, the pursuit of endless consumption, the withdrawal of all collective, communal and social responsibility – undermines everything for which indigenous culture, tradition and history stand.

Local cultural production becomes at best marginalised, at worst totally suppressed. Indigenous music has to be torn away from its context and Westernised to be acceptable to those who are supposed to be its inheritors. Consider, for example, the case of Quawwali, the devotional music of India, Pakistan and Bangladesh. Of mystical Sufi origins, it is sung to the simple rhythm of traditional drums and hand-clapping in praise of God, Prophet Muhammad, Ali the fourth Caliph of Islam and classical Sufi masters. In its 'new, improved' form, the form in which it has become acceptable to the cool youth of the Subcontinent, it has gone funky and is sung to a syncopated rock beat generated by synthesisers. What was originally designed to induce mystical ecstasy is now used to generate disco dancing. Similarly, Indian film songs, which traditionally had a high poetic content, now mirror the meaningless lyrics of American pop songs. Given the dominance of English in global cultural products, local languages acquire the image of inferiority. In other words, the production of indigenous culture acquires the sense of backwardness; its themes and concerns are not those to which the growing generation can relate. No wonder the politics of identity has become so important in most developing countries.

Language is the prime tool of cultural expression. So it should not surprise us to discover that the decline of indigenous cultures is also having a serious effect on the languages of the world. Indeed, an indigenous language disappears every two weeks. It is estimated that by the end of the 21st century, 5,500 of the current 6,000 languages now spoken will simply be as dead as Ancient Greek and Latin. Behind each language is a culture, the expressive richness of a living tongue and its infinite capacity to reflect a distinct mode of thought. So, when a language dies, it truly diminishes the capacity of our world to think, to know, to be and to do differently – to be truly other than the dominant culture. As John Sutherland pointed out in the *Independent on Sunday*:

There is no mystery about the root cause of the linguistic holocaust that we're living through. Take a holiday anywhere in the world. Your airline pilot will, as you listen to the safety instructions (in English), be communicating with ground control in English. Signs in the airport, whatever country you are in, will be duplicated in one of the world's top twenty languages – most likely English. You'll see Coca-Cola logos. MTV will be playing on the screen. Muzak will be crooning Anglo-American lyrics as you walk through the concourse to baggage reclaim. At the hotel, the desk clerk will speak your language, as well, probably, as the bellhop. (His tip depends on being polyglot.) Go to any internet café and the keyboard code that will get you best results is what you are reading now: English – the *lingua franca* of our time … The spread of English is the product of naked linguistic superpower.[31]

Sutherland adds that a favourite axiom among linguists is: 'A language is a dialect with an army behind it.' Follow the big armies (Roman, Norman, Chinese, Russian) and you will find the 'world languages'. The most potent army, in 2008, flies the stars and stripes. It is not just English, but American, the dominant English dialect, that is killing indigenous languages everywhere. It is a colonialism, notes Sutherland, far more sinister than any practised in history: '[O]nce we just took their raw materials. Now we invade their minds, by changing the primary tool by which they think: "their" language.'[32]

Hamburgers are not just culture and economy – they also entail a location. We can eat them almost anywhere, but most are eaten on the run. Every half a mile or so in the US, a drive-up window ready to sell burgers to people on the move can be found. So burgers are associated with an architecture and a geographical space. When McDonald's opens a branch in Red Square in Moscow, or the Forbidden City in Beijing, or in the Holy City of Mecca, it changes the architecture as well as the spatial dynamics of the city. The city – any city – is an expression of a culture's values and ideals, hopes and aspirations, social outlook and behaviour. As such, cities are far more than mere form – more than roads and buildings, bricks and mortar; they are images of a society's perception of its destiny. So the appearance of numerous American fast food restaurants in a city transforms the cityscape as well as its inhabitants' perceptions of themselves. American-led globalisation, by imposing a single set of American standards, is increasingly transforming the cities of developing countries into monuments to the American will to power. Traditional architecture is bulldozed to be replaced by featureless brickworks, multi-lane roads, shopping malls, hotels and fast food joints. Most cities in the more affluent parts of the Third World either look like Dallas or theme-parked extensions of Los Angeles. The change in architecture, use of space and spatial relationships has profound knock-on consequences in the electricity-guzzling, fossil fuel-consuming and motorised transport-dependent products and services required for their upkeep; not to mention the constraints this puts on how people actually exist and interact with one another in these spaces. What results is entire environmental realignment of a way of life.

Jeddah in Saudi Arabia, for example, was a historic city with a distinctive character that always impressed visitors. It consisted of a network of remarkable tall houses that made ingenious use of the local meteorological conditions: the uppermost floors were designed to catch the sea breeze, which created upward draughts with regular temperature differentials; the overarching, open, louvered windows filtered out the sun's glare but allowed air to circulate freely in the rooms; the surrounding flat terraces with wooden grilles permitted the movement of any cool air currents on the hottest of summer nights. These traditional houses showed what the power of imagination and craftsmanship in indigenous building could achieve. American influence and big business brought American city planning and architecture to Saudi Arabia; and soon Jeddah became a poor replica of Houston. Narrow streets and alleyways gave way to huge, wide, sun-baked roads and over-heated concrete monstrosities. Traditional architecture, age-old souks, Saudi cafés – all disappeared to be replaced by shopping malls, fast food restaurants, theme parks and hotels. Americanisation has meted out an even worse fate to Mecca, the holiest city of Islam, where there are no streets left for anyone to walk on. American planners, consultants and architects have turned Mecca – which is, of course, the focus for the 1.3 billion Muslims of the planet who face towards the city during their five daily prayers – into a third-rate American city in which tunnels, flyovers, spaghetti junctions and multi-lane motorways compete for attention with gaudy hotels and the ubiquitous shopping malls. The hatred of America that many Saudis exhibit has little to do with the often-cited American military presence in 'holy areas' – in fact, American troops were based hundreds of miles to the north of what are traditionally considered the holy areas, the cities of Mecca and Medina. The actual withdrawal of US troops, announced in 2003, has been gradual, and considerable numbers of US government and defence contractor personnel remain. The real problem stems more from the fact that the fabric of traditional Saudi life has been torn apart by Americanisation and replaced with centralised, mass-produced monotony. Saudi cities do not reflect the history, culture, tradition or values of the Arabian Peninsula – they sing solemn homilies to the American way of life.

Much the same can be said about many other cities in the developing world. For example, on a visit to Singapore, the cyberpunk author William Gibson found that:

> the sensation of trying to connect psychically with the old Singapore is rather painful, as though Disneyland's New Orleans Square had been erected on the site of the actual French Quarter, obliterating it in the process but leaving in its place a glossy simulacrum. The facades of the remaining Victorian shop-houses recall Covent Garden on some impossibly bright London day … there was very little to be seen of previous realities: a joss stick smouldering in an old brass holder on the white painted column of a shop-house; a mirror positioned above the door of a supplier of electrical goods, set to snare and deflect the evil that travels in a straight line; a rusty trishaw, chained to a freshly painted iron railing. The physical past, here, has almost entirely vanished.[33]

After America itself, Singapore is perhaps the most pathologically Americanised place on earth, and it represents the future of many Asian and Latin American cities.

Such cultural hyper-imperialism creates a deep resentment of the US, even in countries that are supposed to be close allies. Among the minjung (populist) community of South Korea, for example, abhorrence of American cultural products is intense. The minjung consists of a broad alliance of people, including labourers, farmers and the urban poor, who see themselves as stalwarts of traditional Korean culture and who define themselves as victims of US global culture and capitalism. They feel physically, culturally, geographically – and hence psychologically – alienated and dislocated by the Americanisation of South Korea. US-sponsored economic policies uprooted autonomous minjung rural communities, destroyed their traditional lifestyles and forced them to participate subserviently in the maelstrom of Americanised modernity. They believe that Americanisation has produced inequity, exploitation, cultural violence and alienation; and that American culture actually threatens the Korean language itself, which, some suggest, may die off in the next three decades. Indeed, they consider the US to be an occupying power, and are disgusted at the presence of tens of thousands of American troops on their soil for over five decades. Hardly surprising, then, that they demonstrate against the USA, and burn the stars and stripes, with seasonal regularity.

'It will be wrong,' says Steve Fuller, the American academic who occupies the chair of sociology at the University of Warwick, 'to think of American-led globalisation as a form of cultural imperialism. The idea of cultural imperialism implies a much more planned and directed impact on the native culture – what used to be called "ideological warfare", in which people are explicitly told, or forced, to give up their traditional customs and adopt Western ones. But this is not really America's style. Indeed, unlike European cultural imperialism, the US government is rarely directly involved in the most pervasive forms of cultural terrorism, such as McDonaldization.' The desirability of American cultural products – which are perceived to be superior, modern, the wave of the future – means that the 'victims' themselves play an important role in the spread of American culture. Fuller suggests that to really understand what America is doing to the rest of the world, we need to think of US cultural practices in terms of 'bioterrorism', which is almost the exact opposite of the classical form of warfare and cultural imperialism.

> First, [bioterrorism] has no clear goal or point. One does not win a bioterrorist campaign: one simply hopes that the spread of the germ or virus will be as disruptive to society as possible. This may then lay the condition for achieving some other goal. Second, the bioterrorists themselves only start the campaign. Most of the actual 'warfare' is conducted by the victims themselves, who infect each other with the germ or virus in their day-to-day interactions. Third, as the bioterrorist campaign spreads, and the effects of the germs and viruses are combined with other effects, it becomes virtually impossible to find any single responsible agent, since by that point almost all the victims have become complicit in its spread.
>
> McDonald's illustrates this sense of cultural terrorism beautifully. Consider the sign in front of every Golden Arches: 'Billions served'. Notice it is not: 'Billions fed'. From a marketing standpoint, this is a very striking slogan. It points to no goal other than the proliferation of burgers, and it makes no reference to the response of those to whom the burgers are served. But, as we know, the proliferation of burgers has had a devastating effect on most of the world – from forcing the natives to adopt the practices of American culture to blighting their cultural and physical landscapes. In fact, when the natives start behaving more like the burger giants, and start infecting themselves with their attitudes and behaviour (impatience, obesity, heart disease etc.), they become even more susceptible to even more American interventions. By the time serious damage has been done, enough of the natives will have personally benefited from the intervention that it will be very difficult to undo.[34]

While the 'biological terrorism' of the ubiquitous hamburger culture has reduced the cultural geography of the world to a totalising American space, killing the languages, architecture, film industries, television programming, music and art of most of the developing world, American cultural space itself is free from 'contamination'. The open door of 'free trade' in the cultural sphere swings just one way; it projects power and influence outward but springs back to deter and deflect 'foreign' access. Try getting an Iranian film or a Chinese television series released in the US. Even the best British, Canadian and Australian films – which share the same language and much of the same cultural history – hardly ever play in more than a few art-house cinemas Stateside. With the odd very rare exception, US network television screens nothing but US products. Only on cable channels such as the Sundance and Independent Film Channels will foreign films be found, with British dramas and documentaries screened on PBS. 'If something truly irresistible turns up from a foreign land, the standard American response is to buy up the rights and remake it in a US version', says Margaret Wertheim. It is part of a long tradition, as old as Hollywood itself. 'The American repackaging machine reduces all experiences, no matter what their cultural context, to American experience', Wertheim notes.[35] And in doing so it invariably renders them down to bland, insubstantial fare with no trace of origin, no communicative value in acquainting Americans with the wider world. America's mainstream media in prime time venerates the mass audience, and the production decisions it makes reflect a market-tested idea of what Americans want to know about the world.

Thus, while the rest of the world is suffocating under the weight of American cultural products, Americans themselves are insulated from non-American cultures. 'The musical scene is almost as uniform as its televisual cousins – an unbroken vista of American pop, hip-hop and country broken only by the occasional breakthrough of a big British band. Mention Om Kalsoum, the transcendent Egyptian singer beloved throughout the Arab world or Lata Mangashtar, the Indian female vocalist who has sold more records than anyone ever, including Michael Jackson and the Beatles, and the average American music lover will stare in blank incomprehension', says Wertheim. Of course, this situation is not restricted to America – it is symptomatic of a more general problem in the West as a whole, where there is little awareness of non-Western arts and cultures. But America seems a worse offender, being a nation of immigrants with more potential than any other to know the world, and because its cultural exports are so uniquely, uniformly monocultural and so globally dominant – and it is, moreover, as ignorant of European culture as it is of any other.

It is the failure not just to recognise and acknowledge but to empathise that evokes resentment of America. As Wertheim notes: '[T]hey seem not to be able to imagine life itself in any guise other than the one they themselves are enmeshed in. And how could they, when their cultural landscape is so thoroughly mono-toned? It is quite unrealistic to expect that someone brought up on a diet of exclusively American media should comprehend the dynamics of Arab culture or appreciate the struggle needed to survive in an African village. If we have here a failure of the collective American imagination, that lack has at least some of its roots in the abject failure of the American cultural production industries which resolutely refuse to open their doors to anything foreign.'[36] In short, Americans themselves become the victims of, and are strangulated by, American cultural hyper-imperialism.

The question thus arises: if the majority of Americans are ignorant of other cultural possibilities and modes, are they therefore innocent of their own culture's increasingly virulent hyper-imperialism? What, then, of American innocence? Can ignorance of the bioterrorism of their culture be excused? Should Americans be let off the hook for the consequences visited on the rest of the world simply because they choose to remain distracted or unaware? With the resources at their disposal, pleas of ignorance appear to be essentially wilful. As Margaret Wertheim points out: '[T]oo few Americans seem to want to know about other cultural options; too few are prepared to engage with other people's choices, others' ways of being. In the land of the free, the underlying ethic of too much discourse is that one is free only to do things "our way" ... Ignorance may be bliss – though in the wake of 9-11 even that old faith has been called into question. As American-led globalisation decimates the cultures of the world, the responsibility rests with American citizens to preserve what we might call cultural biodiversity. American citizens can no more evade that responsibility and retain moral integrity than they can evade their duty to participate in preserving actual biodiversity. Continued evasion can only result in more hatred abroad and more retaliation at home.'[37]

America's predicament is not the work of one administration. Nor is a zealous group of ideologues within and around one administration solely responsible for the problems amassed by America's response to 9-11. America's problems and the world's problems with America have been long in the making and they place the burden of full spectrum responsibility on the American public. Debating and determining how to change the perils and consequences of dominance will be the true measure of whether America is the democratic brand it claims to be. For America to change means taking responsibility for the multi-layered ingredients that make up the idea of America and the full spectrum of effects this has on American life as well as the living standards, way of life and aspirations of the rest of the world. Real change requires Americans to see through the golden arches and recognise the realities they have made in the world out there. It is time for America to consider that it has come to a fork in the road; there are still ways less travelled that Americans can elect to follow, and which would make all the difference. But history suggests that America is most adept at opting for continuity while naming it change, the harbinger of the future.

Conclusion: The Road Less Travelled

Has the Iraq debacle already changed America? Have the consequences of that lethal three-trillion-dollar distraction achieved what a presidential election might not – the need for America to engage with the world in a different way? Have events delivered a post-American world without the need for public opinion or actual voters to make difficult choices? According to the former British prime minister Harold MacMillan (PM from 1957–63), there is only one iron law of politics: 'Events, dear boy, events.' Will the events of the years post-9-11 produce a more modest, accommodating and chastened America? There were many voices predicting the end of empire as America embarked upon its adventure of democracy-building in the Middle East by means of regime change in Iraq. It was an exercise in imperial hubris, many argued, the kind of overstretch typical of a great power rushing to meet its own decline. But such predictions have themselves been overtaken by a new kind of analysis: not the end of empire but the resumption of history. The end of history, declared by Francis Fukuyama, was the assertion that America had won the ideological contest and vanquished communism with the demise of the Soviet Union. Restarting the march of time, now declared by Robert Kagan, in many ways a response to post-9-11 events, means that the American moment is already past. The US has ceased to be the lone hyperpower; once again a multi-polar world exists. The colossus has been bound, but will need to be reanimated, by the rise of new centres of global economic power – China, India and Brazil – and the return of a basic cleavage between competing systems. Instead of a clash of civilisations, the predicted consequence of the end of the Cold War, we are already immersed in a rivalry between democracy and autocracy, represented by Russia, China and Iran. And that makes all the difference.

In either formulation – end of empire or return of history – there is an implicit suggestion that change has already happened. Therefore, in the words of Tony Blair's mantra, it is 'time to move on'. Britain's former prime minister was also fond of saying 'we are where we are' – by which he meant in the grip of events which leave no opportunity or indeed necessity for reflection on the past, on how we arrived at the changed present. The fortuitous beneficiary of this way of looking at the world is the American electorate. Americans are thus freed from the responsibility of analysing the mess their government has created. All that American voters need worry about is insisting that their politicians restore the abundance and ease of American lifestyles. The problem, however, is that clamour for protection of American living standards has consequences for the well-being of everyone on the planet, as does the profligacy of how America finances its way of living. Keeping the wealthiest nation on earth in its comfort zone can literally take food from the mouths of the poorest and most vulnerable people in the world. And maintaining the American Dream, however illusory for increasing numbers of Americans, usually leads to calls for public acquiescence in the maintenance of US dominance, justified by the inherent threat posed by the competing poles of global power. In which case change, the new era already upon us, can be used to ensure that everything continues as before. The crimes and misdemeanours, the failures of knowledge and judgement of the years since 9-11, will be made irrelevant as America prepares to confront new circumstances filled with all the perils of dominance that led it into the Iraq war.

Events have happened. Changed circumstances already engulf Americans. But has this really made the need to understand and examine the past redundant? Should voters concentrate on how to, or who can best, restore the nation to what America defines as its proper status at home and abroad instead of investigating the causes and meaning of the events which have overtaken their country? Failure to scrutinise the context of what is called change is the root from which fear and vulnerability are nurtured to overshadow Americans' view of the world until the phantasms acquire old familiar patterns. Instead of change the result is more of the same. We have made a case for continuity, that America maintains a way of looking at and responding to events with the self-same set of ideas, means, strategy and reflexes rooted in the idea of America. How America thinks about itself conditions what it knows about the rest of the world, a perspective governed solely by American self-interest which determines all judgements about how to engage with the rest of the world. Our case is not that nothing changes. Things have changed many times. We argue the more depressing proposition that without more informed and critical interest in the antecedents of change, without a changed perspective on America's own and everyone else's past – nothing has improved.

It is certainly the case that the consequences of the Iraq war are no improvement for America, the global community or ordinary people wherever they live. Most of all, war has brought no improvement to Iraq. There are no accurate figures for how many ordinary Iraqis paid with their lives for the boon of democracy that military action was supposed to deliver, or why their deaths were so vital to the security of the American homeland. Nor are there accurate figures for the toll of those maimed or stricken by disease, directly or indirectly resulting from military action – from the bombing of water treatment, sewage and electricity plants to the inability to access inadequate medical facilities. Controversy surrounds any of the available estimates because Iraqi deaths are not appalling human tragedies for which culpability must be apportioned and accepted. In the scale of geopolitical strategic thinking, the calculations of dominance, they are collateral misfortunes attendant on matters of high purpose and thus highly politicised. To leave that proposition in place would be perhaps the greatest inhumanity of America's war. It is the callous proposition of every colonial war and imperial endeavour there has ever been: it denies the reverence, equal dignity and respect for human worth that should be due to all Other people. It is the meaning of America's thesis that we fight them over there – where other people whom we don't have to worry too much about will die and have their lives destroyed – so we don't have to fight them here at home. But when the supposed enemy was not in Iraq in the first place, surely this most basic failure of information and judgement demands self-critical reassessment not just of one administration but of the entire way of thinking that galvanised rapid public endorsement of unleashing such murderous devastation half a world away.

The legacy of war is that Iraq is not stable; it is not a free and independent country; it has not been reconstructed to ameliorate the legacy not just of invasion but of the long years of sanctions that eroded living conditions before the additional devastation of invasion. And before that there is the legacy of the bombing and internal reprisals consequent on the Gulf war, and indeed the legacy of the proxy war that Iraq was encouraged to lose in common with Iran. More than four million Iraqis are estimated to have fled the country since the American invasion. Those best placed to flee are the skilled and educated, draining away the expertise the country will need to rebuild itself. More than three million Iraqis are displaced within the country, a continuing humanitarian disaster inadequately addressed under current conditions and storing up problems for the future. Torture, vicarious violence, corruption and a plethora of civic ills attendant on ethnic and communal tensions were not eradicated but intensified by America's invasion. But before any of these events, Iraq's history had made it only too aware of the subtle and not so subtle meaning of invasion and the consequences of being swallowed by imperial powers. How America acquits itself in that comparison is what really matters for the global future.

Former secretary of state Colin Powell's widely reported stricture about the invasion of Iraq – you break it, you own it – and how America resolves that responsibility is crucial. If America operates as if it has indeed bought and paid for Iraq and therefore is entitled to settle the fate of the country, its government and natural resources for its own benefit, then whether it removes its troops from the country or not will be of little moment. The illegal invasion of a sovereign nation that posed no immediate, or indeed foreseeable, direct threat to America is the ultimate demonstration of the projection of US power and long-term influence. It will compound the legacy of distrust, animosity and latent tension in the Middle East, where America continues to be the prop for profoundly undemocratic governments that are even more out of tune with the sentiments of their populace than ever.

The Iraq war, like the Vietnam war before it, was sold to the American people as an essential element of a grand strategy. So what has become of the global war on terror? The grand strategy endures, and no insight has been gained from the failures of information and judgement made in Iraq. In 1958 the authors of *The Ugly American* fictionalised what they saw as the classic failure of America's grand anti-communist strategy; they summed it up as 'a condition of avoidable ignorance'.[1] The vital question is what constitutes avoidable ignorance and how this is to be distinguished from, and not compounded by, centuries of knowledgeable ignorance about the religion, culture and society of Islam. Muslim organisations that engage in terrorism certainly exist; animosity and disaffection among Muslim populations certainly exists, indeed has become ever more rife in response to the Iraq war; and America has been a target for such organisations. But wherever one looks, these organisations have their own specific history and agenda, and their prime target is local and regional. Terrorism exists in default of a political process capable of resolving the legacy of local and regional histories. For example, the Taliban are not al-Qaeda. However pernicious the ideas and actions of the Taliban, they arise from the particular culture and history of Afghanistan and their focus is and always has been on determining the future of Afghanistan. Switching focus to concentrate on military defeat of the Taliban is a recipe for further devastation of a country that has known nothing but war and its devastation for four decades, with a history of seeking to be independent and fiercely resisting foreign interference inspired by geopolitical strategy that goes back centuries. Wherever one looks around the Muslim world, similar cases can be made. The commonalities of radical rhetoric and resort to religious warrant do not make identikit Islamic extremists. The ideology of al-Qaeda is new and aberrant, and the greatest mistake is to foist it onto organisations and groups in simplistic mistaken identity.

The greatest avoidable ignorance has been America's failure to appreciate how widespread and pointed is dissent from, and condemnation of, the tactics and ideology of al-Qaeda among the world's Muslims. The prosecution of the war on terror has alienated, terrorised and marginalised the very constituency that has the means not just to defeat al-Qaeda but to eradicate the very basis on which it depends. An even greater avoidable ignorance is to be blithely unaware that, despite all provocations, the ideology of terror is being vanquished at its roots without a shot being fired. In reality, the war on terror has no military solution, yet the power to oppose radical extremism does exist in the heart of traditional Islam. What is necessary is the knowledge to appreciate who could achieve a genuine moral victory over a scourge which has victimised Muslims more than America.

In May 2008 a conference on 'Anti-Terrorism and Global Peace', held in Delhi, launched the campaign most likely to eradicate the extremists. It was organised by Darul Uloom ('House of Knowledge') Deoband, a religious seminary based in a small town in Uttar Pradesh, India, to announce that: 'In Islam, creating social discord or disorder, breach of peace, rioting, bloodshed, pillage or plunder and killing of innocent persons anywhere in the world are *all* considered most inhuman crimes.' Further, it declared that those who use the Qur'an or the sayings of the Prophet Muhammad to justify terrorism are perpetuating a lie. The very purpose of Islam, it was said, is 'to wipe out all kinds of terrorism and to spread the message of global peace'. Therefore, Muslims should not cooperate with people who spread the lie of terrorism; those who do are 'committing sin or oppression'.[2]

The declaration was presented to the conference in the form of a fatwa, the term for the legal opinion of an individual Islamic scholar. But this fatwa was signed not just by Maulana Habibur Rehman, the Grand Mufti of Deoband, but also by his three deputies. It is the opinion of an institution, not an individual. In the theological universe of Islam it is more akin to a Supreme Court ruling on a constitutional principle. Darul Uloom Deoband in the Muslim world is second in importance and prestige only to Al-Azhar in Cairo. Estimates of the numbers who attended the conference to discuss the fatwa vary from 10,000 to 70,000, and they included all the main Muslim organisations and virtually all the Muslim sects, including Wahabis, Sufis and Barelvis, in India. This vast assembly of beards declared that jihad and terrorism have no connection. Terrorism targets innocent people and is destructive; jihad is constructive, its ultimate aim is to build peace. The very idea of a terrorist glorying in violence and describing himself as a Jihadi was denounced as an abomination. The conference saw terrorism as the greatest threat facing Muslim societies today. Finally, all the mullahs present publicly swore and signed an oath of allegiance: 'we are bound by the fatwa of Darul Uloom Deoband and undertake that we shall condemn terrorism and spread Islam's message of global peace.'

The significance of the event rests on the credentials of Deoband. The scholars who established Deoband as a religious teaching centre led the 1857 revolt against the British, more commonly known as the Indian Mutiny; though in India it is the first war of independence. Over the last century, the institution has played a leading role in fighting all the 'isms', from imperialism and communism to neo-colonialism, but most especially all those who seek to oppress Islam. Thus it attracts all who aspire to fight the West for its real and imaginary persecution of Muslims. The 'foreign Jihadis' fighting in Iraq claim to be inspired by Deobandi teachings. Pakistani militant groups such as Josh-e-Muhammad and Harkat-e-Islam, accused of kidnapping and suicide bombings, follow the Deobandi school of thought. The Taliban, both in Afghanistan and Pakistan, were educated in Deobandi seminaries. When aspiring terrorists go to Pakistan to study 'Islam', they go to Deobandi establishments. In Britain, the Deobandis are the second-largest group of South Asian Muslims. They control numerous mosques, some of which, allegedly, harbour young militants. What Deobandi scholars say about terrorism resonates and reaches the hearts and minds that military response cannot influence. Deoband is the voice of Muslim tradition talking to its own in terms and language they understand. It may take time, but Deoband's stand will percolate through the grassroots of the worldwide Muslim community. Deoband's fatwa provides demonstrable proof that Islam has within itself the will and resources to combat terrorism. Here is a road less travelled that offers a real prospect of moving beyond the impasse of stereotype and misinformation that dominate the cultural conventions and output of America's domain of the popular. It points in a more hopeful direction, but will require a more informed relationship with the Muslim world. It is evidence of the existence of a multi-polar world – but not the kind that preoccupies the latest fashionable strategic analysis.

A multi-polar world should be a positive direction for all to travel, but for America it is characterised as harbouring inherent threats and is regarded as a source of new fears and vulner-ability. America's greatest avoidable ignorance is to withhold from the rest of the world what we encountered at the outset as the paramount value preached by the voice of American liberal-ism in *The West Wing*: pluralism. Events happen, things change, but they can improve only when there is time and space for dif-ferent countries and peoples to find their own diverse ways to their own vision of a better future. There is no better example of the pitfalls of American dogmatism than its response to the demise of the Soviet Union. For nearly two decades America has been intent on punishing the corpse of its supposedly dead com-petitor/enemy. The result has been to provoke the growth of Russian nationalism and revitalise the theory of great power rivalry with all its attendant dangers for everyone.

The demise of communism, the collapse of the Warsaw Pact and the break-up of the Soviet Union, was hailed as an American triumph. The nations of Eastern Europe were embraced. But the Russian Federation was a different matter. It was allotted ritual humiliation, bullied, brow-beaten and starved of the kind of cooperation that might have secured full spectrum improvement. It had to follow immediately and com-pletely the only prescription that America knows how to hand out. There could be no intelligent transition by gradual reform of the behemoth of state socialism. Complete, instantaneous lib-eralisation devastated the already meagre living standards of the vast majority of the people of the Russian Federation. What arose was a kleptocracy. Criminality seemed to be the only growth industry – the Russian mafia quickly became a new cul-tural convention in the domain of the popular referenced end-lessly on American television – and the selling-off of state resources produced the immense fortunes and consequent power and power struggles of the oligarchs. Ordinary Russians were as anxious as any East Europeans to partake of openness and participate in governance in new, liberated forms. But this is not the same as saying that they wished to abandon and disown all the values they had been raised with, which communism had honoured mostly in the breach. Communism eroded under the weight of its own arrogance from the inside out. But the new world order into which the Russian Federation was ushered was no improvement. On the one hand, it produced the wooing of Vladimir Putin and the total silence in the West about Russia's annihilation of Chechnya. An entire country, and untold numbers of its people, was pulverised back to the Stone Age without a murmur as Russia was welcomed into the club making G7 G8. The silence was heard everywhere around the Muslim world as resounding proof of double standards. Yet, on the other hand, there has been the consistent advance of the US-led and US-determined expansion of NATO, an organisation that has lost any discernible purpose except that defined by Bush Snr, who in remarks made in The Hague on 9 November 1991 saw this military alliance as the means to 'enrich our peoples, create new opportunities and fuel growth' – in other words to fulfil the enduring underpinnings of American foreign policy. NATO has encroached ever closer to the borders of the Russian Federation. To this has been added the provocation of coercing compliant governments to agree to host American Star Wars bases and their array of armaments on Russia's borders, despite popular opposition. Russian history has been shaped by defensive para-noia, fear of the threat of invasion. Pavlovian response is a learned reaction to repeated stimulus. Pavlov was, of course, a Russian scientist whose work predicted what has come to pass: more of the same begets more of the same. It is patent avoidable ignorance to claim that release from Russian dominance has created thriving democracies everywhere in the former Soviet Union and Warsaw Pact countries. The ills of corruption, pol-itical gridlock and authoritarian leaders none too punctilious on human rights, but exonerated because pro-Western, stand behind many of the colour-coded revolutions. America, as is its wont, is less than particular in its scrutiny of the new friends and willing clients it cultivates and supports. Lip service to the signs and symbols and use of the rhetoric of democracy, liberty and freedom are what matter, and what continue to make all the difference.

And then there is China, the other bastion of autocracy. America was an accident found on the route to China. The consistent lodestone of American foreign policy since it became a nation has been opening doors to get access to the markets of China. But one must always be careful what one wishes for – in America's case it is found to harbour a host of new fears and vulnerabilities. China's political autocracy coupled with its liberalised economy looms large in American thinking. It is the outsourcing cuckoo sucking away American jobs, soaking up American money in huge trade imbalances as it becomes the workshop of cheaply-produced goods, the engine of American consumerism; and, swollen with the proceeds, it is competing to buy up the natural resources of the world. It is also, like the rest of the world's surplus economies, underwriting US debt, the credit-driven living beyond your means that has become the norm for the US government as much as ordinary households.

China, like India and the Muslim world, has always been seen through the prism of Orientalist stereotypes. Orientalism has always fostered fear and animosity; it is the avoidable ignorance that promotes failures of information and judgement. It is perfectly true that China has become a model for the Third World, especially those countries from whom it buys natural resources and basic commodities. But Americans would do well to consider why this is true. The Chinese come to buy, not to impose their views or their system on other countries. Chinese aid and investment is made in infrastructure and amenities of direct relevance and benefit to its trading partners, usually side-by-side with its investment in extracting raw materials. The Chinese who operate and oversee their projects live alongside the local workers they employ in similar conditions. China is a model because it has succeeded in lifting hundreds of millions of its people out of poverty, and that is a source of hope in the underdeveloped places of the globe. China comes to buy without the baggage associated with nations of the West: colonial domination, dollar diplomacy and the legacy of enduring poverty they have left in place. True, China is not an open society; its record on human rights leaves much to be desired. But America has created, installed, sponsored and supported tyrants and dictators who have behaved just as badly, if not worse, towards their own people with impunity. China's industrialisation is following the route already pioneered by Western nations. The huddled masses who flocked to Britain's towns lived in hellish conditions, polluting and polluted, and worked in even worse conditions. The huddled masses who made it to America served their time in sweatshops and polluting factories, and still do. If the American lifestyle is non-negotiable, and Americans continue to pollute and degrade the global environment at a greater rate than any other nation, why are China and India the impediment to global environmental cooperation? In the process of becoming the richest nation on earth, America protected its industries as it preached, demanded and broke open doors to trade around the globe. And accumulated wealth continues to confer privileges that America will not forgo. To protect the richest cotton farmers on earth, America ensured the failure of the Doha Development Round, supposedly aimed at liberalising global trade. It did so to prevent India protecting some of the poorest cotton farmers on earth, in a move supported by governments desperate to secure a sustainable livelihood for their impoverished cotton farmers, squeezed out of world markets by American subsidies. The rapacious need for raw materials and the rising living standards of Chinese and Indians is regularly presented as having sinister potential for the American way of life. But a leaked report prepared for the World Bank, and not published to spare the blushes of the US government, shows that it is maintaining the non-negotiable American lifestyle that is taking food from the poorest.[3] The report, written by Don Mitchell, a senior economist at the

World Bank, tracked detailed month-by-month figures for the global surge in food prices, which have risen 75 per cent and pushed 100 million people worldwide below the poverty line, provoking riots in many poor and middle-income countries. The report concluded that there was a causative link between three factors, all connected to America's need for cheap fuel. First, grain has been diverted from food to the production of biofuel; over a third of US corn is now used to produce ethanol, and about half of vegetable oils in the EU go to producing biodiesel. Second, farmers in America are being encouraged to set aside land for biofuel production rather than food production. Third, these factors have provoked financial speculation in grains on commodity markets, driving prices ever higher. America's insatiable appetite for cheap oil, around which its built environment and lifestyle has been constructed, in effect impoverishes and takes food from the mouths of the poor. And American power is such that the global institution that America founded and dominates, the World Bank, is afraid to tell anyone why this is happening. There have to be better ways to travel to a mutually sustaining future that is not content to beggar its neighbours.

A former French foreign minister, Hubert Vedrine, observed: 'America can inspire the dreams and desires of others thanks to its dominance of global images.' The cultural power and influence of the US, however, comes encoded not just with images of material abundance, American values and the idea of America, but also with the nightmare fears that infest its view of the rest of the world. The greatest military power the world has known has the armaments to crush the massed forces of any combination of conventional armies, yet perennially feels so vulnerable that it must spend ever-increasing sums on ever more sophisticated weaponry deployed around the world and into the stratosphere; and it still seems incapable of securing peace of mind. What America understands, what the idea of America has come to mean, is dominance – that is the road it has travelled consistently. And the dominance it requires regards militarism as the essential answer to all problems. Difference and diversity are threats to dominance, undermining America's ability to maintain a world order conducive to its security and prosperity. These are roads that lead us back to insecurity, danger and the shrinking of the freedom of nations and peoples to choose the course most appropriate to their own history, sentiments and aspirations.

Will America change? Can America be changed and embrace plurality? It is not the failings of the Bush administration alone, nor that of a particular coterie of zealots, that have constructed the idea of America and its implicit view of, and way of engaging with, the rest of the world. Change would require America to tackle its avoidable ignorance so that it can seriously debate whether it really wants to maintain the full spectrum dominance that precludes any real partnership or meeting of minds with other societies and peoples. Imperial powers cast fond shadows only when their control over other people has been removed. An empire, even a non-conventional one such as America's, cannot expect to be loved while it inhibits, constrains and circumscribes the autonomous independent choices of other people. It is avoidable ignorance to ignore the fact that America impinges on the lives of ordinary people everywhere just by maintaining its own lifestyle.

America has come to a fork in the road and stopped to contemplate the question of change many times. It has never yet selected the road less travelled, that of trusting global plurality, building cooperation, embracing mutual trust and the need to listen to and learn from other people rather than cocooning itself in the illusory belief that its way is the last best hope for everyone. Hope begins with seeing possibility in the plurality of the human imagination, ideas and experiences; peace and mutual security will be found by creating the conditions for this plurality to flourish in open and equitable relationships. Our differences and diversity suggest that there are multiple ways to solve our common human problems and enhance our future prospects – this should be the first best hope in which all nations place their trust, the new road taken.

Whether America *will* change is the most crucial question and vital concern for the global future. But whether America *can* change is difficult to foresee. Opening his history of Vietnam, Stanley Karnow began with a reflection on the meaning of the Vietnam Memorial in Washington DC:

> The names of the dead engraved on the granite record more than lives lost in battle: they represent a sacrifice to a failed crusade, however noble or illusory its motives. In a larger sense they symbolise a faded hope – or perhaps the birth of a new awareness. They bear witness to the end of America's absolute confidence in its moral exclusivity, its military invincibility, its manifest destiny. They are the price paid in blood and sorrow for America's awakening to maturity, to the recognition of its limitations. With the young men who died in Vietnam died the dream of an 'American Century.'[4]

The thought was published first in 1983. By the time the book was in the shops, Ronald Reagan was in the White House and beginning his successful campaign to make America fall in love with its military again and embrace its power to influence and shape the lives of countries near and far to be conducive to American interests. He would do so by ensuring the greatest-ever peacetime expansion of American military spending; and as the Great Communicator he used the soft power of making America afraid of the world out there.

The Reagan years laid the basis for the policies by which his successor George H.W. Bush conceived a new world order whose strings would remain firmly in the hands of America. The projection of American military power and influence linked the policies of the Republican Bush Snr with those of his Democrat successor, Bill Clinton. And during the Clinton years the Project for the New American Century was being developed, founded on full spectrum dominance of the global future, which duly delivered the policies of George W. Bush. The Iraq war will be overtaken by new formulations of fear and vulnerability about the return of a multi-polar world. America has come to the fork in the road many times without ever taking the road less travelled. Will America change direction this time? It requires ordinary Americans to take a new level of responsibility and accountability for how they think about themselves and what they know about the rest of the world. And that would make all the difference.

Notes

CHAPTER ONE

1. *Groundhog Day*, Columbia Pictures Corporation, 1993. Directed by Harold Ramis and starring Bill Murray.
2. Entry in Ambrose Bierce, *The Devil's Dictionary* (London: Bloomsbury, 2003); originally published in 1906 as *The Cynic's Word Book*.
3. T.S. Eliot, *Murder in the Cathedral* (London: Faber and Faber, 1976).
4. Falwell made his comment on CBS's *60 Minutes*, 1 October 2002. After worldwide protests he apologised a week later. Pat Robertson said that terrorists are 'carrying out Islam' on Fox Network's *Hannity and Colmes* programme on 18 September 2002.
5. Victor Davis Hanson, 'Defending the West: Why the Muslims Misjudge Us', *City Journal*, 25 February 2002; www.opinionjournal.com
6. Originally an email to friends written on 14 September 2001, it subsequently appeared as 'An Afghan American Speaks' on www.Salon.com
7. www.aaiusa.org/pressroom/3141/aaizogby-poll
8. Chalmers Johnson, *Blowback: The Cost and Consequences of American Empire* (London: Little Brown and Co., 2000); *The Sorrows of Empire: Militarism, Secrecy and the End of the Republic* (New York: Metropolitan Books, 2004); *Nemesis: The Last Days of the American Republic* (New York: Metropolitan Books, 2006).
9. Amy Chua, *World On Fire: How Exporting Free Market Democracy Breeds Ethnic Hatred and Global Instability* (New York: Doubleday, 2003).
10. Anne McLennan, 'War on Terror', *London Free Press* (Canada), 5 November 2001, p. 8.

CHAPTER TWO

1. www.newamericancentury.org
2. William Kristol and Donald Kaplan, *War Over Iraq* (New York: Encounter Books, 2003).
3. William J. Lederer and Eugene Burdick, *The Ugly American* (New York: W.W. Norton, 1958).
4. George Ball, a senior state department official under Presidents Kennedy and Johnson, quoted in Stanley Karnow, *Vietnam: A History*, revised edition (London: Pimlico, 1991), p. 24.
5. Rajiv Chandrasekaran, *Imperial Life in the Emerald City: Inside Baghdad's Green Zone* (London: Bloomsbury, 2007).
6. *The Ugly American*, p. 21.
7. Quoted in Karnow, op. cit., p. 163.
8. Ho Chi Minh, *Selected Works* (Hanoi, 1960–62), vol. 3.
9. See Christopher Bayly and Tim Harper, *Forgotten Wars: The End of Britain's Asian Empire* (London: Allen Lane, 2007).
10. Both quotes in Karnow, op. cit., p. 22.
11. Gareth Porter, *Perils of Dominance: Imbalance of Power and the Road to War in Vietnam* (Berkeley: University of California Press, 2005).
12. Ibid., p. 272.
13. Ibid., p. 273.
14. Ibid., p. 272.
15. *The Ugly American*, p. 30.
16. William R. Polk, *Understanding Iraq* (London: I.B. Taurus, 2006).
17. Jonathan Steele, *Defeat: Why America and Britain Lost Iraq* (London: I.B. Taurus, 2008).
18. Charles Tripp, *A History of Iraq*, new edition (Cambridge University Press, 2000), p. 39.
19. Writing as president of the Air Council, 1919. Quoted in Rory Bremner, John Bird and John Fortune, *You*

Are Here: An Updated Dossier (London: Phoenix, 2005), p. 75.

20. Quoted in Bremner, Bird and Fortune, op. cit., p. 74.

21. Muhammad Heikal, *Illusions of Triumph: An Arab View of the Gulf War* (London: Fontana, 1993), quoted in Steele, op. cit., p. 35.

22. See Porter, op. cit., pp. 13, 22–3.

23. Quoted in Porter, op. cit., p. 86.

24. Polk, op. cit., p. 113.

25. Ibid., p. 115.

26. Ibid., p. 119.

27. Ibid., p. 128.

28. Available at www.nsarchive.org

29. Polk, op. cit., p. 132.

30. Quoted in ibid., p. 141.

31. Polk, op. cit., p. 152.

32. Speech at Andover, MA, 15 February 1990.

33. Quoted in Polk, op. cit., p. 153.

34. Dilip Hiro, *Iraq: A Report From the Inside* (London: Granta, 2003); the American edition was published by Thunder Mouth Press/Nation Books in 2002.

35. Ghassan Salame, *American Policy for the Arabs*, p. 7, quoted in Steele, op. cit., p. 35.

36. *The Ugly American*, p. 145.

37. Ibid., p. 81.

38. *The Iraq Study Group Report: The Way Forward – A New Approach* (New York: Vintage Books, 2006).

39. Chandrasekaran, op. cit., p. 25.

40. Ibid., p. 15.

41. Ibid., p. 103.

42. *The Ugly American*, p. 162.

43. Quoted in Chandrasekaran, op. cit., p. 171.

44. Ibid., p. 116.

45. *The Guardian*, 28 April 2008.

46. Ibid.

47. Steele, op. cit., p. 63.

48. Ali A. Allawi, *The Occupation of Iraq: Winning the War, Losing the Peace* (New Haven: Yale University Press, 2007).

49. Steele, op. cit., p. 53.

50. Ibid., p. 44.

51. Ibid., pp. 44–5.

52. Ibid., p. 44.

53. *The Guardian*, 27 March 2008.

54. Interviewed on *Newsnight*, BBC TV, 25 March 2008.

55. Tarik Barkawi, 'Globalization, Culture and War: On the Popular Mediation of "Small Wars"', *Cultural Critique*, 58, Fall 2004, pp. 115–47.

56. Ibid., p. 115.

CHAPTER THREE

1. Interviewed by Jon Stewart on *The Daily Show*, 7 May 2008.

2. Franco Cardini, *Europe and Islam* (Oxford: Blackwell, 1999), p. 143.

3. Ruth Vasey, *The World According to Hollywood, 1918–1939* (Exeter: University of Exeter Press, 1997), p. 58.

4. For an extended discussion, see Merryl Wyn Davies and Ziauddin Sardar, *Framing Muslims: Freeze Frames of the Western Imagination* (forthcoming), and Ziauddin Sardar, *Orientalism* (Buckingham: Open University Press, 1999).

5. Barkawi, op. cit.

6. Cardini, op. cit., p. 81.

7. Ibid., p. 79.

8. Joshua Prawer, *The Crusaders' Kingdom: European Colonialism in the Middle Ages* (London: Phoenix Press, 2001), p. 469.

9. Barkawi, op. cit., p. 116.

10. Donald Rumsfeld, 12 February 2002, department of defence news briefing.

11. Quoted in Michael Hirsh, 'Bernard Lewis Revisited', *Washington Monthly*, November 2004.

12. Richard W. Bulliet, *The Case for Islamo-Christian Civilization* (New

York: Columbia University Press, 2004).

13. Dr David Kay, hearing of the Senate Armed Services Committee, 28 January 2004; transcript at www.ceip.org

14. Quoted in Stuart C. Millar, *Benevolent Assimilation: The American Conquest of the Philippines 1899–1903* (New Haven, CT: Yale University Press, 1982), p. 211.

15. 'A Nation Challenged: Public Relations; Pentagon Plays Role in Fictional Terror Drama', *New York Times*, 31 March 2002.

16. Karnow, op. cit., p. 55.

17. Ibid., p. 55.

18. *New York Times*, 31 March 2002, op. cit.

19. Ibid.

20. 'Letter from Hollywood: Whatever it Takes; The politics of the man behind *24*', Jane Mayer, *The New Yorker*, 19 February 2007.

21. *Democracy Now!*, 3 April 2008; available at www.democracynow.org

22. Ibid.

23. Quoted in 'US Military tells Jack Bauer: Cut out the torture scenes … or else!', *The Independent*, 13 February 2007.

24. *The New Yorker*, 19 February 2007, op. cit.

25. Ibid.

26. Quoted in a film review in *Al Ahram Weekly*, 479, 27 April 2000.

CHAPTER FOUR

1. Robert Kagan, *Of Paradise and Power: America and Europe in the New World Order* (New York: Knopf, 2003), p. 85.

2. Ibid., p. 86.

3. Clyde Prestowitz, *Rogue Nation* (New York: Basic Books, 2003), p. 41.

4. Ibid., p. 36.

5. Quoted in Barton Gellman, 'Aim of Defense Plan Supported by Bush', *Washington Post*, 12 March 1992.

6. Andrew J. Bacevich, *American Empire: The Realities and Consequences of US Diplomacy* (Cambridge, MA: Harvard University Press, 2002), pp. 45–6.

7. John Rolfe's letter to Sir Thomas Dale, from the Ashmole MS reprinted in Phillip L. Barbour, *Pocahontas and Her World* (Boston, MA: Houghton Mifflin, 1970), Appendix III, pp. 247–52.

8. John Winthrop, *A Modell of Christian Charity*, 1630 (Boston, MA: Collections of the Massachusetts Historical Society, 1838), third series, 7, pp. 31–48.

9. Jimmie Durham, 'Cowboys and …', *Third Text*, 12, Autumn 1990, pp. 5–20.

10. Ibid.

11. Peter Mathiesson, Foreword to Oren Lyons et al., *Exiled in the Land of the Free* (Santa Fe, NM: Clear Light Publishers, 1992), p. xi.

12. Cited in Lewis Hanke, *Aristotle and the American Indians* (Bloomington, IN: Indiana University Press, 1975), p. 16.

13. Cited in ibid., p. 112.

14. Cited in ibid., p. 100.

15. Vince Deloria Jr, 'Indian Law and the Reach of History', *Journal of Contemporary Law*, 4, 1977–8, pp. 1–13.

16. Durham, op. cit., pp. 5–20.

17. Ibid.

18. Arthur M. Schlesinger Jr, *The Disuniting of America: Reflections on a Multicultural Society* (New York, Whittle Books, 1998), p. 134.

19. See Richard Slotkin, *Regeneration Through Violence: The Mythology of the American Frontier 1600–1860* (Middletown, CT: Wesleyan Uni-

versity Press, 1973); *The Fatal Environment: The Myth of Frontier in the Age of Industrialization 1800–1890* (Norman, OK: University of Oklahoma Press, 1998); and *Gunfighter Nation: The Myth of Frontier in Twentieth-Century America* (Norman, OK: University of Oklahoma Press, 1998).

20. John L. O'Sullivan, 'Annexation', *United States Magazine and Democratic Review*, August 1845. Cornell University maintains a searchable archive of this journal at http://cdl.library.cornell.edu

21. John L. O'Sullivan, 'The Great Nation of Futurity', *United States Magazine and Democratic Review*, November 1835.

22. Slotkin, *Regeneration Through Violence*, op. cit., p. 25.

CHAPTER FIVE

1. Madeleine Albright on NBC's *Today* show, 19 February 1998.

2. Bacevich, op. cit., 2002, p. 33.

3. Andrew J. Bacevich, *The New American Militarism: How Americans are Seduced by War* (Oxford: Oxford University Press, 2005), p. 4.

4. Jedidiah Morse, *American Geography* (1789), p. 467.

5. Quoted in Sidney Lens, *The Forging of the American Empire*, new edn (London: Pluto Press, 2003), p. 163.

6. Ibid., p. 165.

7. Quoted in ibid., p. 280.

8. Charles A. Beard, *American Government and Politics*, rev. edn (New York: Macmillan, 1914), p. 331.

9. Cited in Gore Vidal, *The Decline and Fall of the American Empire* (Chicago: Oldonian Press, 2000), p. 18.

10. Quoted in Lens, op. cit., p. 178.

11. Quoted in ibid., p. 212.

12. Quoted in ibid., p. 215.

13. William Appleman Williams, *America Confronts a Revolutionary World, 1776–1976* (New York: Morrow, 1976), p. 43.

14. William Appleman Williams, *Empire as a Way of Life* (New York: Oxford University Press, 1980), p. 128.

15. Prestowitz, op. cit., p. 170.

16. US Commission on National Security, *New World Coming* (Washington, DC, 1999), p. 128.

17. George H.W. Bush and Brent Scowcroft, *A World Transformed* (New York: Knopf, 1998), p. 491.

18. Bacevich, op. cit., 2002, p. 74.

19. Ibid., p. 88.

20. Address by Madeleine Albright, 2 October 1998.

21. Bacevich, op. cit., 2002, p. 121.

22. Joshua Muravchik, *The Imperative of American Leadership: A Challenge to Neo-isolationism* (Washington, DC: AEI Press, 1996), p. 135.

23. William Cohen, 'US Must Remain Active in Post-Cold War Foreign Affairs', Foreign Policy Association, New York, 2 April 1998.

24. General John M. Shalikashvili, 'Joint Vision 2010' (Washington, DC, 1996), p. 2.

25. Paul Kennedy, 'The Eagle Has Landed', *Financial Times* Weekend section, 3 February 2002.

26. Bremner, Bird and Fortune, op. cit., p. 135.

27. Michael Sherry, *In the Shadow of War: The United States Since the 1930s* (New Haven, CT: Yale University Press, 1995), p. x.

28. Charles A. Beard, *The Open Door At Home* (New York: Macmillan, 1935), pp. 125–6.

29. Ibid., p. 241.

CHAPTER SIX

1. 'Can Charlotte Beers Sell Uncle Sam?', *Time*, 14 November 2001.

2. 'Charlotte Beer's Toughest Sell', *Business Week*, 17 December 2001.

3. Boutros Boutros-Ghali, *Unvanquished: a US–UN Saga* (New York: Random House, 1999).

4. William Blum, *Rogue State* (London: Zed Press, 2001), pp. 185–97.

5. John Bolton in a speech to the Global Structures Convention, New York, 3 February 1994.

6. Blum, op. cit., p. 198.

7. Cited in Andrew Simms, Tom Big and Nick Robins, *It's Democracy, Stupid* (London: New Economic Foundation, 2000), p. 6.

8. *Financial Times*, 15 August 2001.

9. *Economist*, 18 September 1999.

10. Ed Mayo, interviewed by the authors, 20 March 2002.

11. Andrew Simms, interviewed by the authors, 20 March 2002.

12. Mayo, op. cit.

13. Jimmy Carter, *Christian Science Monitor*, 29 December 1999.

14. 'Debt Relief is down: Other ODA rises slightly', Development Co-operation Directorate, available at www.oecd.org

15. All quoted in Peter Schwartner's 'Read My Lips' column, 'Kyoto Treaty: Dead or Comatose?', at www.theglobalist.com

16. Andrew Kimbrell, *The Human Body Shop: The Engineering and Marketing of Life* (Penang: Third World Network), 1993.

17. 'Mexico Confirms GM Maize Contamination', Science and Development Network, 18 April 2002, at www.scidev.net

18. Quoted in BBC TV *Earth Report*, 13 November 2004, available at www.bbc.co.uk/news

19. Quoted in ibid.

20. Jim Dator, interviewed by the authors, 28 February 2002.

21. Ben Bagdikian, *The Media Monopoly* (Boston, MA: Beacon Books, 1983).

22. Mark Crispin Miller, *The Nation*, 7 January 2002.

23. Interviewed on BBC TV *Newsnight*, 6 June 2002; transcript available at www.bbc.co.uk/newsnight (archive).

24. Robert W. McChesney, 'Global Media, Neoliberalism and Imperialism', *Monthly Review*, 52, 17 March 2001.

25. Naomi Klein, 'America is not a hamburger', *Guardian*, 13 March 2002.

26. George Ritzer, 'Obscene from any angle: fast food, credit cards, casinos and consumers', *Third Text*, 51, Summer 2000, pp. 17–28.

27. Margaret Wertheim, email interview with the authors, 12 December 2001.

28. Ibid.

29. Ibid.

30. 'Youth: The Wilder Ones', *Asiaweek*, 25 May 1994, pp. 24–33.

31. John Sutherland, 'Linguicide: the death of language', *Independent on Sunday*, Life Etc. section, 10 March 2002, p. 1.

32. Ibid.

33. William Gibson, 'Disneyland With a Death Penalty', *Observer*, Life section, 14 August 1994.

34. Steve Fuller, email interview with the authors, 3 April 2002.

35. Wertheim, op. cit.

36. Ibid.

37. Ibid.

CONCLUSION

1. *The Ugly American*, p. 278.

2. See Ziauddin Sardar, 'Fatwa Against Terrorism', *New Statesman*, 19 June 2008.

3. *The Guardian*, 4 July 2008.

4. Karnow, op. cit., p. 9.

Select Bibliography

Achcar, Gilbert, trans. Peter Ducker. *The Clash of Barbarisms: September 11 and the Making of the New World Disorder* (New York: Monthly Review Press, 2002).

Ansari, Ali M. *Confronting Iran* (London, Hurst, 2006).

Araeen, Rasheed, Sean Cubitt and Ziauddin Sardar (editors). *The Third Text Reader on Art, Culture and Theory* (London: Continuum, 2002).

Barber, Benjamin R. *Fear's Empire* (New York: W.W. Norton, 2003).

Barber, Benjamin R. *Jihad vs McWorld: Terrorism's Challenge to Democracy* (London: Corgi, 2003).

Berman, Paul. *Terror and Liberalism* (New York: W.W. Norton, 2003).

Bobbitt, Philip. *The Shield of Achilles* (London: Allen Lane, 2002).

Boot, Max. *The Savage Wars of Peace: Small Wars and the Rise of American Power* (New York: Basic Books, 2002).

Bovard, James. *Terrorism and Tyranny: Trampling Freedom, Justice, and Peace to Rid the World of Evil* (New York: Palgrave Macmillan, 2003).

Brzezinski, Zbigniew. *Choice: Global Domination or Global Leadership* (New York: Basic Books, 2004).

Bush, George W. *We Will Prevail* (New York: Continuum, 2003).

Chomsky, Noam. *Hegemony or Survival: America's Quest for Global Dominance* (Metropolitan Books, 2003).

Clarke, Richard. *Against All Enemies* (New York: Free Press, 2004).

Costa-Gavras. 'Resisting the Colonels of Disney', *New Perspective Quarterly* 12 (4), Fall 1995, pp. 4–7.

Cubitt, Sean. *The Cinema. Effect* (Cambridge, MA: MIT Press, Massachusetts, 2004).

Daalder, Ivo H. and James M. Lindsay (editors). *America Unbound: The Bush Revolution in Foreign Policy* (Washington: Brookings Institution Press, 2003).

Daniel, Norman. *Islam and the West: The Making of an Image*, revised edn, (Oxford: One World, 1993, first published by University of Edinburgh Press, 1960).

Fukuyama, Francis. *The End of History and the Last Man* (London: Hamish Hamilton, 1992).

Garrison, Jim (editor). *American Empire: The Realities and Consequences of US Diplomacy* (Cambridge, MA: Harvard University Press, 2002).

Garrison, Jim. *America as Empire: Global Leader or Rogue Power?* (Berrett-Koehler Publishers, 2004).

Gehring, Verma V. (editor). *War After September 11* (Lanham: Rowman and Littlefield, 2003).

Giroux, Henry A. 'Global Capitalism and the Return of the Garrison State', *Arena Journal*, 19, 2002, pp. 141–60.

Giroux, Henry A. 'Living in the Shadow of Authoritarianism: Proto-Fascism, Neoliberalism, and the Twilight of Democracy', *Third Text*, 2004.

Glassner, Barry. *The Culture of Fear* (New York: Basic Books, 1999).

Grandin, Greg. *Empire's Workshop* (New York: Metropolitan, 2006).

Hardt, Michael and Antonio Negri. *Empire* (Cambridge, MA: Harvard University Press, 2000).

Hauerwas, Stanley and Frank Lentricchia (editors). *Dissent from the Homeland: Essays After September 11* (Durham: Duke University Press, 2003).

Huntington, Samuel P. *The Clash of Civilizations and the Remaking of World Order* (London: Simon and Schuster, 1997).

Huntington, Samuel P. *Who Are We? The Challenge to America's National Identity* (New York: Simon and Schuster, 2004).

Ignatieff, Michael. 'The American Empire: The Burden', *New York Times Magazine*, 5 January 2003, section 6.

Ikenberry, G. John (editor). *America Unrivaled: The Future of the Balance of Power* (Ithaca: Cornell University Press, 2002).

Jensen, Robert. *Citizens of the Empire* (San Francisco: City Light Books, 2004).

Joxe, Alain (trans. Ames Hodges, ed. Sylvère Lotringer). *Empire of Disorder* (Cambridge, MA: Semiotexte, MIT Press, 2002).

Kagan, Robert. 'The Benevolent Empire', *Foreign Policy*, Summer 1998, pp. 24–34.

Kagan, Robert. *Paradise and Power* (New York: Alfred A. Knopf, 2003).

Kinzer, Stephen. *Overthrow: America's Century of Regime Change from Hawaii to Iraq* (New York: Times, 2006).

Krugman, Paul. *The Great Unravelling* (New York: W.W. Norton, 2003).

Kupchan, Charles. *The End of the American Era: US Foreign Policy and the Geopolitics of the Twenty-First Century* (New York: Knopf, 2002).

Kurtz, Stanley. 'Democratic Imperialism: A Blueprint', *Policy Review*, April/May 2003, pp. 3–20.

Landau, Saul. *The Pre-Emptive Empire* (London: Pluto Press, 2003).

Lewis, Jon (editor). *The End of Cinema As We Know It* (London: Pluto Press, 2001).

Lifton, Robert Jay. *Superpower Syndrome: America's Apocalyptic Confrontation with the World* (New York: Nation Books, 2003).

Magdoff, Harry. *The Age of Imperialism: The Economics of US Foreign Policy* (Monthly Review Press, 1969).

Mahajan, Rahul. *Full Spectrum Dominance: US Power in Iraq and Beyond* (Seven Stories Press, 2003).

Mann, Michael. *Incoherent Empire* (London: Verso Books, 2003).

May, Ernest R. *Imperial Democracy: The Emergence of America as a Great Power* (New York: Imprint, 1961).

Maynes, Charles William. 'The Perils of (and for) an Imperial America', *Foreign Policy*, Summer 1998, pp. 36–47.

Mead, Walter Russell. *Mortal Splendor: The American Empire in Transition* (Houghton Mifflin, 1988).

Mearsheimer, John. *The Tragedy of Great Power Politics* (New York: W.W. Norton, 2003).

Moosa, Ebrahim. 'Inside the Madrassa', *Boston Review*, 24 January 2007, available at www.bostonreview.net

Muldoon, James. *Popes. Lawyers and Infidels: The Church and the Non-Christian World 1250–1550* (Philadelphia: University of Pennsylvania Press, 1979).

Pfaff, William. *Barbarian Sentiments: America in the New Century* (New York: Hill and Wang, 2000).

Progressive Policy Institute, 'Progressive Internationalism: A Democratic National Security Strategy', Washington DC, 30 October 2003; available from www.ppionline.org/

Project for the New American Century, 'Rebuilding America's Defences: Strategy, Forces and Resources for a New Century', September 2000, available from www.newamericancentury.org

R.W. Southern. *Western Views of Islam in the Middle Ages* (Cambridge, MA: Harvard University Press, 1962).

Rogers, Paul. *A War on Terror* (London: Pluto Press, 2004).

Ryan, David. *US Foreign Policy in World History* (London: Routledge, 2000).

Sardar, Ziauddin and Merryl Wyn Davies. *American Dream Global Nightmare* (Cambridge: Icon Books, 2004).

Sardar, Ziauddin and Merryl Wyn Davies. *No Nonsense Guide to Islam* (Oxford: New Internationalist, 2004).

Sardar, Ziauddin and Merryl Wyn Davies. *Why Do People Hate America?* (Cambridge: Icon Books, 2002).

Sardar, Ziauddin. *Balti Britain* (London: Granta, 2008).

Sardar, Ziauddin. *Orientalism* (Buckingham: Open University Press, 1999).

Sardar, Ziauddin. *Postmodernism and the Other* (London: Pluto Press, 1998).

Schudson, Michael. *The Good Citizen: A History of American Civic Life* (Cambridge, MA: Harvard University Press, 1998).

Shaheen, Jack G. *Reel Bad Arabs: How Hollywood Vilifies a People* (New York: Olive Branch Press, 2001).

Sim, Stuart. *Fundamentalist World* (Cambridge: Icon Books, 2004).

Singer, Peter. *The President of Good and Evil* (London: Granta, 2004).

Sklar, Robert. *Movie Made America: A Cultural History of American Movies*, revised edn (New York: Vintage Books, 1994).

Smith, Julian. *Looking Away: Hollywood and Vietnam* (New York: Charles Scribner, 1975).

Smith, Neil. *American Empire: Roosevelt's Geographer and the Prelude to Globalization* (Berkeley: University of California Press, 2003).

Soros, George. *The Bubble of American Supremacy: Correcting the Misuse of American Power* (New York: Public Affairs, 2004).

Stiglitz, Joseph E. and Linda Bilmes. *The Three Trillion Dollar War: The True Cost of the Iraq Conflict* (London: Allen Lane, 2008).

Stiglitz, Joseph E. *Globalization and Its Discontents* (New York, W.W. Norton, 2002).

Todd, Emmanuel. *After the Empire: The Breakdown of the American Order* (Cambridge: Cambridge University Press, 2003).

Vidal, Gore. *Inventing A Nation: Washington, Adams, Jefferson* (New Haven: Yale University Press, 2003).

Vidal, Gore. *The Decline and Fall of the American Empire* (Chicago: Odonian Press, 2000).

Wallerstein, Immanuel. *The Decline of American Power* (New York: New Press, 2003).

Wood, Ellen Meiksins. *Empire of Capital* (London: Verso Books, 2003).

Woodward, Bob. *Plan of Attack* (New York: Simon and Schuster, 2004).

Yew, Leong. *The Disjunctive Empire of International Relations* (Aldershot: Ashgate, 2003).

Zakaria, Freed. *The Future of Freedom: Illiberal Democracy at Home and Abroad* (New York: W.W. Norton, 2003).

Zimmerman, Warren. *First Great Triumph: How Five Americans Made Their Country a World Power* (Farrar, Straus and Giroux, 2002).

Index